James King

Anglican Hymnology

James King

Anglican Hymnology

ISBN/EAN: 9783744649216

Printed in Europe, USA, Canada, Australia, Japan

Cover: Foto ©Thomas Meinert / pixelio.de

More available books at **www.hansebooks.com**

Anglican Hymnology

*BEING AN ACCOUNT OF THE 325 STANDARD HYMNS
OF THE HIGHEST MERIT ACCORDING TO
THE VERDICT OF THE WHOLE
ANGLICAN CHURCH*

BY

Rev. JAMES KING, M.A.

AUTHORISED LECTURER TO 'THE PALESTINE EXPLORATION FUND'
VICAR OF ST. MARY'S, BERWICK-UPON-TWEED

LONDON
HATCHARDS, PICCADILLY
1885

Edinburgh University Press:
THOMAS AND ARCHIBALD CONSTABLE, PRINTERS TO HER MAJESTY.

CONTENTS.

	PAGE
INTRODUCTION,	v
LIST OF HYMNALS COLLATED,	xiii

CHAPTER I.

HISTORY OF ANCIENT AND MEDIÆVAL HYMNOLOGY,   1

CHAPTER II.

FIRST RANK HYMNS: INDEX, SUMMARY, AND ACCOUNT OF EACH HYMN, ... 41

CHAPTER III.

SECOND RANK HYMNS: INDEX, SUMMARY, AND ACCOUNT OF EACH HYMN, ... 200

CHAPTER IV.

THIRD RANK HYMNS: INDEX, SUMMARY, AND ACCOUNT OF EACH HYMN, ... 264

CHAPTER V.

GENERAL SUMMARY AND INDEX OF STANDARD HYMNS, . 305

INTRODUCTION.

IN the English language there are about *twenty thousand* hymns and versions of the Psalms—composed almost entirely during the last three hundred years, by fifteen hundred authors. The greater number of these hymns are poor when judged by the ordinary laws of sacred poetry, and the compilers of Church Hymnals have no easy task in making judicious selections from the vast stores of hymnology. Many hymns of little intrinsic merit have obtained an undue notoriety, either from some happy associations, or from the excellent music to which they have been wedded ; and considerable diversity of opinion exists with respect to the relative merits of hymns in general.

If a hundred persons were each to write a list of a dozen favourite hymns, the probability is that no two lists of the hundred would be alike ; so greatly is each individual influenced by natural temperament, education, and associations. Amid much diversity of individual opinion, however, there is a general agreement as to what constitutes real excellence, and the verdict of the whole Church, could such be determined, may be accounted a safe guide in deciding the question of relative merit. In order to find out the verdict of the whole Anglican Church, the writer adopted the following method. He collected and collated with much labour fifty-two representative Hymnals used in the Church of England at home and abroad. These included Hymnals of the Scottish Episcopal, American, and Colonial Church in communion with the Anglican. They also in due proportion represented the various parties in the Church—namely, the Ritualistic, High, Broad, and Evangelical. All the fifty-two have, moreover, been published, with one exception, within the last twenty-one years, extending from 1863 to 1885—that is, during the lifetime of all who have now attained their majority, and consequently they represent the taste of the present generation.

By means of these Hymnals he put to the test all hymns of acknowledged merit, in order to find out those that have received what has been aptly called 'the broad seal of approval of the whole Anglican Church.'

Introduction. ix

The fifty-two were regarded as a committee, each member of which could, as it were, give one vote for each approved hymn. Thus, if a hymn was found in fifteen Hymnals, then it was credited with fifteen votes or marks of approval; if found in twenty Hymnals, twenty marks; if in thirty Hymnals, thirty marks; if in fifty Hymnals, fifty marks; and so on.

For instance, taking a few well-known hymns commencing with the letter A as the initial letter of the first line, the question was asked—How many of you have 'Abide with me, fast falls the even-tide'? Forty-nine answer, 'I have.' This hymn was therefore credited with forty-nine marks, because it was found in forty-nine books.

The six best-known hymns in A, after being duly tested, are found to stand in the following order of merit :—

Order.	Hymns.	Marks.
1.	All praise to Thee, my God, this night,	51
2.	Abide with me, fast falls the even-tide,	49
3.	Awake, my soul, and with the sun,	49
4.	All people that on earth do dwell,	44
5.	All hail, the power of Jesus' Name,	37
6.	As with gladness men of old,	34

Perhaps a dozen individuals would have arranged the above hymns in a dozen different ways; but it must be admitted that, as regards authority, the verdict of fifty-two representative Hymnals towers high above individual opinion, inasmuch as they represent the voice of the whole Anglican Church.

Two thousand of our best-known hymns have thus been tested, and those that have obtained most marks have been selected and classified on the following principle :—

1. All hymns found in thirty Hymnals and upwards have been classified as *first rank* hymns.
2. All hymns found in twenty Hymnals and upwards, and in fewer than thirty, have been classified as *second rank* hymns.
3. All hymns found in fifteen Hymnals and upwards, and in fewer than twenty, have been classified as *third rank* hymns.
4. All hymns found in fewer than fifteen Hymnals have been regarded as not having received the general approval of the Anglican Church.

According to this principle 105 hymns were found to be entitled to be placed in the first rank, 110 in the second rank, and 110 in the third rank; making a total of 325 approved by the voice of the whole Church of England.

These 325 standard hymns have been arranged in order of merit, according to the marks of approval awarded to each; and it is interesting

Introduction. xi

to notice the relative position assigned to the universal favourites.

It is startling to find that of the twenty thousand hymns existing in the English language, not a single one is to be found in all the fifty-two Hymnals, and it is somewhat remarkable that only 325 are found in fifteen Hymnals and upwards.

Many excellent hymns have doubtless failed to attain even to the third rank, simply because they lack age. As a general rule, a period of time from twenty to fifty years is required before a hymn becomes adequately appreciated and finds its way into our modern Hymnals.

A list of thirty hymns of comparatively recent date is given on pp. 310, 311. These hymns are rapidly finding their way into modern Hymnals, and in the future they will probably take rank as 'standard hymns.'

LIST OF HYMNALS COLLATED.

THE following is a list of the fifty-two Hymnals collated :—

1. *The Church of England Hymn-book.* Edited by Godfrey Thring, and published by Skeffington and Son in 1882. It contains 730 hymns.

2. *Church Hymns.* Edited by Arthur Sullivan, and published by the S.P.C.K. in 1874. It contains 592 hymns.

3. *The People's Hymnal.* Re-issued by Masters and Co. in 1868. It contains 600 hymns, and may be regarded as an exponent of the Ritualists.

4. *Hymns Ancient and Modern.* Revised and enlarged edition. Edited by the late Sir Henry W. Baker and a committee of compilers, and published in 1874 by Clowes and Son. It contains 473 hymns, and has obtained the widest circulation of all Hymnals.

5. *The Hymnal Companion.* Edited by the Rev. Edward H. Bickersteth, and published by Sampson Low, Marston, Searle, and Rivington. The revised and enlarged edition of this excellent Hymnal contains 550 hymns.

List of Hymnals collated.

6. *Church Hymnal.* Published in 1876 by permission of the General Synod of the Church of Ireland. This admirable collection has obtained a very wide circulation.

7. *Hymns for Divine Service.* Approved and sanctioned by the Episcopal Synod of the Church in Scotland. It contains 236 hymns, and is published by Grant and Son, Edinburgh. This Hymnal may be accounted as the general exponent of the Scottish Episcopal Church.

8. *The Parish Hymnal.* Published by Bell and Daldy in 1873. Contains 222 hymns.

9. *The Church Psalter and Hymn-book.* Re-arranged in 1864 by the Rev. William Mercer, and generally known, therefore, as Mercer's Hymnal; is published by Nisbet and Co., and contains 591 hymns.

10. *The Year of Praise.* Edited by the late Dean Alford, and published by Strahan in 1867. Contains 326 hymns for Sundays and Holy-days of the Christian Year.

11. *The Canterbury Hymnal.* Selected and arranged by the Rev. R. H. Baynes, and published by Houlston and Wright. It contains 285 hymns.

12. *A Church Psalter and Hymnal.* Edited by the Rev. Edward Harland, and published, with an Appendix, in 1875, by Routledge and Sons. It contains 584 hymns.

List of Hymnals collated. xv

13. *The New Church Hymn-book.* Edited by the late Rev. Charles Kemble, and published by Shaw and Co. The new edition of 1873 contains 510 hymns.

14. *The New Metre Hymnal.* Founded on Psalms and Hymns; edited as early as 1836 by Rev. W. J. Hall. This Hymnal, published by Rivingtons in 1875, contains 202 hymns.

15. *Hymnal Noted.* An exponent of the Ritualists, was originally published by G. J. Palmer. A revised and greatly enlarged edition, with Supplement and Appendix, containing 588 hymns, was printed by Home and Macdonald, Edinburgh, in 1882.

16. *The Hymnal*, edited by the Rev. R. R. Chope, was published by W. Mackenzie, London, and contains 300 hymns.

17. *Psalms and Hymns, together with Hymns for Mission Services.* Published by the Religious Tract Society. Contains 258 hymns.

18. *Hymns for Public Worship.* Published by the Society for Promoting Christian Knowledge. The new and enlarged edition contains 490 hymns.

19. *Hymns for Christian Worship.* Published by the Religious Tract Society. Contains 500 hymns.

20. *A Hymnal for use in the English Church.* Published by Mozley and Smith in 1879. Contains 260 hymns.

xvi   *List of Hymnals collated.*

21. *The Church Hymnal.* Published by Bell and Daldy. The new edition of 1870 contains 289 hymns.

22. *The Daily Service Hymnal.* Published by Rivingtons in 1864. Contains 306 hymns.

23. *A Selection of Psalms and Hymns for the Public Service of the Church of England.* Published by James Nisbet and Co. in 1868. Contains 421 hymns.

24. *The Church and Home Metrical Psalter and Hymnal.* Edited by the Rev. William Windle, and published by Routledge and Sons. Contains 547 hymns.

25. *Introits and Hymns: adapted to the Seasons of the Christian Year.* Published by Joseph Masters in 1870. Contains 194 hymns.

26. *Common Praise: for use in the Church of England.* Published by the Church of England Book Society. The new edition of 1882 contains 822 hymns.

27. *The Sarum Hymnal*—edited by Earl Nelson and others—was published in 1868 by Simpkin, Marshall, and Co. It contains 320 hymns, and was founded on the Salisbury Hymn-book.

28. *The Anglican Hymn-book.* Edited by the Rev. R. Singleton and E. G. Monk. Published by Simpkin, Marshall, and Co. in 1871. Contains 404 hymns.

29. *The Book of Praise Hymnal.* Chiefly taken from the *Book of Praise* by Sir Roundell Palmer (Lord

List of Hymnals collated. xvii

Selborne). The Hymnal was compiled by that eminent hymnologist in 1867, and contains 320 hymns. It is published by Macmillan and Co.

30. *Hymns for the Church and Home.* Edited by the Rev. W. Fleming Stevenson. Published by Henry King and Co. in 1873. It contains 652 hymns.

31. *A Selection of Hymns suited to the Services of the Church of England.* Edited by the late Rev. Hugh Stowell. Published by Powlson and Sons, Manchester. A recent edition, published with a Supplement in 1877, contains 489 hymns.

32. *The Parochial Psalter and Hymn-book.* Edited by Rev. J. Robinson. Published by S. Lucas, Weber, and Co. The new and enlarged edition of 1883 contains 546 hymns.

33. *Songs of Grace and Glory.* Edited by Rev. C. B. Snepp. Published by J. Nisbet and Co. in 1871. The edition of 1880 contains 1094 hymns.

34. *The Temple Church Hymnal.* Published in 1869 by Metzler and Co. Contains 321 hymns.

35. *Hymnologia Christiana: or Psalms and Hymns selected and arranged in the order of the Christian Seasons.* By Rev. B. H. Kennedy. Published by Longman, Green, and Co. Contains 1500 hymns.

36. *Psalms and Hymns for Public Worship.* Edited by the late Rev. John Hampden Gurney and others. This admirable Hymnal contains 300 hymns.

37. *The Hymnary: a Book of Church Song.* Edited by the Rev. W. Cooke and Rev. B. Webb. Published by Novello, Ewer, and Co. The 1876 edition contains 646 hymns.

38. *Hymns for the Church of England.* Published in 1874. Contains 226 hymns.

39. *The Book of Common Praise.* Published in 1872 by J. T. Hayes. Contains 208 hymns.

40. *Lyra Britannica.* Edited by the Rev. Charles Rogers. Published by Longmans and Co. in 1867. Contains 660 hymns.

41. *Hymnal of the Protestant Episcopal Churches in the United States of America.* Was published in America in 1872, and contains 520 hymns. 'By the Bishops, the Clergy, and the Laity of the Protestant Episcopal Church in the United States, held A.D. 1871, it was resolved that this Hymnal be authorised for use.'

42. *Select Hymns for Church and Home.* Edited by the Rev. Robert Brown-Borthwick. Published in 1871 by Edmonston and Douglas, Edinburgh. It contains 168 hymns.

43. *Hymns for the Church Catholic.* Edited by the Rev. J. B. Whiting. Published in 1882 by Hodder and Stoughton. It contains 510 hymns.

44. *Psalms and Hymns for the Church, School, and Home.* Edited by the Rev. D. T. Barry. Published by W. Mackenzie. The latest edition of this excellent Hymnal contains 471 hymns.

List of Hymnals collated. xix

45. *Hymns for the Cathedral and Collegiate Church, Isle of Cumbrae.* Founded upon *Hymns Ancient and Modern.* Was published in 1876, and contains 561 hymns.

46. *Hymnal of St. John the Evangelist and St. Margaret's, Aberdeen.* Published by Brown and Co., Aberdeen, in 1870. Contains 255 hymns.

47. *Psalms and Hymns.* Edited by the Rev. T. B. Morrell, D.D., Coadjutor-Bishop of Edinburgh, and the Right Rev. W. W. How, Bishop of Bedford. Published by William Wells and Gardner, London. The 200th thousand was issued in 1866, and contained 258 hymns.

48. *The New Zealand Hymnal.* Published in 1872 by William Collins and Company. Contains 307 hymns.

49. *Hymns fitted to the Order of Common Prayer.* Published in 1869 by Hamilton, Adams, and Co. Contains 267 hymns.

50. *Psalms and Hymns for Divine Worship.* Published in 1875 by James Nisbet and Co. Contains 521 hymns.

51. *English Hymnology.* By the Rev. L. Coutier Biggs. Published by Mozleys in 1873.

52. *The Westminster Abbey Hymn-book.* Edited by the Rev. John Troutbeck. Published in 1883 by Novello, Ewer, and Co. This recent collection contains 400 hymns.

CHAPTER I.

History of Ancient and Mediaeval Hymnology.

OLD TESTAMENT HYMNOLOGY.

'The morning stars sang together, and all the sons of God shouted for joy' at the creation of the world, and since that time songs of praise have never ceased to ascend from earth to Heaven. In Eden there was the melody of grateful hearts, but when our first parents fell from primeval innocence, thus bringing 'death into the world, and all our woe, with loss of Eden,' then must the song of the human heart have been one of sorrow and sadness. From the Fall to the Bondage in Egypt the ear catches no sound of jubilant song.

'The first wave of promise which flowed in to cover the first wave of sin must have found its response in the heart of man; but after the first universal hymn of Eden was broken, and the music of creation fell into a minor, whilst the wail of human sin and sorrow ran across all its harmonies, a long silence reigns in the hymn-book of the Church universal; and through all the records of violence and judgment from the flood and the ark—from patriarchal tent and Egyptian kingdom—the only song which has reached us is the wail of a murderer echoing the curse of Cain. We feel sure, however, that those who walked in the light, like Enoch and Abraham, must have had their hearts kindled into music. But from the green earth rising out of the flood; from the shadow of the great oak at Mamre; from the fountains and valleys and upland pastures of the Promised Land, where the tents of the patriarchs rose amid their flocks; from the prisons and palaces of Egypt, we catch no sound of sacred song. So far the stream flows for us underground.'

The first hymn recorded in the Sacred Word is the song of victory sung by Moses and the Israelites by the shores of the Red Sea, as the utterance of a national thanksgiving for deliverance from their Egyptian oppressors. 'Then sang Moses and the children of Israel this song unto the Lord, and spake, saying, I will sing unto the Lord, for He hath triumphed gloriously: the horse and his rider hath He thrown into the sea.'

That song of victory hath never ceased to be sung, and the grand chant of the Mighty Deliverer is still echoed by the celestial shores of the sea of glass, for the ransomed of the Lord 'sing the song of Moses the servant of God, and the song of the Lamb, saying, Great and marvellous are Thy works, Lord God Almighty; just and true are Thy ways, Thou King of saints.' In the days of the Judges, the triumphal song of Deborah and Barak is a strain of lofty poetic beauty: 'Praise ye the Lord for the avenging of Israel, when the people willingly offered themselves. Hear, O ye kings; give ear, O ye princes; I, even I, will sing unto the Lord; I will sing praise to the Lord God of Israel. Lord, when Thou wentest out of Seir, when Thou marchedst out of the field of Edom, the earth trembled, and the heavens dropped, the clouds also dropped water. The mountains melted from before the Lord, even that Sinai from before the Lord God of Israel. . . . The kings came and fought; then fought the kings of Canaan in Taanach by the waters of Megiddo; they took no gain of money. They fought from heaven; the stars in their courses fought against Sisera. The river of Kishon swept them away, that ancient river, the river Kishon. O my soul, thou hast trodden down strength. . . . So let all Thine enemies perish, O Lord: but let them that love Him be as the sun when he goeth forth in his might.'

The hymn of Hannah is the prototype of the Virgin Mary's 'Magnificat,' while the Book of Job may fitly be described as a hymn of immortality. David's touching lamentation when Saul and Jonathan were slain on the mountains of Gilboa is one of the most plaintive dirges ever written: 'The beauty of Israel is slain upon thy high places: how are the mighty fallen! Tell it not in Gath, publish it not in the streets of Askelon; lest the daughters of the Philistines rejoice, lest the daughters of the uncircumcised triumph. Ye mountains of Gilboa, let there be no dew, neither let there be rain upon you, nor fields of offerings: for there the shield of the mighty is vilely cast away, the shield of Saul, as though he had not been anointed with oil. From the blood of the slain, from the fat of the mighty, the bow of Jonathan turned not back, and the sword of Saul returned not empty. Saul and Jonathan were lovely and pleasant in their lives, and in their death they were not divided: they were swifter than eagles, they were stronger than lions. . . . How are the mighty fallen in the midst of the battle! O Jonathan, thou wast slain in thine high places. I am distressed for thee, my brother Jonathan: very pleasant hast thou been unto me: thy love to me was wonderful, passing the love of women. How are the mighty fallen, and the weapons of war perished!'

The Psalms of King David, the sweet singer of Israel, form the first hymnal of the universal Church, while Solomon's mystical Song of Songs will receive its full significance at the great marriage-supper of the Lamb, when Christ can say to the Church Triumphant, 'Arise, my love, my fair one, and come away; the winter is past, the rain is over and gone; and the time of the singing is come.'

'The Songs of Zion,' though not heard by the ears of the oppressors, were deeply graven on the hearts of the Jewish exiles, as they sat weeping by the waters of Babylon. After the Babylonian Captivity, the ransomed of the Lord returned with gladness to the land of their fathers, and came to Zion with songs and everlasting joy upon their heads. At the dedication of the restored wall of Jerusalem, 'the singers sang loud, and rejoiced, for God had made them rejoice with great joy; the wives also and the children rejoiced, so that the joy of Jerusalem was heard afar off.'

In exalted strains of glowing imagery, the prophets of old sang the glories of the new and brighter day of the Messianic kingdom, when 'the Sun of Righteousness' would rise ' with healing in His wings.'

These prophetic strains were but the prelude to the celestial anthem sung on the first Christmas morn by the pastures of Bethlehem, where, in the exquisite language of St. Luke, 'there were in the same country shepherds abiding in the field, keeping watch over their flock by night. And lo, the angel of the Lord came upon them, and the glory of the Lord shone round about them : and they were sore afraid. And the angel said unto them, Fear not : for, behold, I bring you good tidings of great joy, which shall be to all people. For unto you is born this day, in the city of David, a Saviour, which is Christ the Lord. . . . And suddenly there was with the angel a multitude of the heavenly host praising God, and saying, Glory to God in the highest, and on earth peace, good-will toward men.'

NEW TESTAMENT HYMNOLOGY.

The first recorded Christian hymn is the 'Magnificat,' sung by the Virgin Mary in the home of her cousin Elisabeth ; the second is the 'Benedictus,' sung by Zacharias at the circumcision of his son, John the Baptist; while the third is the 'Nunc Dimittis,' sung by the aged Simeon in the courts of the Temple.

This first triad of Christian hymns, sung in connection with the birth of Christ, are but varied strains of the great Song of Redemption, and they have fittingly been retained in the daily services of the Anglican Church. Paul and Silas sang praises to God at midnight in the prison of Philippi. In the Revelation of St. John the ear catches sweet fragments of celestial songs, chanted by the general assembly and church of the first-born: 'They sing the song of Moses the servant of God, and the song of the Lamb, saying, Great and marvellous are Thy works, Lord God Almighty; just and true are Thy ways, Thou King of saints.' 'The four-and-twenty elders fell down before the Lamb, and they sang a new song, saying, Thou art worthy to take the book, . . . for Thou wast slain, and hast redeemed us to God by Thy blood out of every kindred, and tongue, and nation, and people.' And many angels, 'ten thousand times ten thousand, and thousands of thousands, say with a loud voice, Worthy is the Lamb that was slain, to receive power, and riches, and wisdom, and strength, and honour, and glory, and blessing.'

The true fountain of Christian song is to be found on Calvary, and from this fountain has flowed forth a never-failing stream of triumphant praise which from age to age has unceasingly refreshed and gladdened the Church of God. Of this flood of song it may be said, 'There is a river, the streams whereof shall make glad the city of God, the holy place of the tabernacles of the Most High.' 'The wilderness and the solitary place shall be glad for them; and the desert shall rejoice, and blossom as the rose; for in the wilderness shall waters break out, and streams in the desert.'

LITURGY HYMNOLOGY.

The second triad of Christian hymns are three songs of noblest praise dating from a very early period, and these have been incorporated into our Liturgy. The 'Tersanctus' or 'Thrice Holy' is the triumphal hymn in the Communion Service, beginning 'Holy, holy, holy, Lord God of Hosts,' etc. It is found in all the earliest Liturgies. Secondly, the 'Gloria in Excelsis'—'Glory be to God on high, and on earth peace'—is a glorious hymn of Greek origin, and appears as early as the fourth century. It is probably the composition of some anonymous Greek hymnist, and appears to have been highly esteemed throughout the Eastern Church.

The 'Te Deum laudamus.' is a magnificent hymn of triumphant praise, familiar to English ears as a grand canticle of the daily service. It holds the same position in the Western Church as the 'Gloria in Excelsis' does in the Eastern. The 'Te Deum' is generally ascribed to St. Ambrose and St. Augustine, and would thus date from the last part of the fourth century. It probably, however, sprang from some earlier Oriental morning hymn, or grew out of fragments of sacred songs sung in the Eastern Church in very ancient times.

Several hymns by Greek anonymous writers have come down to us from early ages. Amongst them are hymns on the Nativity, Baptism, and Resurrection of Christ, and an Oriental doxology as follows: 'God is my hope, Christ is my refuge, the Holy Spirit is my vesture: Holy Trinity, glory to Thee.'

8   *Ancient and Mediæval Hymnology.*

Clement of Alexandria is the earliest Christian hymn-writer whose name has come down to us. He was a teacher at Alexandria; but in consequence of a persecution of Christians he was obliged to, flee for his life. Probably about 200 A.D. he composed his 'Hymn of the Saviour Christ,' which for the most part consists of a catalogue of Scriptural images applied to Christ. These images must indeed have been very precious to him, for, writing amid terrible perils, he says, 'Daily martyrs are burnt, beheaded, and crucified before our eyes.'

EARLY HYMNISTS.

CLEMENT—EPHRAEM—GREGORY.

CLEMENT OF ALEXANDRIA—DIED A.D. 217.

Clemens Alexandrinus, one of the earliest Christian hymn-writers, was born at Athens about the middle of the second century. In philosophy he was first a Stoic and then an Eclectic. He spent much of his life at Alexandria—hence his name—and there he was converted to Christianity. He became a teacher and presbyter of the Alexandrian Church.

Clement was a voluminous writer, his works being for the most part on Christian evidences, and they are highly commended by the Christian Fathers, especially by Eusebius and Jerome. Of his hymns the best known is that beginning 'Shepherd of tender youth,' a free rendering of Clement's Greek verses.

EPHRAEM SYRUS—DIED 381 A.D.

Ephraem Syrus, or Ephraim the Syrian, a monk of Mesopotamia, one of the earliest Christian hymn-writers, was born near Nisibis, in Mesopotamia, in the beginning of the fourth century. Several of his hymns have of late years been translated from the Syriac, in which language the originals were written, and appeared in Dr. Burgess's *Hymns of the Ancient Syrian Churches*. He lived more than a century after the days of Clement of Alexandria, and is the next hymn-writer whose name is known. The chief hymns of this writer that have come down to us are, 'The Children in Paradise,' 'On Palm Sunday,' 'On the Triumphal Entry of Jesus into Jerusalem,' 'The Star of Bethlehem,' 'Lament of a Father on the death of his little Son.'

Sweet is the sacred singing of this monk of Mesopotamia; and the following golden saying of his ought to be kept in remembrance: 'In the very moment when thou prayest a treasure is laid up for thee in heaven.'

GREGORY—326-389 A.D.

Gregory of Nazianzus is so named from Nazianzus, a town of Cappadocia, where he was born in 326. His father was Bishop of the place, and his mother was a pious lady named Nonna. Gregory rose to be Bishop of Constantinople, and amid countless heresies continued steadfastly to preach the Deity of Christ. He died at his native place in 389. Several of his hymns, written among numerous toils and troubles, have come down to us; prominent amongst them are a 'Hymn to Christ,' 'An Evening Hymn,' and 'Light in Adversity.'

St. Ambrose and the Ambrosian Hymns.

Ambrose, the eminent ecclesiastic of the fourth century, was born at Treves, in Gaul, in 340 A.D. He was educated at Rome, and studied law in Milan. He was raised to be Prefect of Liguria, and distinguished himself for his talent and justice. Renouncing secular pursuits, he was, by universal consent, promoted to be Bishop of Milan,—an office in which he enjoyed both celebrity and considerable personal authority. In the great Arian controversy of his day Ambrose stoutly contended for the purity of Christian doctrine, and boldly refused the request of the Empress Justina, when she asked the use of one church in Milan where Arian doctrine might be taught. When, moreover, Theodosius, Emperor of the East, had permitted the massacre of the Thessalonians, the Bishop denied to the imperial offender the privileges of the Church, and so highly was Ambrose esteemed by the people that the multitude supported him in his opposition to the imperial will. He died at Milan in 397, and was buried in the great church which still bears the name of 'Basilica Ambrosiana.' The hymns of Ambrose mark a new stage in the history of sacred song. Ephraem the Syrian wrote in Syriac, a language akin to the old Hebrew, in which the Israelites chanted the Song of Moses by the shores of the Red Sea; while Clement of

Early Hymnists.

Alexandria, Gregory of Nazianzus, and the earliest hymnists of the Eastern Church, wrote in Greek, the language of Evangelists and Prophets. The Ambrosian hymns, on the other hand, were the first written in Latin, and thus in them sacred song passed from the original languages of the Inspired Word, and henceforth in the Western Church hymns were written in Latin. Thus the stream of psalmody in the fourth century flowed from the tongue of Homer, Plato, and the New Testament into the stately Roman, the language of Virgil and Cicero. On this account the Latin hymns of the fourth and fifth century form a link of connection between the classical Greek of the early Christian Church and the Latin hymnology of the Middle Ages.

'In the days of Ambrose the Latin language had not gathered around it the spiritual and ecclesiastical associations of centuries. It had to come into the Church fresh from the market, the battle-field, the court of justice, with no sacred laver of inspiration to baptize it from the stains and dust of secular or sinful employment. Yet there is a calm and steady glow in these early Latin hymns, a straightforward plainness of speech, and an unconscious force, which grow on you wonderfully as you become more acquainted with them. If they have not the sublime simplicity of a faith which sees visions, and leaves it to fancy to scatter flowers, or the fervency of an outburst of solitary devotion, the regular beauty of Greek art, or the imagination and homely pathos of Teutonic sacred ballads, they have a Roman majesty of their own, the majesty of a national anthem, the subdued fire of the battle-song of a disciplined army. The imperial dignity of the great language of law and of war has passed into them ; they are the grand national anthems of the Church militant, and their practical plainness, their healthy objective life, are bracing as mountain air.' The Ambrosian period of hymnology embraces the Latin hymns of the fourth and fifth centuries. Amongst the conspicuous hymnists of this era were Ambrose, Augustine, Hilary, and Prudentius.

Twelve hymns have been attributed to Ambrose, and although these hymns are austere in simplicity and devoid of rhyme, yet their unadorned sublimity is very striking. Archbishop Trench says of Ambrose's hymns that 'although his almost austere simplicity seems cold and displeasing after the rich sentiment of some later writers, yet we cannot but observe how truly these poems belonged to their time and to the circumstances under which they were produced; how suitably the faith which was in actual conflict with and was just triumphing over the powers of this world found its utterance in hymns such as these, wherein is no softness, perhaps little tenderness, but a rock-like firmness, the old Roman stoicism transmuted and glorified into that nobler Christian courage which encountered and at length overcame the world.'

The following are well-known renderings from St. Ambrose's hymns :—

1. Above the starry spheres.   Jam Christus astra ascenderat.
2. Before the ending of the day.   Te lucis ante terminum.

3. Come, Holy Ghost, who ever one. — Nunc Sancte nobis Spiritus.
4. Creator of the stars of night. — Conditor alme siderum.
5. Jesu, the virgins crown do Thou. — Jesu corona virginum.
6. Light's glittering morn bedecks the sky. — Aurora lucis rutilat.
7. Now that the daylight fills the sky. — Jam lucis orto sidere.
8. O Christ, who art the light and day. — Christe qui lux es et dies.
9. O God, Thy soldiers' great reward. — Deus tuorum militum.
10. O Jesu, Lord of light and grace. — Splendor paternae gloriae.
11. O Lord, most high eternal King. — Aeterne Rex altissime.
12. O Trinity, most blessed light. — O lux beata Trinitas.
13. Redeemer of the nations, come. — Veni, Redemptor gentium.

All the above are attributed to St. Ambrose, but the authorship of some is doubtful. One of them, viz., 'Creator of the stars of night,' has attained a place among the 325 Standard Hymns, being number 259. Another Standard Hymn, 239, 'Hark! a thrilling voice is sounding,' belongs to the Ambrosian era.

AURELIUS CLEMENS PRUDENTIUS.
BORN 348—DIED ABOUT 413 A.D.

Prudentius, the early Christian hymnist, was born in Spain in 348 A.D. He became in course of time a civil and criminal judge, and was subsequently promoted by the Emperor Honorius to be the head of the imperial bodyguard. In the fifty-seventh year of his age his mind seems to have passed through some remarkable experiences, for he suddenly realised that the honours of the world could not satisfy the yearnings of his soul. Accordingly he renounced his post of dignity, and returning to his native land devoted himself forthwith to religious works and the composition of sacred songs. His character is perhaps too highly commended by Barth, who says of Prudentius, 'Poeta eximius, eruditissimus et sanctissimus scriptor; nemo divinius de rebus Christianis unquam scripsit.' (An excellent poet, a most learned and pious writer; no one has ever written on Christian matters in a more sublime strain.)

Archbishop Trench considers that Prudentius was by nature possessed of the gift of sacred poetry, and accounts for the reputed impurity of his Latinity by the fact that the poet tried to charge the Latin used by people of a sunken taste with the purity of Christian thought. He died about 413, and was therefore a contemporary of St. Augustine and St. Ambrose.

The two renderings from Prudentius that are most widely known are—

    1. Earth has many a noble city.   O sola magnarum urbium.
    2. Of the Father's love begotten.   Corde natus ex Parentis.

The latter has attained a place among Standard Hymns, being No. 227.

The three chief hymnists of the Ambrosian era—that is, of the fourth and fifth centuries—were St. Ambrose, Prudentius, and St. Hilary, Bishop of Poitiers, who died in 367 A.D.

ANTE-MEDIÆVAL ERA.

GREEK HYMNISTS.

The chief Greek hymnists of this period are SS. Andrew of Crete, Cosmas, John Damascene, Stephen, Joseph of the Studium, and Metrophanes of Smyrna.

ST. ANDREW OF CRETE was a Greek hymn-writer of the eighth century. He was a native of Damascus, and rose to be Archbishop of Crete, from which diocese he receives his name. His best-known work is the excellent Lenten hymn rendered by Dr. Neale—

Christian! dost thou see them? Οὐ γὰρ βλέπεις τοὺς ταράττοντας.

This has attained to the second rank in Standard Hymns. (See Hymn 205.)

ST. COSMAS—DIED 760 A.D.

Χριστὸς γεννᾶται, δοξάσατε.
Christ is born! Tell forth His fame!
Christ from heaven! His love proclaim!

This hymn for Christmas Day is Dr. Neale's translation from the Greek of St. Cosmas, and appeared in 1862 in his *Hymns of the Eastern Church.*

St. Cosmas of Jerusalem, surnamed the Melodist, was born at Jerusalem about the end of the seventh or beginning of the eighth century. He is regarded as the most learned of the Greek Fathers, and the second best poet of the Greek Church. Left an orphan in youth, he was adopted by the father of John of Damascus, and the two foster-brothers being brought up together cemented a lifelong friendship. They incited each other in hymn-writing, and in friendly rivalry undertook to write on the same Scriptural subjects. Both became monks of Mar Saba, and subsequently, while John Damascene was ordained a priest of Jerusalem, Cosmas was consecrated Bishop of Maiuma near Gaza. For fifteen years he discharged the duties of the See with faithfulness and holy zeal, and departed this life about 760 A.D. His memory is cherished in the Greek Church, and in a preface to his life occurs the following laudatory couplet :—

> Where perfect sweetness dwells is Cosmas gone :
> But his sweet lays to cheer the Church live on.

His chief works on sacred song comprise Canons on the Nativity, Epiphany, the Transfiguration and Purification. His Canon for Christmas Day is generally regarded as his masterpiece, and may justly be preferred to the Canon of John Damascene on the same subject. The above Christmas hymn is the first ode of Cosmas's Christmas Canon.

> Χορὸς 'Ισραήλ.
>
> The choirs of ransomed Israel,
> The Red Sea's passage o'er,
> Upraised the hymn of triumph
> Upon the further shore.

This hymn is a translation by Dr. Neale from the Greek of St. Cosmas, and is indeed a cento from the four first odes of Cosmas's Canon on the Transfiguration.

St. John Damascene—died about 780.

'Αναστάσεως ἡμέρα.

'Tis the Day of Resurrection, From Death to Life Eternal,
Earth! tell it out abroad! From this world to the sky,
The Passover of gladness, Our Christ hath brought us over
The Passover of God! With hymns of victory.

This 'glorious old hymn of victory,' as it is fitly named, is a translation by Dr. Neale from the Greek of John of Damascus, and first appeared in 1862 in Neale's *Hymns of the Eastern Church*. St. John Damascene, or John of Damascus, was born about the beginning of the eighth century, and, according to Gibbon, was the last of the Fathers of the Greek Church. To him belongs the high honour of being unanimously esteemed the greatest poet of the Eastern Church. Unfortunately little is known of his life. He was born at Damascus of good family, and early distinguished himself in eloquence and philosophy. For some time he held office under the Caliph of Bagdad. He retired to the monastery of Mar Saba, situated in the valley of the Kedron, midway between Jerusalem and the Dead Sea, and there enjoyed the society of Cosmas and his nephew Stephanos, both sons of the monastery. At a comparatively late period of life he was ordained a priest of the Church of Jerusalem. During his life raged the bitter controversy respecting the use of icons or images. John, by his learned and eloquent writings, stoutly opposed the Iconoclasts or Image-breakers, and proved himself to be a most able advocate of images. In consequence of his able defence of icons, he has received the title of 'The Doctor of Christian Art.' He died at Mar Saba, probably about 780 A.D., and his tomb is still pointed out in the monastery.

As a sacred poet his chief works consist of three great Canons, respectively for Easter, Ascension, and St. Thomas's Sunday. A Canon on sacred song is a term employed in the Greek Church to denote a long poem consisting of nine odes or canticles. John Damascene's Canon for Easter Day has from its general excellence been named the 'Golden Canon' and the 'Queen of Canons.' The above hymn is the first ode of this celebrated Canon, and is a hymn of victory designed to be sung at the first hour of Easter morn.

Ἀσωμεν πάντες λάοι.
Come, ye faithful, raise the strain
Of triumphant gladness!
God hath brought His Israel
Into joy from sadness.

This hymn for St. Thomas's Sunday is a translation by Dr. Neale from the Greek of St. John Damascene, and appeared in 1862 in his *Hymns of the Eastern Church*. The original forms the first ode in John Damascene's Canon for St. Thomas's Sunday.

Τὰς ἑδρὰς τὰς αἰωνίας.

Those eternal bowers	Who may hope to gain them
Man hath never trod,	After weary fight?
Those unfading flowers	Who at length attain them
Round the throne of God :	Clad in robes of white?

This sweet hymn for 'All Saints' Day' is Dr. Neale's rendering from the Greek of St. John of Damascus,

Ante-Mediæval Era. 19

and appeared in 1862 in *Hymns of the Eastern Church*. The original was probably composed in the monastery of Mar Saba in the third quarter of the eighth century, and is therefore eleven centuries old. It has very nearly attained a place among Standard Hymns.

'The Day of Resurrection' has attained a place among 'third rank' of Standard Hymns. (See Hymn 223.)

St. Stephen the Sabaite—725-794 A.D.

St. Stephen the Sabaite was a Greek hymn-writer of the eighth century. He was nephew to John Damascene, and spent all his life in the monastery of Mar Saba, situated in the valley of the Kedron, about ten miles from Jerusalem. His best-known hymn, rendered by Dr. Neale, is—

Art thou weary, art thou languid?   Κόπον τε καὶ κάματον.

It has attained a place in the first rank of Standard Hymns. (See Hymn 101.)

St. Joseph of the Studium—9th Century.

> Stars of the morning so gloriously bright,
> Filled with celestial resplendence and light.

This hymn, known as 'The Stars of the morning,' is a cento by Dr. Neale founded on some Greek verses in the 'Canon of the Bodiless Ones' by St. Joseph of the Studium. It first appeared in 1862 in Neale's *Hymns of the Eastern Church*.

The Canon referred to was appointed to be sung

once in eight weeks in the Abbey Church of the Studium, the chief monastery in Constantinople, in honour of the angels.

St. Joseph, the hymn-writer of the Greek Church, was a native of Sicily. He became a monk of the Studium during the ninth century. He composed a great number of hymns, but only a few renderings are familiar to the Anglican Church.

THE RETURN HOME.

Safe home, safe home in port,   And only not a wreck:
Rent cordage, shattered deck,   But oh! the joy upon the shore
Torn sails, provisions short,   To tell our voyage perils o'er.

This hymn, by Dr. Neale, was suggested by some Greek verses of St. Joseph of the Studium, and appeared in *Hymns of the Eastern Church*, 1862.

Τῶν ἱερῶν ἀθλοφόρων.
Let our choir new anthems raise,
Wake the morn with gladness;
God Himself to joy and praise
Turns the martyrs' sadness.

This hymn is a cento by Dr. Neale founded on the Greek of St. Joseph of the Studium, and appeared in 1862 in *Hymns of the Eastern Church*. The original is from a long Canon for SS. Timothy and Maura, a deacon of Constantinople and his wife, both of whom suffered martyrdom. The story of their sufferings is beautifully told in Charles Kingsley's *Santa Maura*.

Ante-Mediæval Era.

Metrophanes of Smyrna—died about 910 a.d.

Metrophanes of Smyrna was Bishop of the town from which he takes his name. He is best known by eight Canons which he composed in honour of the Holy Trinity. From one of those Canons Dr. Neale made the well-known rendering—

O Unity of threefold light.   Τριφεγγὴς Μονὰς Θεαρχική.

LATIN HYMNISTS.

The commencement of the Middle Ages proper is almost coincident with the Norman Conquest of England. Before, however, the consolidation of the Feudal System, the introduction of Gothic art, the campaigns of the Crusades, and the days of chivalry—all distinguishing features of that period—there elapsed some centuries of struggle for supremacy between the peoples of the decaying Roman Empire and the more modern races. This era of strife, which may be regarded as a borderland between the Roman Empire and the Middle Ages, produced many lyric poets and hymnists, whose compositions are remarkable rather for rich boldness than for peaceful sublimity. Amongst the writers of sacred song the most distinguished in the Western Church were Gregory the Great, Venantius Fortunatus, the Venerable Bede, and St. Theodulph.

Gregory the Great—550-604 a.d.

Gregory the Great was born of noble family in Rome in 550 A.D. He was possessed of distinguished talents, and from being a senator was promoted by the Emperor to be Prefect of the Eternal City. The bent of his mind was religious, and, longing for spiritual retirement, he became a monk, and thus sought to withdraw from public life. On the death of Pelagius, Gregory by general consent was raised to be Pope, and for fourteen years discharged the duties of that high office with earnestness and ability.

The best-known rendering from Gregory is—

Father of mercies, hear.   Audi, benigne Conditor.

The 'Veni, Creator Spiritus,' so excellently rendered by Bishop Cosin, and retained in the Prayer-Book Ordination Service, is thought by some to be by Gregory :—

Come, Holy Ghost, our souls inspire,   Veni, Creator Spiritus,
And lighten with celestial fire.   Mentes tuorum visita.

This magnificent hymn is ascribed by Mone in his *Hymni Latini Medii Ævi* to Gregory the Great, although, as has been pointed out, it is popularly ascribed to Charlemagne, although without good authority.

VENANTIUS FORTUNATUS—530-609 A.D.

Venantius Fortunatus, an Italian by birth, was born in the province of Venetia in 530. His hymns form the connecting link between the hymnology of the Ambrosian period and that of the Middle Ages. He seems to have distinguished himself early in poetry and oratory, and so extensive was his learning that he obtained among his contemporaries the epithet of 'scholasticissimus.' His youth and early manhood were spent in gaiety and pleasure; but while making a pilgrimage, in the thirty-fifth year of his age, to the tomb of the holy Martin of Tours, he was aroused to a religious fervour which had a marked influence upon his future career. He obtained the friendship of the celebrated Gregory, Bishop of Tours, and that also of the holy and accomplished Queen Rhadegund, who had just then founded a large monastic institution at Poitiers. Through the influence of these two distinguished persons Fortunatus was induced to enter the priesthood, and in the sixtieth year of his age he was promoted to be Bishop of Poitiers. The following renderings from the Latin of Fortunatus are best known :—

The royal banners forward go,	Vexilla regis prodeunt,
The Cross shines forth in mystic glow.	Fulget Crucis mysterium.

This favourite hymn on the Passion of our Lord is a translation by Dr. Neale from the Latin of Fortunatus. The translator says of it : 'This world-famous hymn, one of the grandest in the treasury of the Latin Church, was composed by Fortunatus on occasion of the reception of certain relics by S. Gregory of Tours and S. Rhadegund, previously to the consecration of a church at Poitiers. It is therefore strictly and primarily a processional hymn, though very naturally afterwards adapted to Passion-tide.' It will be noticed that the Cross is here honoured as the sacred symbol of Christ's victory over death and the grave, while the earlier Christian hymns regard it with horror as the instrument of the Saviour's Passion and ignominy, and therefore speak of it as the accursed tree. In the Roman Breviary the last two verses of Fortunatus's hymn are replaced by these words: 'Hail, Cross, only hope in this season of the Passion! give to the pious justice, to the guilty give pardon.' The banners of the Cross are by some understood to mean the scourge, the crown of thorns, the nails, and the spear, the emblems of the Saviour's Passion.

Sing, my tongue, the glorious battle,	Pange, lingua, gloriosi
With completed victory rife.	Proelium certaminis.

The above hymn is a translation by Dr. Neale from the Latin of Fortunatus. The translator regards this as worthy to take rank in the very first class of Latin hymns, and thinks that its original beauty has suffered from ill-judged corrections in the Roman Breviary. Another translation of the Latin stanzas, by the Rev. Francis Pott, appears in *Church Hymns*, and commences

>Sing, my tongue, the Saviour's glory,
>Tell His triumph far and wide.

Venerable Bede—672-735 A.D.

The Venerable Bede, one of the brightest ornaments of the Anglo-Saxon Church, was born at Jarrow in 672, and brought up in the monastery of Monk Wearmouth. Subsequently he was appointed head of the Jarrow monastery, where he spent his life in writing hymns and sacred literature. He writes: 'I have used all diligence in the study of the Holy Scriptures, and in the

Ante-Mediæval Era. 25

observance of the conventual rules, and the daily singing in the church: it was ever my joy to learn or to teach or to write something.'

The last days of his life show what great influence the ancient hymns of the Church had on Christian men during that period. In his last sickness 'he lived joyfully, giving thanks to God day and night, yea, at all hours. . . . Every day he gave lessons to us his pupils, and the rest of his time he occupied in chanting psalms. He sang the words of the apostle Paul. He sang much besides from the Holy Scriptures, and also many Anglo-Saxon hymns. He sang antiphons according to his and our custom, the ancient custom which Ambrose had introduced among the people from the East.' He dictated to a monk a translation of the Gospel of St. John. When the last sentence was finished Bede said, 'Raise my head on thy hand, for it will do me good to sit opposite my sanctuary where I was wont to kneel down to pray.' So he seated himself down on the ground of his cell and sang the Glory to Thee, O God, Father, Son, and Holy Ghost, and when he had named the Holy Ghost he breathed his last breath.' Such was the calm deathbed of Bede eleven centuries ago.

Eleven hymns have been attributed to the Venerable Bede, but doubts exist on the authenticity of these. The following two are best known:—

1. A hymn for martyrs sweetly sing.   Hymnum canentes martyrum.
2. The great forerunner of the morn.   Praecursor altus luminis.

St. Theodulph—died 821 A.D.

St. Theodulph was a Latin hymnist of the ninth century. He was born in Italy, became Abbot of a Benedictine monastery in Florence, and died Bishop of Orleans in 821. The best-known rendering from this author is—

    All glory, laud, and honour.   Gloria, laus, et honor.

This hymn has attained to the first rank of Standard Hymns. (See Hymn 100.)

Godescalcus—died c. 868 A.D.

Few particulars are known of the life of Godescalcus. As a hymn-writer his best known is Dr. Neale's rendering of what is called the 'Alleluiatic Sequence:'

    The strain upraise of joy and praise, Alleluia!
    Cantemus cuncti melodum. Alleluia!

This favourite hymn has attained to the first rank of Standard Hymns. (See Hymn 69.)

St. Fulbert of Chartres—died c. 1029 A.D.

St. Fulbert is one of the hymn-writers of the tenth century. He was educated at Rheims, and became Bishop of Chartres, a town in Brittany about forty miles south-west of Paris. His best-known hymn is that rendered by Robert Campbell in 1850, viz.—

    Ye choirs of New Jerusalem.   Chorus novae Hierusalem.

This has attained a place in the third rank of Standard Hymns. (See Hymn 325.)

Robert II., King of France—972-1031 A.D.

| Come, thou Holy Spirit, come, | Veni, Sancte Spiritus, |
| And from Thy celestial home. | Et emitte coelitus. |

This hymn, known as the 'Golden Sequence,' is a translation from the Latin by the Rev. Edward Caswall. The original is the work of Robert II., King of France, who ascended the throne about 1000 A.D. Archbishop Trench, in his *Sacred Latin Poetry*, describes it as 'the loveliest of all the hymns in the whole circle of Latin poetry.' The hymn refers to the sorrows and troubles of his turbulent reign. This king was in the habit of going frequently to the cathedral of St. Denis, and there in his royal robes, along with the monks, he took part in the singing. According to one authority Robert was a weak-minded king, but others describe him as pious, learned, and musical.

Peter Damiani—988-1072 A.D.

Peter Damiani, a contemporary of Robert II., king of France, and one of the most distinguished hymn-writers of the eleventh century, was born at Ravenna, 1002. He became a pious priest, and rose to be Cardinal Bishop of Ostia and coadjutor to Gregory VII. Late in life he retired to the Abbey of Sta. Croce d'Avellano, and spent the remainder of his life in devotion and sacred song. The way in which he realised the hour of death is shown by a Commendatory Prayer, which he composed as a letter to a dying friend, and which has ever since his day been used in the Roman Church. It thus begins : 'To God I commend thee, beloved brother, and to Him whose creature thou art I commit thee.' His sacred song is described by Dr. Neale as the lovely painting of Damiani. He died in 1072 at the age of seventy.

Amongst his best-known hymns are—

    For the fount of life eternal,   Ad perennis vitae fontem,

a bold translation by Rev. John Dayman. 'The Dies Irae of individual life,' a remarkable piece rendered by Dr. Neale in his *Mediæval Hymns and Sequences*. It begins

    O what terror in thy forethought,
    Ending scene of mortal life,

and is an awful hymn of great force and sublimity. Another rendering in the same collection is the hymn,

    O Cross, whereby the earth is blest,   Crux mundi benedictio,

a piece of great beauty and quaintness.

MEDIÆVAL HYMNS.
GOLDEN ERA.

The twelfth century has aptly been called the 'harvest-field of mediæval hymns,' the Latin hymns of an earlier period being regarded as first-fruits, while those of a later period are after-gleanings. The five great hymnists of this golden era are St. Bernard of Clairvaux, Bernard of Cluny, Adam of St. Victor, Archbishop Hildebert, and Peter the Venerable.

St. Bernard—1091-1153 A.D.

St. Bernard of Clairvaux, whom Luther calls 'the best monk that ever lived,' was son of a nobleman of

Mediæval Hymns.

Burgundy. He became a Cistercian monk, and founded the new monastery of Clairvaux, of which he became Abbot. He died in 1153. Three renderings from St. Bernard have found a place among the Standard Hymns, viz. 'Jesu, the very thought of Thee'—found among first rank hymns,—'O Jesu, King most wonderful,' and 'Jesu! the very thought is sweet'—found in third rank hymns. Other renderings worthy of notice are—

| O Jesu! Thou the beauty art | Jesu! decus angelicum |
| Of angel-worlds above | In aure dulce canticum |

—portion of a Latin poem by St. Bernard of Clairvaux, written about 1140 A.D., and rendered into English by Edward Caswall, M.A., in 1849. It forms Part III. of Hymn 178 in *Hymns Ancient and Modern*. The three parts consist of fifteen stanzas, but as the original poem known as 'Jubilus rhythmicus de nomine Jesu' ('Jubilee rhythm on the name of Jesu') contains forty-eight stanzas, it appears that the three portions of the English hymn include scarcely one-third of the Latin poem.

| Jesu! Thy mercies are untold | Amor, Jesu dulcissimus |
| Through each returning day | |

—portion of St. Bernard's 'Jubilee rhythm on the name of Jesu,' 1140, rendered by Edward Caswall in 1848. It is properly a cento, and the above corresponds with stanza 12 of the original poem. Four of Caswall's well-known hymns are translations from St. Bernard's 'Jubilee rhythm.'

A full account of St. Bernard will be found under Hymn 59, 'Jesu! the very thought of Thee.'

Bernard of Cluny.

Bernard, the celebrated monk of the monastery of Cluny, is accounted one of the five great hymn-writers of the twelfth century. His great work is 'De Contemptu Mundi,' a Latin poem of 3000 lines. A large portion of this poem was translated by Dr. Neale; and portions of this translation form some of our favourite hymns. Three such hymns have attained to the first rank of the Standard Hymns, namely, 'Jerusalem the golden,' 'Brief life is here our portion,' 'For thee, O dear, dear country.' A full account of Bernard and his celebrated Rhythm will be found under Hymn 7, 'Jerusalem the golden.'

> The world is very evil,   Be sober and keep vigil,
> The times are waxing late,   The Judge is at the gate.
> Hora novissima, tempora pessima sunt, vigilemus,
> Ecce minaciter imminet arbiter ille supremus.

This hymn, consisting of ten stanzas of four lines each, includes the opening part of the 'Rhythm of Bernard of Cluny,' translated from the Latin by Dr. Neale. The moral darkness and fearful corruption of the age caused the Cluniac monk to believe that the cup of iniquity was full, and that the day of judgment was nigh at hand. The opening lines of his noble poem 'De Contemptu Mundi' are those given above.

Peter the Venerable—Died 1156 A.D.

Of Bernard's contemporaries, 'Peter the Venerable' was born of a noble family of Auvergne in 1094 A.D. In

1122 he was elected Abbot of Cluny, then in the meridian of its monastic fame. For the long period of thirty-four years he ruled the monastery with gentle sceptre, and it is thought that his talents and personal influence were second only to those of the illustrious St. Bernard. By a strange coincidence these two bright ornaments of the Church of France were contemporaries, so that while Peter the Venerable was the head of Cluny, St. Bernard was Abbot of the neighbouring monastery of Clairvaux. It was Peter who received the excommunicated Abelard into Cluny, and effected a reconciliation between that philosopher and his theological opponent St. Bernard. He also caused the Koran to be translated into Latin for the first time. He wrote many sacred songs, and is accounted one of the five great Latin hymn-writers who adorned the French Church in the first half of the twelfth century.

ARCHBISHOP HILDEBERT—DIED 1133 OR 1134 A.D.

Hildebert, one of the five great hymnists of the twelfth century, was born of humble parents in Vendôme in 1057. He became Bishop of Mans and Archbishop of Tours, the diocese of Bishop Gregory five centuries before Hildebert's time. He was a wise and gentle prelate, but courageous also when the cause of truth required vindication. He was a prolific hymnist, and it is calculated that he must have composed above ten thousand sacred verses. Hildebert died in 1133 or 1134, when about fourscore years of age.

ADAM OF ST. VICTOR—DIED 1192.

Adam of St. Victor, one of the great hymnists of the twelfth century, is called in history a Briton, but it is uncertain whether he was a native of Great Britain or of Brittany. In 1130 he entered the hermitage of St. Victor, a religious house then in the suburbs of Paris, but now the spot is included within the walls of that city.

In this institution Adam spent sixty years of his life, and here he died in 1192. Little is known of his life, but his extensive poetical works show that he was a man of literary attainments and high poetic genius. Indeed, some writers regard him as the greatest of all sacred poets, for out of a hundred pieces which he composed fifty at least are of rare excellence. The religious house of St. Victor produced many hymnists during the twelfth and thirteenth centuries, and its children evidently remained faithful to the cultivation of sacred song. Archbishop Trench in his *Sacred Latin Poetry* says: 'Of the life of St. Victor, the most fertile and, in my judgment, the greatest of the Latin-hymnologists of the Middle Ages, little is known. His profound acquaintance with the whole circle of the theology of his day, and eminently with its exposition of Scripture, the abundant and admirable use which he makes of it, delivering as he thus does his poems from the merely subjective cast of those of St. Bernard, beautiful as they are: the exquisite art and variety with which for the most part his verse is managed and his rhymes disposed—their rich melody multiplying and ever deepening at the close—the strength which often he concentrates into a single line, his skill in conducting a story, and, most of all, the evident nearness of the things which he celebrates to his own heart,—all these and other excellencies render him, as far as my judgment goes, the foremost amongst the sacred Latin poets of the Middle Ages. He may have no single poem to vie with the austere grandeur of the " Dies Irae," nor yet with the tearful passion of the "Stabat Mater," but then it must not be forgotten that these stand wellnigh alone in the names of their respective authors, while from his ample treasure are a multitude of poems, all of them of considerable, some of the very highest, merit. Indeed, were I disposed to name any one who might dispute the palm of sacred Latin poetry with him, it would not be one of these, but rather Hildebert, Archbishop of Tours.'

Of Adam's hymns the best known are those translated by Dr. Neale for the *Hymnal Noted*. These are 'The Church on earth, with answering love, echoes her mother's joys above' ('Supernae Matris gaudia'), and 'The praises that the blessed know' ('Harum laudum praeconia'). Of the former Neale says, 'This Sequence, to my mind, is one of the loveliest Adam ever wrote.'

THIRTEENTH CENTURY.

As regards hymnology, the thirteenth century was distinguished by the writings of four Latin hymnists of considerable fame. These were St. Bonaventura, St.

Thomas Aquinas, Thomas of Celano, and Jacobus de Benedictis.

St. Bonaventura—1221-1274 A.D.

Bonaventura was an Italian, born in Tuscany in 1221. He became in youth a friar of the Order of St. Francis of Assisi, and went to Paris, where he spent many years. He proved himself a theological writer of considerable power, and exercised a great personal influence. He was raised to be Bishop of Albano, and died in 1274. Two beautiful hymns by this Latin author are—

In the Lord's atoning grief.	In passione Domini.
Praise of the Cross.	Recordare sanctae crucis.

The former English rendering is by Canon Frederick Oakeley, made in 1841. It has attained a place in the third rank of Standard Hymns. (See Hymn 313.)

St. Thomas Aquinas—1227-1274 A.D.

Thomas of Aquino, in the kingdom of Naples, was the son of the Count of Aquino, who was nephew to the Emperor Frederic I. Thomas was educated at Monte Casino and Naples. At fifteen years of age he joined the Order of Dominican preaching friars. He lived for many years at Cologne and Paris, where he wrote his famous work, *Defence of the Monastic Life*. He died in 1274, and shortly afterwards was canonised by the Romish Church. His voluminous works are favourites with Roman Catholics, and he is styled the

'Angelic Doctor.' His best-known hymns that have come down to us are those rendered by Dr. Neale, viz.—

Now, my tongue, the mystery telling.	Pange lingua gloriosi.
Humbly I adore Thee, hidden Deity.	Adoro Te devote, latens Deitas.

THOMAS OF CELANO.

This Latin hymn-writer of the thirteenth century was born at Celano, near Naples, from which he takes the name of Thomas of Celano. He was an intimate friend of St. Francis of Assisi, and became a member of the Order of Minorites. He wrote the Life of St. Francis, a work held in high honour by the Order.

The work, however, by which Thomas is best known is his magnificent Latin hymn, 'Dies Irae,' by many considered to be the finest of mediæval hymns.

There are several excellent renderings of 'Dies Irae, dies illa,' viz., 'That day of wrath, that dreadful day,' rendered by Sir Walter Scott, which has attained a place among 'first rank' hymns; while Dr. Irons's rendering, 'Day of wrath, O day of mourning,' and Newton's 'Day of judgment, day of wonders,' have attained a place among 'second rank' hymns.

For full account of 'Dies Irae' see Hymn 96 in Standard Hymns.

JACOBUS DE BENEDICTIS—DIED 1306.

At the cross her station keeping,	Stabat Mater dolorosa,
Stood the mournful Mother weeping,	Juxta crucem lacrymosa,

Where He hung, the dying Lord,	Dum pendebat Filius,
For her soul, of joy bereavèd,	Cujus animam gementem,
Bowed with anguish, deeply grievèd,	Contristantem et dolentem,
Felt the sharp and piercing sword.	Pertransivit gladius.

The above is the first stanza of the grand Latin hymn, the 'Stabat Mater.'

Jacobus de Benedictis, familiarly known as Jacopone, was a native of Todi, in Umbria.

Several accurate sketches of his life have been made recently, and it appears that he was a person of remarkable character. The date of his birth is unknown, but as he died in 1306 at an advanced age, he was probably born in the second quarter of the thirteenth century, about the time that his illustrious compeer, Thomas of Celano, author of 'Dies Irae,' departed this life. Jacobus was born of noble parents, followed the profession of a lawyer, and led a secular life, until he experienced a deep affliction. His pious wife, to whom he was much attached, met with a violent death through an accident at a theatre, and this untoward circumstance made such a decided impression upon his mind that he resolved to withdraw from the world, and devote himself exclusively to the services of the religious life. Accordingly he joined the Order of St. Francis, and became a lay brother. Although the Franciscan Order had then been established for little more than half a century, yet it numbered 200,000 members, possessed thousands of monasteries throughout Christendom, and enjoyed the highest reputation for humility and sanctity. As a hymnist Jacobus composed numerous spiritual songs, which indicate surpassing poetic talent. His chief work, however, was the world-renowned 'Stabat Mater dolorosa,' one of the most pathetic of mediæval poems, and, next to the 'Dies Irae,' the masterpiece of Latin hymnology.

It appears from a recently published biography by Ozanam that Jacobus wrote also a 'Stabat Mater' of the Blessed Virgin by the cradle of Bethlehem, as well as the 'Stabat Mater' by the Cross of Calvary. The former, although little known, possesses much poetic beauty, but it is nevertheless far inferior to his better-known masterpiece.

The 'Stabat Mater dolorosa,' consisting originally of ten stanzas of six lines each, appears in the Roman Missal as a 'Mass on the seven griefs of the Blessed Virgin Mary.'

It was composed towards the end of the thirteenth century, and therefore about fifty years after the 'Dies Irae.' As in the case of other sacred songs, it has been ascribed to different authors. Some say it was the work of Bernard; others that of certain Popes. The whole matter of authorship has been carefully investigated of late years by Daniel, and the result shows that to Jacobus belongs the sole honour of this sacred piece.

The 'Stabat Mater' was set to exquisite music by Rossini, and this fact has largely contributed to extend the fame of the poem, more especially such portions as 'Cujus animam,' and 'Sancta Mater.'

To the English it is best known through the above translation, found in *Hymns Ancient and Modern*, the work of Bishop Mant, slightly altered by the compilers of the Hymnal. The rendering consists of five stanzas, and represents, therefore, only half of the original.

Jacobus was a keen humorist, and his satires, exposing as they did the moral corruption of the age, did much to reform the religious abuses of that period, although they exposed the writer to charges of buffoonery and madness. He seems, however, to have permitted himself to be considered a fool that he might make others wise. Many anecdotes are related illustrative of his profound piety. On one occasion his eyes were observed to be suffused with tears, and on being asked the cause of his grief he replied, 'Because He who is Love is not loved.'

A monument was erected to his memory at his native Todi in 1596, that is, about three centuries after his death. The epitaph on the stone furnishes the key to Jacobus's character:—' Ossa B. Jacoponi de Benedictis, Tudertini, qui, stultus propter Christum, novâ mundum arte delusit et caelum rapuit.' (The bones of B. Jacobus de Benedictis, of Todi, who, a fool for Christ's sake, deluded the world by this strange wile and seized heaven.)

'PARIS BREVIARY' HYMNISTS.

SEVENTEENTH AND EIGHTEENTH CENTURIES.

SANTOLIUS MAGLORIANUS—1628-1684.

Santolius Maglorianus was the elder brother of Santolius Victorinus, and was born in Paris in 1628.

He became a secular monk of Magloire, a celebrated religious college of Paris, from which he took the name Maglorianus, his real name being Claude de Santeul. He wrote many beautiful hymns, which found a place in the Paris Breviary. Amongst them is

Now, my soul, thy voice upraising.   Prome vocem mens canoram.

The English rendering is by John Chandler and Sir H. W. Baker, Bart.

SANTOLIUS VICTORINUS—1630-1697.

Santolius Victorinus was a Frenchman, born in Paris in 1630. His real name was Jean Baptiste de Santeul. He became a regular canon of St. Victor, a celebrated religious house in Paris, and distinguished himself both as an author and hymn-writer. His best hymns are to be found in the Paris and Cluny Breviaries. Amongst them are—

Disposer supreme.   Supreme quales Arbiter.
    Rendered by ISAAC WILLIAMS, 1839.
Christ's everlasting messengers.   Christi perennes nuntii.
    Rendered by ISAAC WILLIAMS.
The Heavenly Child in stature grows. Divine crescebas Puer.
    Rendered by JOHN CHANDLER, 1837.
O Sion, open wide thy gates.   Templi sacratas pande Syon fores.
    Rendered by EDWARD CASWALL.
Not by the martyr's death alone.   Non parta solo sanguine.
First of martyrs, Thou whose name.   O qui tuo, dux martyrum.

CHARLES COFFIN—1676-1749.

Charles Coffin was a Frenchman, born in 1676. He was a scholarly person, and became Principal of the

University of Paris, a post he held for about forty years, till his death in 1749. It is said that under his influence the University rose to the highest pitch of honour and success. He was one of the most distinguished of the Breviary writers, and his Latin hymns, distinguished for pure Latinity and sublimity of thought, were composed in 1736 for the Paris Breviary. The best-known translations of Coffin's hymns are—

Creator of the world, to Thee,	*Rendered by*	JOHN MASON NEALE.
The advent of our King,	,,	JOHN CHANDLER.
On Jordan's bank the Baptist's cry,	,,	,,
As now the sun's declining rays,	,,	,,
What star is this with beams so bright,	,,	,,
Once more the solemn season calls,	,,	,,
O Saviour, who for man hast trod,	,,	,,
Great Mover of all hearts, whose hand,	,,	ISAAC WILLIAMS.
Lo! from the desert homes,	,,	,,

CHAPTER II.
First Rank Hymns:
INDEX, SUMMARY, AND ACCOUNT OF EACH.

INDEX OF FIRST RANK HYMNS.

List of the 105 First Rank Hymns, arranged in order of merit, with names of Authors, Dates, and Number of Marks of Approval.

Order.	Hymns.	Authors.		Marks.
1.	All praise to Thee, my God, this night,	Bp. Ken,	1697-1709.	51
2.	Hark! the herald angels sing,	C. Wesley,	1739.	51
3.	Lo! He comes with clouds descending,	{ C. Wesley, Madan,	1758. 1760. }	51
4.	Rock of Ages, cleft for me,	Toplady,	1776.	51
5.	Abide with me: fast falls the eventide,	Lyte,	1847.	49
6.	Awake, my soul, and with the sun,	Bp. Ken,	1697-1709.	49
7.	Jerusalem the golden,	Neale, 1851, *from* Bernard of Cluny,	1150.	49
8.	Jesu, Lover of my soul,	C. Wesley,	1740.	49
9.	Sun of my soul, Thou Saviour dear,	Keble,	1827.	49
10.	When I survey the wondrous cross,	Watts,	1709.	49
11.	Holy! Holy! Holy! Lord God Almighty,	Heber,	1811.	48
12.	Jesus Christ is risen to-day,	Anon.,	1750.	47
13.	Nearer, my God, to Thee,	Adams,	1840.	47
14.	Hark! the glad sound, the Saviour comes,	Doddridge,	1735.	46
15.	How sweet the name of Jesus sounds,	Newton,	1779.	46
16.	Jerusalem, my happy home,	F. Baker,	1590.	46
17.	From Greenland's icy mountains,	Heber,	1819.	45
18.	Great God, what do I see and hear,	Ringwaldt,	1585.	45
19.	O God, our help in ages past,	Watts,	1719.	45
20.	Saviour, when in dust to Thee,	Sir R. Grant,	1815.	45
21.	All people that on earth do dwell,	W. Kethe,	1561.	44

Index of First Rank Hymns.

Order.	Hymns.	Authors.		Marks.
22.	Brief life is here our portion,	Neale, 1851, *from* Bernard of Cluny,	1150.	44
23.	Come, Holy Ghost, our souls inspire,	Cosin,	17th cent.	44
24.	My God, my Father, while I stray,	Elliott,	1834.	44
25.	Hail the day that sees Him rise,	C. Wesley,	1739.	43
26.	Hail to the Lord's Anointed,	Montgomery,	1831.	43
27.	Hosanna to the living God,	Heber,	1811.	43
28.	Oft in danger, oft in woe,	Kirke White,	1827.	42
29.	Thou whose almighty word,	Marriott,	1813.	42
30.	Come let us join our cheerful songs,	Watts,	1674-1748.	41
31.	Glorious things of thee are spoken,	Newton,	1779.	41
32.	O worship the King,	Grant,	1839.	41
33.	The Son of God goes forth to war,	Heber,	1827.	41
34.	Christ, whose glory fills the skies,	C. Wesley,	1740.	40
35.	Lord, when we bend before Thy throne,	Carlyle,	1802.	40
36.	Sweet the moments, rich in blessing,	Allen and Shirley,	1759, 1774.	40
37.	Christ the Lord is risen to-day,	C. Wesley,	1739.	39
38.	For thee, O dear, dear country,	Neale, 1851, *from* Bernard of Cluny,	1150.	39
39.	God that madest earth and heaven,	{ Heber, { Whately,	1827. 1855.	39
40.	Jesus shall reign where'er the sun,	Watts,	1719.	39
41.	My God, and is Thy table spread,	Doddridge,	1775.	39
42.	O Thou from whom all goodness flows,	Haweis,	1800.	39
43.	When our heads are bowed with woe,	Milman,	1827.	39
44.	Where high the Heavenly Temple stands,	Bruce,	1767.	39
45.	While shepherds watched their flocks by night,	N. Tate,	1696.	38
46.	All hail, the power of Jesus' name,	Perronet,	1780.	37
47.	Come, ye thankful people, come,	Alford,	1844.	37
48.	Father of Heaven, whose love profound,	Cooper,	1808.	37
49.	God moves in a mysterious way,	Cowper,	1773.	37
50.	How bright these glorious spirits shine,	{ Watts, { Cameron,	1709. 1781.	37
51.	Jesus lives, no longer now,	{ Gellert, { Cox,	1757. 1841.	37
52.	O Lord, turn not Thy face from me,	Mardley,	1562.	37
53.	Our blest Redeemer, ere He breathed,	Auber,	1829.	37
54.	Through the day Thy love has spared us,	Kelly,	1806.	37
55.	Children of the Heavenly King,	Cennick,	1742.	36
56.	Glory be to Jesus,	Caswall,	1858.	36
57.	Go to dark Gethsemane,	Montgomery,	1820.	36
58.	Guide me, O Thou great Jehovah,	W. Williams,	1760.	36

Index of First Rank Hymns.

Order.	Hymns.	Authors.		Marks.
59.	Jesu, the very thought of Thee,	Caswall, 1840, *from* St. Bernard,	1150.	36
60.	O God of Bethel! by whose hand,	Doddridge,	1727.	36
61.	Ride on, ride on, in majesty,	Milman,	1827.	36
62.	Songs of praise the angels sang,	Montgomery,	1819.	36
63.	Through all the changing scenes of life,	Tate and Brady,	1696.	36
64.	Just as I am, without one plea,	Elliott,	1836.	35
65.	New every morning is the love,	Keble,	1822.	35
66.	Praise, my soul, the King of heaven,	Lyte,	1834.	35
67.	Praise the Lord; ye heavens, adore Him,	Anon.,	1809.	35
68.	Soldiers of Christ, arise,	Wesley,	1749.	35
69.	The strain upraise of joy and praise,	Neale, 1863, *from* Godescalcus,	950.	35
70.	There is a land of pure delight,	Watts,	1709.	35
71.	Thou art gone up on high,	Toke,	1853.	35
72.	Ye servants of the Lord,	Doddridge,	1755.	35
73.	As with gladness men of old,	Dix,	1859.	34
74.	Love divine, all love excelling,	C. Wesley,	1747.	34
75.	O come, all ye faithful,	Oakeley, 1841, *from* Bonaventura, 13th cent.		34
76.	O help us, Lord, each hour of need,	Milman,	1837.	34
77.	Thou art the way, to Thee alone,	Doane,	1824.	34
78.	Forth in Thy name, O Lord, I go,	C. Wesley,	1749.	33
79.	Lord, dismiss us with Thy blessing,	Shirley,	1772.	33
80.	Lord of mercy and of might,	Heber,	1812.	33
81.	When gathering clouds around I view,	Grant,	1806.	33
82.	Brightest and best of the sons of the morning,	Heber,	1811.	32
83.	Christians, awake! salute the happy morn,	Byrom,	1763.	32
84.	Lord of the worlds above,	Watts,	1709.	32
85.	O for a closer walk with God,	Cowper,	1779.	32
86.	Rejoice, the Lord is King,	Wesley,	1748.	32
87.	The Lord shall come, the earth shall quake,	Heber,	1827.	32
88.	Angels from the realms of glory,	Montgomery,	1825.	31
89.	As pants the hart for cooling streams,	Tate and Brady,	1709.	31
90.	Come, gracious Spirit, Heavenly Dove,	Browne,	1720.	31
91.	For Thy mercy and Thy grace,	Downton,	1843.	31
92.	Lead us, Heavenly Father, lead us,	Edmeston,	1821.	31
93.	Lord, as to Thy dear Cross we flee,	Gurney,	1838.	31
94.	Lord, in this Thy mercy's day,	I. Williams,	1840.	31
95.	O God, unseen, yet ever near,	Osler,	1837.	31
96.	That day of wrath, that dreadful day,	Scott,	1805.	31
97.	The day is past and over,	Neale, 1862, *from* St. Anatolius, 5th cent.		31

Summary of First Rank Hymns.

Order.	Hymns.	Authors.		Marks.
98.	The roseate hues of early dawn,	Alexander,	1848.	31
99.	When all Thy mercies, O my God,	Addison,	1712.	31
100.	All glory, laud, and honour,	Neale, *from* Theodulph of 9th century.		30
101.	Art thou weary, art thou languid,	Neale, *from* Stephanos of 8th century.		30
102.	Before Jehovah's awful throne,	Watts, J. Wesley,	1719. 1741.	30
103.	God of our life, to Thee we call,	Cowper,	1779.	30
104.	In token that thou shalt not fear,	Alford,	1832.	30
105.	Now thank we all our God,	Winkworth, *from* Rinkart,	1586-1649.	30

SUMMARY OF FIRST RANK HYMNS.

All hymns found in thirty Hymnals and upwards have been classified as hymns of the *first* rank.

Of these there are 105, composed by 54 hymn-writers, of whom—

35 authors contribute	1 hymn each	=	35 hymns.
9	,,	2	,,	18	,,
4	,,	3	,,	12	,,
2	,,	4	,,	8	,,
2	,,	7	,,	14	,,
1	,,	8	,,	8	,,
1	,,	10	,,	10	,,
54 authors.				105 hymns.

Arranging the hymn-writers according to the number of hymns contributed by each, they stand as follows:—

C. Wesley,	10	Milman,	3	Lyte,	2
Watts,	8	Tait and Brady,	3	Newton,	2
Heber,	7	Alford,	2	Shirley,	2
Neale,	7	Anon.,	2	Adams,	1
Doddridge,	4	Caswall,	2	Addison,	1
Montgomery,	4	Elliott,	2	Alexander,	1
Cowper,	3	Keble,	2	Auber,	1
Grant,	3	Ken,	2	Baker, F.,	1

Summary of First Rank Hymns.

Browne,	. . 1	Doane,	. . 1	Oakeley,	. . 1
Bruce,	. . 1	Downton,	. . 1	Osler,	. . 1
Byrom,	. . 1	Edmeston,	. . 1	Perronet,	. . 1
Cameron,	. . 1	Gurney,	. . 1	Ringwaldt,	. . 1
Carlyle,	. . 1	Haweis,	. . 1	Rinkart,	. . 1
Cennick,	. . 1	Kelly,	. . 1	Scott,	. . 1
Cooper,	. . 1	Kethe,	. . 1	Toke,	. . 1
Cosin,	. . 1	Kirke White,	. 1	Toplady,	. . 1
Cox,	. . 1	Mardley,	. . 1	Williams, I.,	. 1
Dix,	. . 1	Marriott,	. . 1	Williams, W.,	. 1

Arranging the above 105 hymns according to the initial letter of the first word it is found that

12	commence with T	8	commence with H	3	commence with N
11	,,	O	8	,,	J	3	,,	R
10	,,	A	6	,,	W	2	,,	M
9	,,	L	5	,,	F	2	,,	P
8	,,	C	5	,,	S	1	,,	I
8	,,	G	3	,,	B	1	,,	Y

None commence with the letters D, E, K, Q, U, V, Z.

Number of First Rank Hymns found in the chief Hymnals.

Of the best-known Hymnals now used in the Church of England it is interesting to notice how many hymns of the first rank are found in each. Thus out of 105 hymns aforenamed—

1. The Hymnal Companion . . . contains 103
2. The Church of England Hymn-Book ,, 102
3. Church Hymnal (Irish) . . . ,, 99
4. The Westminster Abbey Hymn-Book ,, 98
5. Church Hymns (S.P.C.K.) . . ,, 97
6. Hymns Ancient and Modern . . ,, 90
7. Hymnal Noted . . . . . ,, 82
8. The People's Hymnal . . . . ,, 65

Hymns of the First Rank omitted.

The *Hymnal Companion* omits 2—
   56. Glory be to Jesus.
   76. O help us, Lord, each hour of need.

The *Church of England Hymn-Book* omits 3—
    41. My God, and is Thy table spread.
    59. Jesu! the very thought of Thee.
    60. O God of Bethel! by whose hand.

Church Hymnal (Irish) omits 6, viz.—
    25. Hail the day that sees Him rise.
    72. Ye servants of the Lord.
    87. The Lord shall come, the earth shall quake.
    88. Angels from the realms of glory.
    96. That day of wrath, that dreadful day,
    105. Now thank we all our God.

The *Westminster Abbey Hymn-Book* omits 7, viz.—
    32. O worship the King.
    36. Sweet the moments, rich in blessing.
    56. Glory be to Jesus.
    84. Lord of the worlds above.
    87. The Lord shall come, the earth shall quake.
    88. Angels from the realms of glory.
    103. God of our life, to Thee we call.

Church Hymns (S.P.C.K.) omits 8, viz.—
    59. Jesu! the very thought of Thee.
    87. The Lord shall come, the earth shall quake.
    85. O for a closer walk with God.
    90. Come, gracious Spirit, Heavenly Dove.
    93. Lord, as to Thy dear cross we flee.
    96. That day of wrath, that dreadful day.
    99. When all Thy mercies, O my God.
    102. Before Jehovah's awful throne.

Hymns Ancient and Modern omits 15, viz.—
    31. Glorious things of thee are spoken.
    55. Children of the Heavenly King.
    60. O God of Bethel! by whose hand.
    70. There is a land of pure delight.
    74. Love divine, all love excelling.
    79. Lord, dismiss us with Thy blessing.
    80. Lord of mercy and of might.
    84. Lord of the worlds above.

Account of First Rank Hymns.

   87. The Lord shall come, the earth shall quake.
   81. When gathering clouds around I view.
   88. Angels from the realms of glory.
   82. Brightest and best of the sons of the morning.
   85. O for a closer walk with God.
   99. When all Thy mercies, O my God.
  102. Before Jehovah's awful throne.

Hymnal Noted omits 23 hymns.
The *People's Hymnal* omits 40 hymns.

---

1. All praise to Thee, my God, this night,
   For all the blessings of the light.

This much-prized Evening Hymn was composed by Bishop Ken, and appeared in his edition of *A Manual of Prayers*, published in 1700.

The original consisted of twelve stanzas, including the Doxology, but seven of these are usually omitted in our present Hymnals. In the edition of Ken's hymns for 1709 we find the Bishop's latest corrections and improvements.

In earlier editions the first line of the first stanza was 'Glory to Thee, my God, this night.' It was in 1709 corrected to ' All praise,' etc. Again, the third stanza was corrected from

        Teach me to die, that so I may
        Triumphing rise at the last day,

to

        To die, that this vile body may
        Rise glorious at the awful day.

The 'Midnight Hymn' is comparatively seldom seen, although it is generally considered to be equal in sentiment and poetic beauty to match the other two.

The original consists of thirteen stanzas. The seventh is perhaps the best known, and runs thus:—

> All praise to Thee, in light arrayed,
> Who light Thy dwelling-place hast made;
> A boundless ocean of bright beams
> From Thy all-glorious Godhead streams.

Thomas Ken was born in 1637 at Berkhampstead, Hertford, where, a century afterwards, the hymnist Cowper also was born. Ken lost his parents when but a youth, and his early education was directed by his eldest sister Ann—the lady who afterwards became the wife of Izaak Walton, author of *The Complete Angler*. At thirteen years of age he was sent to Winchester College, where he studied for five years, after which he entered Oxford, and was ordained a clergyman at the age of twenty-four. In 1666 Ken was elected to a Fellowship in the College of Winchester, and forthwith he manifested great interest in the spiritual interest of the scholars. The next year he became rector of Brighstone in the Isle of Wight, a place famous as the village where William Wilberforce wrote his well-known *Practical Christianity*. In 1674 Ken wrote a small book entitled *A Manual of Prayers*, designed primarily for the use of Winchester scholars. This volume proved useful to George Whitefield, and as it still exists, it may be commended as a fitting companion to any young man. A quarter of a century afterwards he appended to this Manual his well-known Morning, Midnight, and Evening Hymns. In the edition of the *Manual* published in 1700, the three hymns are printed, and mentioned in

Account of First Rank Hymns. 49

the title of the book, with the words 'not in the former editions by the same author.'

The hymns and prayers are alike in the clearness and simplicity of their sentiments. It is moreover thought that the hymns were known many years before they were embodied in the *Manual of Prayers*, and that on broadsheets they were hung against the wall in the sleeping apartments of the Winchester scholars.

'How many thousands on thousands of every following generation throughout the Christian world have found each day a devout bias given to their souls by his Morning Hymn, "Awake, my soul, and with the sun"! How many a family circle has finished the day in peace while singing his Evening Hymn, "All praise to Thee, my God, this night"! And how many a lonely wakeful saint, and many a band of holy watchers, have had darkness turned into light by the music of the Midnight Hymn, "Glory to Thee in light arrayed"!' After many changes and preferments, Ken was made Chaplain to King Charles II., and attended that unhappy monarch in his dying hours. In 1684 he was created Bishop of Bath and Wells, but seven years afterwards was deprived of his See, after being committed to the Tower of London, because he refused to read the 'Declaration of Indulgence' introduced by James II. In 1704 he received a pension of £200 a year from Queen Anne, and retired to Longleat in Wiltshire, where, after many years of suffering, he died in 1711. In accordance with the Bishop's dying request, he was buried in the early morn at Frome, 'under the east window of the chancel, just at sun-rising.' It is said, that as the day dawned on his grave, and the sun began to light up the brightening horizon, the friends burst out into the beautiful words of his never-dying hymn, 'Awake, my soul, and with the sun.'

Bishop Ken was a pious, earnest, laborious Christian. Dryden, his contemporary, took him as a model for his 'good parson,' and thus pictures the saintly man :—

> . . . Letting down the golden chain from high,
> He drew his audience upward to the sky :
> And oft with holy hymns he charmed their ears,
> (A music more melodious than the spheres) :
> For David left him, when he went to rest,
> His lyre ; and after him he sung the best.

2. Hark ! the herald angels sing
 Glory to the new-born King.

This noble Christmas hymn is one of the most popular in the English language. It is by Charles Wesley, and first appeared in 1739 in *Hymns and Sacred Poems* by John and Charles Wesley. The author was little more than thirty years old when he wrote it, and about a year before his soul had passed through some remarkable spiritual experience which enabled him to say, 'O taste and see that the Lord is good : blessed is the man that trusteth in Him.' The original consisted of five double stanzas, and is entitled 'A Hymn for Christmas Day.' The last two stanzas are generally omitted in modern Hymnals; but it is no uncommon thing to meet with a fourth stanza made up of parts of the two last stanzas of the original ; thus :—

Account of First Rank Hymns.

> Come, Desire of nations, come,
> Fix in us Thy humble home ;
> Rise, the woman's conquering Seed,
> Bruise in us the serpent's head.

This is first half of fourth stanza.

> Adam's likeness, Lord, efface ;
> Stamp Thy image in its place.
> O to all Thyself impart,
> Form'd in each believing heart.

This is first half of fifth stanza.

Charles Wesley thus commenced the hymn :—

> Hark ! how all the welkin rings
> Glory to the King of kings.

Twenty years afterwards, in 1760, this was altered, either by John Wesley or by Madan, a contemporary hymnist, to

> Hark ! the herald angels sing
> Glory to the new-born King.

This couplet is sung as a refrain at the end of each stanza, and constitutes the most familiar lines. The hymn, in some way unknown, was printed at the end of Tate and Brady's 'New Version of Metrical Psalms,' annexed to the Book of Common Prayer, and this fact has doubtless rendered it more familiar to Churchmen ; but apart from this, there is an intrinsic beauty in the hymn that has rendered it a universal favourite. It is invariably sung in all the Churches at Christmas-tide, and Christmas Day, with its many hallowed associations, is made more joyous by the gladdening strains of

> Hark ! the herald angels sing.

Charles Wesley, the celebrated hymnist of the Wesley family, was the third son of Samuel Wesley, and was born at Epworth in 1708. He was five years younger than his brother John, the founder of the Wesleyan denomination. Educated at Westminster and Oxford, he took holy orders in 1735, and married in 1749 Miss Gwynne, a lady of good family of Brecknockshire. Of their offspring, two sons, Charles and Samuel, became noted musicians.

While John Wesley, by his natural firmness and unwonted zeal, was well fitted to be a religious reformer, Charles was a man of more genial spirit and happy piety, and considered liveliness and laughter quite compatible with religion. It is said that from the year 1740 he continued to write hymns without intermission almost up to the day of his death. He became the sweet hymnist of Wesleyanism, and many of his hymns are justly prized by all Christians. In the Wesleyan Hymn-book, out of 770, Charles Wesley wrote 623, and Isaac Watts 66; so that 700 hymns, save one, were composed by these two hymnists. In the preface to the collection Wesley states the simple truth when he says: 'In these hymns there is no doggerel, no botches, nothing put in to patch up the rhyme, no feeble expletives. There is nothing turgid or bombastic on the one hand, or low and creeping on the other. Here are no cant expressions, no words without meaning. Here are both the purity, the strength, and the elegance of the English language, and at the same time the utmost simplicity and plainness suited to every capacity.'

Besides this collection, Charles published many volumes of hymns, and it is considered that altogether he wrote six thousand hymns. Most of these are

Account of First Rank Hymns. 53

seldom used, but for the most part they are distinguished for poetic beauty and fervent spirituality. Indeed, in the number and excellence of his hymns Charles Wesley is not only pre-eminently the 'Bard of Methodism,' but he is generally regarded as the 'Prince of Hymnists.'

He died in 1788, in the eightieth year of his age.

3. Lo! He comes with clouds descending,
   Once for favoured sinners slain.

This Advent hymn, said to be one of the finest hymns ever written, is for the most part the work of Charles Wesley, and is founded upon Rev. i. 7: 'Behold, He cometh with clouds; and every eye shall see Him, and they also which pierced Him: and all kindreds of the earth shall wail because of Him. Even so, Amen.'

It is generally thought that the germ of this noble hymn was suggested to Wesley by a hymn that appeared in 1752 in a Dublin collection entitled *Sacred Hymns*, written by John Cennick, a contemporary hymnist. Cennick's hymn contains four stanzas, of which the first runs thus:—

> Lo! He cometh, countless trumpets
> Blow to raise the sleeping dead,
> Mid ten thousand saints and angels
> See the great exalted Head.
>   Hallelujah!
> Welcome, welcome! Son of God.

To Cennick's hymn belongs the credit of being the first attempt to render the thoughts and sentiments of the 'Dies Irae' in this fine appropriate measure, the flowing majestic lines first, then the first trumpet-note of the chorus, then the full sounding line at the close; upon which, to change the figure, the whole stanza rests gracefully but firmly. There are many pieces written afterwards upon the same subject in the same metre.

It is evident that Charles Wesley a few years after imitated, both in style and sentiment, Cennick's imitation of the 'Dies Irae,' when he wrote the well-known 'Lo! He comes with clouds descending.' Wesley's hymn appeared in 1758, in his *Hymns of Intercession for all Mankind*, a collection of forty suited to the circumstances of the country. England, and indeed almost all Europe, was in a state of warfare; and consequently this collection contains hymns for the King and all in authority, for soldiers and sailors, as well as for all prisoners and captives. In 1760 Madan, a contemporary hymnist, added two stanzas to Wesley's hymn, commencing respectively 'Every island, sea, and mountain,' and 'Now redemption, long expected.' The four well-known stanzas by Wesley are those respectively commencing—

'Lo! He comes with clouds descending.'
'Every eye shall now behold Him.'
'Those dear tokens of His Passion.'
'Yea, Amen, let all adore Thee.'

There is an erroneous notion that this fine composition is the work of Thomas Olivers, a contemporary of Wesley, but there is no foundation for this opinion, and the popular error probably arose thus. About this time, namely in 1757, an Advent hymn of twelve stanzas was written by Thomas Olivers, a hymn-writer. In measure

Account of First Rank Hymns.

and in sentiment it resembles Wesley's, and, strange to say, commences in the same words, 'Lo! He comes with clouds descending.' Olivers wrote a tune for his own hymn, the melody of which was taken from the music of a street song. This tune suited Wesley's hymn, and was accordingly set to it in Wesley's *Sacred Melody*, published in 1760. The tune for a long time was called 'Olivers,' from its author, and seeing this name in the *Sacred Melody*, the public got the idea that both tune and hymn were by Olivers. The tune is now called 'Helmsley,' and is admirably suited for Wesley's noble composition.

> 4. Rock of Ages, cleft for me,
>   Let me hide myself in Thee.

This world-renowned hymn is from the pen of Augustus Montague Toplady. He was the son of Major Toplady, and was born at Farnham, Surrey, in 1740. In childhood he was brought up under the loving care of a pious mother, and throughout life Toplady retained a deep and lasting sense of his mother's kindness.

In early manhood he wrote several 'Poems on Sacred Subjects,' which gave promise of his poetic ability. At the age of twenty-three he was ordained a clergyman of the Church of England, and six years afterwards became Vicar of Broadhembury, a sequestered village amid the beautiful hills of eastern Devon. Here, by the banks of the Otter stream, and among the peaceful hills, he composed most of his spiritual songs.

The moist air of Devonshire was thought to be injurious to his weak lungs, and at the advice of his medical man Toplady removed to London in 1775, where he preached for more than two years. 'With fast failing health he continued the services, preaching with the solemnity of a voice from the tomb, and the joy of one on the very verge of heaven. At all times an impressive preacher, his peculiar circumstances lent additional weight to his words.' In the closing scene of his life he remarked, 'Sickness is no affliction, pain no curse, death itself no dissolution. I have such an abiding sense of God's goodness, and of the certainty of my being fixed upon the Eternal Rock, Jesus Christ, that my soul is still filled with peace and joy.' 'Upon his doctor informing him, in answer to his inquiry, that his pulse was becoming weaker and weaker, he replied, " Why, that is a good sign that my death is fast approaching ; and, blessed be God ! I can add that my heart beats every day stronger and stronger for glory." And after many other beautiful Christian words, he said, when close to his end, bursting into tears of joy as he spoke, " It will not be long before God takes me, for no mortal man can live after the glories which God has manifested to my soul." He died in the thirty-eighth year of his age, and was thus early called to join the heavenly choirs.'

Montgomery says, 'Toplady evidently kindled his poetic torch at that of his contemporary, Charles Wesley.' In doctrine he was a strict Calvinist, and stoutly opposed the idea of full and free salvation taught by the Wesleys.

His language in controversy was severe, but his hymns are sweet and gentle.

The justly prized hymn 'Rock of Ages, cleft for me,' first appeared in the *Gospel Magazine* for March 1776, with the title, 'A living and dying prayer for the holiest believer in the world.' This title was aimed against the doctrine of 'absolute perfection,' which Toplady erroneously suspected Wesley of preaching. The leading thoughts of the hymn are manifestly founded upon Isaiah xxvi. 4, 'The Lord Jehovah is the Rock of Ages,' and Exodus xxxiii. 22, 'I will put thee in a clift of the rock, and will cover thee with my hand while I pass by.' Dr. Pusey calls it 'the most deservedly popular hymn, perhaps *the* very favourite.' Assuredly it is considered by many to be the finest hymn in the English language. It was a great favourite with the late Prince Consort, and afforded him much comfort in his dying hours.

Dr. Pomeroy, during his pilgrimage in the East, found his way into an Armenian church at Constantinople. The people were singing. The language of their hymn was foreign; but it was evident that the singers were in earnest, and that there was a deep feeling in the words of their song. The music was a simple melody. All sang with closed eyes, but as the strain continued, tears were starting, and trickling down many a cheek. Dr. Pomeroy would fain have joined in the plaintive, tender, yet glowing hymn. What were they singing? The stanzas were translated, and at once were recognised as the world-renowned hymn, 'Rock of Ages, cleft for me.'

5. Abide with me: fast falls the even-tide;
   The darkness deepens; Lord, with me abide.

This well-known hymn was composed by Henry Francis Lyte, born in 1793 at Ednam, near Kelso, the birthplace also of James Thomson, author of *The Seasons*. He took holy orders, and in 1823, when thirty years of age, was appointed perpetual curate of Lower Brixham, Devon, where for about a quarter of a century he laboured amongst the warm-hearted, rough seafaring population. In the autumn of 1847, the increasing weakness of his constitution demanded change and repose, and his medical advisers accordingly urged him to pass the coming winter in a more genial clime. 'They tell me,' said he, 'that the sea is injurious to me. I hope not, for I know of no divorce I would more deprecate than from the lordly ocean. From childhood it has been my friend and playmate, and never have I been weary of gazing on its beautiful face. Besides, if I cannot live by the sea, adieu to poor Berry Head, adieu to the wild birds and wild flowers, and all the objects that have made my old residence so attractive. . . . I am meditating flight again to the South. The little faithful robin is every morning at my window, sweetly warning me that autumn hours are at hand. The swallows are preparing for flight, and inviting me to accompany them; and yet, alas! while I talk of flying, I am just able to crawl, and often ask myself whether I shall be able to leave England at all.' Before taking his journey he made an effort to address his

Account of First Rank Hymns. 59

flock once more, and with a wasted frame and hectic flush he spoke with deep earnestness. His subject was the 'Holy Communion,' and he impressed upon his people the vital importance of close communion with the Saviour :—

'O brethren, I stand here among you to-day, as alive from the dead, if I may hope to impress it upon you, and induce you to prepare for that solemn hour which must come to all, by a timely acquaintance with the death of Christ.' His voice was heard for the last time in the pulpit. With much difficulty he dispensed the sacred elements to his sorrowing communicants. Exhausted with the effort, he was led from the sanctuary, and laid down on his couch at home, in great weakness, but with a soul in sweet repose. As the evening drew on he handed to a dear relative a manuscript, which on being opened disclosed the undying verses, 'Abide with me: fast falls the even-tide,' etc. The hymn is founded upon the touching incident, the journey to Emmaus, when the two disciples constrained Christ to sojourn with them for the night, saying, 'Abide with us, for it is toward evening, and the day is far spent.'

Reclining on his couch, the Christian poet felt that the shadows of death were gathering around him, but with a strong confidence in Christ's presence, he knew that the deepening darkness would only remain 'until the day break and the shadows flee away.' Already could the eye of faith, piercing through the gloom, scan the increasing brightness on the celestial horizon, and triumphantly exclaim, 'Heaven's morning breaks, and earth's vain shadows flee.'

He had expressed the wish, 'Grant me my last breath to spend in song that may not die.' That wish was realised, for this hymn, now a universal favourite, was the last he composed, and was written only two months before his death. He left his home in September 1847 for the south of France, but he returned not again. On reaching Nice his bodily weakness became so extreme that his loving friends saw the end was at hand. Sinking to rest, he pointed upwards, and whispered 'Peace!' 'Joy!' His face brightened, and the shadows of death melted away before the 'Sun of Righteousness.'

> 6. Awake, my soul, and with the sun
> Thy daily stage of duty run;
> Shake off dull sloth, and early rise,
> To pay thy morning sacrifice.

This world-renowned Morning Hymn is the work of Bishop Ken, and, together with the Evening and Midnight Hymns, was embodied in 1700 in his edition of *A Manual of Prayers*, a volume specially written for the use of the scholars of Winchester College (see Life of Ken). The original consists of fourteen stanzas, including the Doxology, but the hymn in our present Hymnals is usually abridged to five stanzas.

The hymn was a favourite with Ken himself, and it is said he was in the habit of singing it in the early morn, before dressing, accompanying himself on the

Account of First Rank Hymns. 61

lute. Probably the tune to which he sang the hymn was that known as 'Tallis's Canon.'

> Praise God, from whom all blessings flow,
> Praise Him, all creatures here below;
> Praise Him above, ye heavenly host,
> Praise Father, Son, and Holy Ghost.

This noble Doxology is by Bishop Ken, and appears as the last stanza both in his Morning and Evening Hymn. No single stanza of poetry has attained to a greater popularity than the above, and it is spoken of by way of pre-eminence as 'The Doxology.' In 1709 Ken changed the words of the third line, 'angelic host,' as it appeared in former editions, to 'ye heavenly host.'

Speaking of this stanza, Montgomery says:—'The well-known Doxology is a masterpiece at once of amplification and comprehension: amplification on the burthen "Praise God," repeated in each line; compression, by exhibiting God as the object of praise in every view in which we can imagine praise due to Him: praise for all His blessings, yea, for *all* blessings, none coming from any other source; praise by every creature, specifically invoked, "here below" and in heaven "above," praise to Him in each of the characters wherein He has revealed Himself in His Word,—Father, Son, and Holy Ghost.' Probably there is no other verse in existence that is so often sung by Christians of all denominations. With this glad utterance of praise to the Triune Jehovah, they have times without number brought to a conclusion their most solemn and most delightful assemblies.

7. Jerusalem the golden,
   With milk and honey blest,
   Beneath thy contemplation
   Sink heart and voice opprest.

   Urbs Syon aurea, Patria lactea, cive decora,
   Omne cor obruis, omnibus obstruis et cor et ora.

This very sweet hymn is portion of the 'Rhythm of Bernard of Cluny on the Heavenly Country,' rendered from the Latin by Dr. Neale in 1852.

The soul of the Cluniac monk seems to have caught a glimpse of ' that great city, the holy Jerusalem, descending out of heaven from God, having the glory of God : and her light was like unto a stone most precious, even like a jasper-stone, clear as crystal ; . . . and the nations of them which are saved shall walk in the light of it, . . . and they shall bring the glory and honour of the nations into it.' Archbishop Trench, in his *Sacred Latin Poetry*, speaks of the above as 'that lovely hymn which within the last few years has been added to those already possessed by the Church. A new hymn, which has won such a place in the affections of Christian people, is so priceless an acquisition that I must needs rejoice to have been the first to recall from oblivion the poem which yielded it.' The sweet strains of 'Jerusalem the Golden' have found their way into the heart of Christendom, and will continue to revive the drooping energies of the Church militant

Till they, who with their Leader   For ever and for ever
  Have conquered in the fight,   Are clad in robes of white.

Account of First Rank Hymns. 63

Writing in 1862, that is, ten years after its translation into English, Dr. Neale says, '"Jerusalem the Golden" has found a place in some twenty Hymnals; and for the last two years it has hardly been possible to read any newspaper which gives prominence to ecclesiastical news without seeing its employment chronicled at some dedication or other festival. It is also a great favourite with dissenters, and has obtained admission in Roman Catholic services. I am yet more thankful that the Cluniac's verses have been permitted to solace the deathbeds of so many of His servants, and not seldom to have supplied them with the last earthly language of praise.'

Bernard is generally known as 'Bernard of Cluny.' He was born of English parents at Morlaix, on the sea-coast of Brittany. Having resolved to become a monk, Burgundy, the 'golden land' of sacred poets during the twelfth century, found for Bernard a cloistered home. A few miles west of the modern town of Macon, and five hundred miles from Morlaix, stood the well-known monastery of Cluny, which in the twelfth century 'was at the very height of monastic reputation. Its glorious church, the most magnificent in France, the fulness and exactness of its ritual, and the multitude of its brethren, raised it to a pitch of fame which perhaps no other house ever attained.'

Bernard became one of its children, and spent the remainder of his life in the tranquil monastery. Cluny was then under the fatherly care of an abbot known as 'Peter the Venerable,' himself a master of spiritual song, who for thirty-four years, from 1122 till 1156, ruled the great abbey with gentle sceptre.

Surrounded by monastic brethren, worshipping in the grandest church in France, joining daily in the most impressive ritual, Bernard soon became enamoured of monastic life. Although living in the quiet retreat of the cloisters, he was not by any means ignorant of the spiritual wickedness of society, and the consequent sorrows and woes of a sinful world. He soon cherished a desire to write a sacred poem, setting forth the fruits of wickedness and the joy of a religious life. The poet himself says: 'Often and of long time I had heard the Bridegroom, but had not listened to Him, saying, "Thy voice is pleasant in mine ears." And again the Beloved cried out, "Open to me, my sister." What then? I arose that I might open to my Beloved. And I said, "Lord, to the end that my heart may think, that my pen may write, and that my mouth may set forth Thy praise, pour into my heart and pen and mouth Thy grace." And the Lord said, "Open thy mouth," which He straightway filled with the spirit of wisdom and understanding, that by one I might speak truly, by the other perspicuously.'

Accordingly he occupied his leisure time in composing a long poem of about 3000 lines, called 'De Contemptu Mundi,' 'On the contempt of the world.' As the title indicates, the greater portion inveighs against the demoralisation of his countrymen and the fearful corruptions of the age; but in contrast with this spiritual darkness he draws a most sublime picture of that

Account of First Rank Hymns. 65

heavenly Jerusalem, the home and hope of God's people. Bernard thus states his own argument: 'The subject of the author is the advent of Christ to judgment; the joys of the saints; the pains of the reprobate. His *intention*, to persuade to the contempt of the world. The *use*, to despise the things of the world; to seek the things which be God's.'

'De Contemptu Mundi,' like the other great religious poems of the period, was written in Latin—the language of the Roman Catholic Church,—and it was probably finished about the middle of the twelfth century.

Not only was Bernard a contemporary of the great St. Bernard, but, by a strange coincidence, the above poem was composed at Cluny while the saint was composing at Clairvaux the equally well-known sacred poem, 'Jubilus rhythmicus de nomine Jesu.' The two monasteries were only about 150 miles from each other; the two Bernards were at the same time, each in his cloistered cell, singing the glories of the Celestial Country; and both departed to their rest about the middle of the twelfth century.

It is also worthy of notice that three other celebrated hymnists were contemporaries of the two Bernards. These were Adam of St. Victor; Hildebert, a monk of Cluny, afterwards Archbishop of Tours; and Peter the Venerable, Abbot of Cluny.

Those great hymn-writers filled the Church with hymns of praise, and made the twelfth century the great era of sacred song.

The 'De Contemptu Mundi' was first edited by Illyricus at the time of the Reformation, and has since been reprinted at least half a dozen times.

Archbishop Trench, in his *Sacred Latin Poetry*, published in 1849, has given a beautiful cento of about 100 lines from Bernard's poem.

The Rev. John Mason Neale, D.D., in 1852 translated into English the greater part of that cento, and the manifest popularity of the translation induced him to make a fuller extract from the Latin, and a further translation into English. Accordingly, in 1859 was published by this author, *The Rhythm of Bernard de Morlaix, Monk of Cluny, on the Celestial Country*, consisting of about 200 lines of the original work, with a very beautifully rendered translation. Trench says: 'No one with a true passion of poetry will deny the breath of a real inspiration to Bernard. . . . The poet, instead of advancing, eddies round and round his subject, recurring again and again to that which he seemed to have thoroughly treated and dismissed. I quote a few lines from Casimir, the great Latin poet of Poland. They turn upon the same theme,—the heavenly homesickness; but with all their classical beauty, and it is great, who does not feel that the poor Cluniac monk's is the more real and deeper utterance; that, despite the strange form which he has chosen, he is the greater poet?'

Dr. Neale says: 'I am more thankful still that the Cluniac's verses should have soothed the dying hours of many of God's servants: the most striking of which I know is related in the memoir published by Mr. Brownlow under the title, *A Little Child shall lead them*, where he says that the child of whom he writes, when suffering agonies which the medical attendants declared to be almost unparalleled, would lie without a murmur or motion while the whole 400 lines were read to him. I have no hesitation in saying that I look upon these verses of Bernard as the most lovely, in the same way that the "Dies Irae" is the most sublime, and the "Stabat Mater" the most pathetic, of mediæval poems. They are even superior to that glorious hymn on the same subject, the "De Gloriâ et gaudiis Paradisi" of S. Peter Damiani.'

From Dr. Neale's 'Rhythm of St. Bernard' many portions have been adapted as hymns in our English Hymnals. The following are the opening lines of those best known:—

1. Brief life is here our portion.   Hic breve vivitur.
2. The world is very evil.   Hora novissima, tempora pessima.
3. For thee, O dear, dear country.   O bona patria.
4. Jerusalem the golden.   Urbs Syon aurea.
5. Jerusalem the glorious.   Urbs Syon inclyta, gloria.
6. Jerusalem exulting.   Urbs Syon inclyta, turris.

These six hymns contain about 200 lines, but, as each line in Latin equals two lines in the English, the above hymns represent only 100 lines of Latin. The original poem consisted of 3000 Latin lines, and therefore Bernard's 'De Contemptu Mundi' is thirty times longer than the united portions that have found their way into our Anglican Hymnals.

8. Jesu, Lover of my soul,
　　Let me to Thy bosom fly.

This hymn was written by Charles Wesley in 1740, and is considered to be one of his best compositions. The original, found in *Hymns and Sacred Poems*, 1742, consists of five double stanzas, of which the third and fourth are usually omitted in modern Hymnals.

Speaking of this hymn a well-known writer says: 'I would rather have written that hymn of Wesley's than to have the fame of all the kings that ever sat upon the earth. It is more glorious. It has more power in it. I would rather be the author of that hymn than to hold the wealth of the richest man. He will die. He will pass after a little while out of men's thoughts. His money will go to his heirs, and they will divide it. And they in turn will die. But that hymn will go on singing until the last trump brings forth the angel band, and then, I think, it will mount up on some lip to the very presence of God. I would rather have written such a hymn than to have heaped up all the treasures of the richest man in the globe.'

Another writer says: 'There are some hymns which make themselves felt at once, as soon as they fall on the ear—hymns which never lose their freshness and power, never cease to widen their influence, until they are acknowledged as things of life, by all souls, in all lands, and over all seas. Such a hymn is that of Charles Wesley, "Jesu, Lover of my soul," a hymn whose music is kept up on both sides of the Atlantic.

Account of First Rank Hymns. 69

It has often been on the lips of departing saints in this land, when, as an aged Christian said, "they see their native land in the distance and the sea intervening,—a sea which none is able to cross unless borne by the Cross of Christ."'

Forty years ago, on a winter's night, a heavy gale set in upon the precipitous rock-bound coast of one of our western counties. A brave little coasting-vessel struggled hard and long to reach some shelter in the Bristol Channel, but the struggle was vain,—one dark, fearful headland could not be weathered; the bark must go on shore, and what a shore it was the fated men well knew. Then came the last pull for life. The boat was swung off and manned, captain and crew united in one more brave effort, but their toiling at the oar was soon over, their boat was swamped. They seem to have sunk together, for in the morning, when the day dawned, they were found lying all but side by side under the shelter of a weedy rock. They might have been saved had they stayed in the ship, for they had been borne in upon a heavy sea close under the cliff, where she was jammed immoveably between two rocks, and in the morning the ebb-tide left her high and dry. There was no sign of life on deck, and below scarcely anything told of late distress. One token of peace there was,—it was the captain's hymn-book still lying on the locker, closed upon the pencil with which he had marked some passages before he left the ship to meet his fate. A leaf of the page was turned down, and several pencil-marks were seen on the margin of Charles Wesley's precious hymn—

>   Jesu, Lover of my soul,
>   Let me to Thy bosom fly
>   While the nearer waters roll,
>   While the tempest still is high!

9. Sun of my soul, Thou Saviour dear!
It is not night if Thou be near.

John Keble, author of *The Christian Year*, is generally regarded as the most popular hymn-writer of the nineteenth century. He was the son of a clergyman, and was born at Fairford, Gloucestershire, in 1792. He was educated at Oxford, and graduated in 1810, on which occasion he took the distinguished honour of a double first. Shortly after he received a Fellowship, and was twice appointed a Public Examiner, and in 1831 Professor of Poetry. Among his fellow-students and friends were Arnold, Whately, Newman, and Pusey. Keble became Vicar of Hursley, near Winchester, in 1835, and there, amid the calm surroundings of a country village, the country parish priest pursued the quiet path of duty till his death in 1866. He died at Bournemouth in the seventy-fourth year of his age.

John Keble, in company with the illustrious men aforenamed, took part in the great religious movement of that day, generally known as 'the Tractarian Movement,' and contributed six of the ninety *Tracts for the Times*.

He was indefatigable in the cause of religion, and his pen never seemed to rest. With Pusey and Newman, Keble edited *The Library of the Fathers* and the

Anglo-Catholic Library. His edition of the *Works of Richard Hooker* and his *Life of Bishop Wilson* are justly regarded as standard works.

As a hymn-writer he will be best known to posterity by his *Christian Year*, a noble work, which reached its ninety-sixth edition before the author's death. It was published in 1827, and when the copyright expired in 1873, the enormous number of 350,000 copies had been sold. Since that year its circulation has immensely increased on both sides of the Atlantic, and it may safely be said that the success of *The Christian Year* is without a parallel in the history of religious poetry. In 1839 appeared his *Psalter, or Psalms of David in English Verse*, but, like all other metrical versions of the Psalms, it was not a success. In 1846 he published *Lyra Innocentium, or Thoughts in Verse for Children, their Ways and their Privileges.* Although without family himself, Keble was very fond of children, and consequently wrote many beautiful hymns for the young. Indeed, many pieces in *Lyra Innocentium* are thought to be of equal excellence with those in *The Christian Year.*

He was a man of deep piety and retiring modesty; and the MS. of *The Christian Year* was reluctantly published at the urgent solicitation of his intimate friends. He says that his plan was 'to go on improving his series all his life, and leave it to come out, if judged useful, only when he should be fairly out of the way;' and again he elsewhere writes: 'I am not without hopes that I shall quite persuade my persuaders to let it stand over *sine die.*' The treasure, however, was not to be kept in secret. His friend Whately had seen the MS. of the hymns, and spoke of their high poetic excellence. Dr. Arnold also had seen them, and wrote to Sir John Coleridge: 'I live in hopes that he will be induced to publish them; and it is my firm opinion that nothing equal to them exists in our language: the wonderful knowledge of Scripture, the purity of heart, and the richness of poetry which they exhibit, I never saw paralleled.' Newman and other high authorities have spoken of them in similar eulogistic terms, and the English public have approved of their judgment. What Wordsworth did for poetry in general, Keble did the same for religious verse; inasmuch as his hymns are distinguished for chaste refinement and deep spirituality. Like Wordsworth and George Herbert, his poetry abounds in allusions to the beauties of Nature, so that Nature and Revelation unite in singing the praises of the Great Governor of all things in heaven and earth. His well-known Evening Hymn is perhaps the most popular of all his poems. It is the second piece in *The Christian Year*, and in the original consists of fourteen stanzas. There is a wide-prevailing notion that the hymn loses much of its beauty by the common omission of the first two stanzas. The sudden turn of thought from the natural sun to the Sun of Righteousness is very effective. Thus—

> 'Tis gone, that bright and orbèd blaze,
> Fast fading from our wistful gaze;
> Yon mantling cloud has hid from sight
> The last faint pulse of quivering light.

> In darkness and in weariness
> The traveller on his way must press,
> No gleam to watch on tree and tower,
> Whiling away the lonesome hour.

> Sun of my soul, Thou Saviour dear!
> It is not night if Thou be near;
> O may no earth-born cloud arise
> To hide Thee from thy servant's eyes!

10. When I survey the wondrous cross
    On which the Prince of glory died.

This admirable hymn, one of the most touching in the English language, was written by Isaac Watts, and appeared in 1709, when the author was thirty-five years old. The original consisted of five stanzas, but the fourth is invariably omitted in modern Hymnals, as being much inferior to the others. It is as follows:—

> His dying crimson like a robe
> Spreads o'er His body on the tree;
> Then am I dead to all the globe,
> And all the globe is dead to me.

The hymn is founded on Gal. vi. 14, 'God forbid that I should glory, save in the cross of our Lord Jesus Christ, by whom the world is crucified unto me, and I unto the world;' and Phil. iii. 7, 'What things were gain to me, those I counted loss for Christ.'

A writer of the *Oxford Essays* in 1858 fixes upon the above as Watts's finest hymn, and by general consent it is selected out of about twenty thousand English hymns to take the highest rank as one of the six best hymns in the English language.

Account of First Rank Hymns.

Isaac Watts, one of the best English hymnists, was the son of a schoolmaster, and was born at Southampton in 1674. His parents were Nonconformists, and eminently pious, so that from infancy the poet was reared in a pious home. In boyhood he gave promise of his superior talents. His education was intrusted to a Southampton clergyman, and continued by an Independent minister in London. Here Isaac injured his constitution through excessive study, and returned for two years to his father's house. During these two years he pursued his poetic studies, and wrote many good hymns. Again he went to London and became a private tutor at Stoke Newington. At this period he entered the ministry, and continued for fourteen years to minister to an Independent congregation. In 1712 he went on a friendly visit to the country seat of Sir Thomas Abney, in Hertfordshire. Sir Thomas was so delighted with Watts that he offered him a permanent home, and for the remainder of his life, a period of thirty-six years, the poet-preacher resided with his patrons, Sir Thomas and Lady Abney.

The rural retreat in Hertfordshire suited his delicate constitution, and afforded him favourable opportunities for pursuing his literary studies. Besides hymns, sermons, and religious works, he wrote treatises on logic, astronomy, and other subjects. In 1720 his works were published in six quarto volumes. In 1728 Watts received his Doctor's degree from the Universities of Edinburgh and Aberdeen. His Catechisms and Divine Songs were written at the request of his patrons. His

Account of First Rank Hymns. 75

rhymes are sometimes poor, and the expressions objectionable; yet Watts 'must always stand high for the comprehensiveness and catholicity of his hymns, for their fulness of Gospel doctrine, and for the numerous instances in which they fulfil all that can be required in a Christian hymn, and in which criticism is forgotten in the joyful consent of the reader's heart.' Dr. Johnson, no mean judge, gives the following high and just estimate of Dr. Watts:—'Few men have left behind such purity of character or such monuments of laborious piety. He has provided instruction for all ages,—from those who are lisping their first lessons to the enlightened readers of Malebranche and Locke; he has left neither corporeal nor spiritual nature unexamined: he has taught the art of reasoning and the science of the stars. His character, therefore, must be formed from the multiplicity and diversity of his attainments, rather than from any single performance; for it would not be safe to claim for him the highest rank in any single denomination of literary dignity; yet perhaps there was nothing in which he would not have excelled, if he had not divided his powers to different pursuits.'

He was a man of great generosity and deep humility, and his Christian character was of the highest order. His catholicity of spirit and his ardent zeal for the truths of the Gospel and the cause of Christ shine out in all his works.

The dying words of this great hymn-writer ought to be remembered by all generations: 'I would be waiting to see what God will do with me. It is good to say, as Mr. Baxter, "What, when, and where God pleases." The business of a Christian is to do and hear the will of God, and if I was in health I could but be doing that, and that I may be now. If God should raise me up again I may finish some more of my papers, or God can make use of me to save a soul, and that will be worth living for. If God has no more service for me to do, through grace "I am ready." It is a great mercy to me that I have no manner of fear or dread of death. I could, if God please, lay my head back and die without alarm this afternoon or night. My chief supports are from my view of eternal things, and the interest I have in them; I trust all my sins are pardoned through the blood of Christ.' In this happy frame the great hymnist entered into his rest in 1748, at seventy-four years of age.

11. Holy! Holy! Holy! Lord God Almighty!
    Early in the morning our song shall rise to Thee.

This grand hymn, which has the noble swell of an anthem, was composed by Bishop Heber, and appeared in 1827 in *Hymns Written and Adapted to the Weekly Church Service of the Year*. It there appears as the hymn for Trinity Sunday, and is founded on the portion of Holy Scripture appointed for the Epistle for that day, and especially on the words, 'They rest not day and night, saying, Holy, holy, holy, Lord God Almighty, which was, and is, and is to come.' The popularity of

Account of First Rank Hymns. 77

the hymn has been increased by the magnificent tune to which it is sung. The tune is called Nicæa, and was composed by Dr. Dykes expressly for Heber's hymn. Nicæa in Asia Minor was the place where the first Christian Ecumenical Council was held in 325. At this Council the Eternal Sonship of Christ and His equality with the Father were established as a dogma, and thus the doctrine of the Holy Trinity, which had been impugned by the Arians, was vindicated.

Reginald Heber, the well-known hymnist, was the son of Reginald Heber, Rector of Malpas, Cheshire, where he was born in 1783. He was educated at Oxford, and in 1801 took the Chancellor's prize for a Latin poem. In 1803, when only twenty years old, he gained the University prize by his beautiful poem 'Palestine,' considered to be the best Oxford prize poem of this century. In 1807 Heber became Rector of Hodnet, Shropshire, where he laboured for sixteen years. In 1823 he was made Bishop of Calcutta, and for two and a half years he laboured in his vast diocese with unflagging zeal. He died suddenly of apoplexy, and his end was very sad. On 3d April 1826 the Bishop was at Trichinopoly, in the south of India. 'After some particular arrangements for the morning,' says his biographer, 'he left me in order to undress and bathe.' 'Some time having elapsed, and the Bishop not returning, his servant became alarmed, opened the door of the bath, and saw his master's lifeless body lying below the surface of the water. Medical assistance was at once procured, but in vain.' It was the opinion of medical men on the spot that disease had been existing for some time, and that under any circumstances his life could not have been a long one, but that the end was hastened by excessive labours and the effects of the climate, and the fatal catastrophe caused by the shock of the cold water on an enfeebled frame.'

12. Jesus Christ is risen to-day, Hallelujah!
    Our triumphant holy day.   Hallelujah!

The author of this noble hymn for Easter Day is unknown. Three stanzas appear in a little work printed at Northampton in 1749, called, *The Compleat Psalmodist*, by John Arnold. Appended to the stanzas are the initials C. B., and it is thought that the hymn may have been the work of one of Doddridge's pupils.

Unfortunately all the old records of the printers of the book were destroyed by fire a few years ago. Philip Doddridge, the sweet hymnist, conducted an academy in Northampton for twenty years, 1730-1750. In this academy he trained young men for the ministry, and about 200 students were trained by him in that period. It is known that some of the students, emulating their master, composed some noble verses, to wit, 'O God of Bethel! by whose hand,' etc. The 'Gloria' often appended to it as a fourth stanza is certainly from the pen of Charles Wesley, and appears in his *Hymns and Sacred Poems*, published in 1743. In a collection of hymns entitled *Lyra Davidica*, published in 1708 at

London, occur 'some verses very much resembling the above Easter Hymn.

They appear to be a translation of a Latin hymn of the fourteenth century beginning, 'Surrexit Christus hodie' ('Christ is risen to-day').

It thus appears that of the four stanzas of the hymn, the first stanza, beginning, 'Jesus Christ is risen to-day,' is a translation by an anonymous writer *circa* 1708. The second and third stanzas, beginning respectively—

> 'Hymns of praise then let us sing,'
> 'But the pain which He endured,'

were re-written about 1749 by C. B.

The fourth stanza, called the 'Gloria,' beginning, 'Sing we to our God above. Hallelujah!' is from the pen of Charles Wesley, about 1743.

> 13. Nearer, my God, to Thee,—
>   Nearer to Thee!
> E'en though it be a cross
>   That raiseth me,
> Still all my song shall be,
> Nearer, my God, to Thee,—
>   Nearer to Thee!

Sarah Flower, author of this favourite hymn, was born at Cambridge in 1805. She was the younger of two sisters, both distinguished for literary ability. On the death of their father they took up their residence in London. In 1834 she married Mr. Adams, the well-known civil engineer, and favourably known also as a literary writer. Mrs. Adams became distinguished for her religious earnestness and the moral influence she exerted over all who came within the sphere of her influence. Her sister died in 1847, and Mrs. Adams's long and unremitting attention to her sister during affliction so enfeebled her own health that she gradually sank, and died in 1849. She was buried at Foster Street, near Harlaw, Essex. In 1840 Mrs. Adams composed the above well-known hymn, which first appears in a volume of *Hymns and Anthems*, published in 1841. The prayer embodied in the hymn had been answered in her own experience. She was a member of a Unitarian congregation, and this accounts for the fact that the hymn, beautiful though it is, never rises to the level of Christianity. The hymn is founded on that part of Jacob's journey to Padan-Aram, when he halted for the night at Bethel, and falling asleep, with a stone for his pillow, dreamt that he saw a ladder let down from heaven to earth, with angels ascending and descending upon it. A few years ago, while journeying through the Holy Land, we visited the scene of the patriarch's halting-place for the night. Two hours over the bleak heights of Benjamin brought us to the venerable ruins of Bethel. Standing by the ruined mounds, we remembered that somewhere near this spot Abraham pitched his tent, and built an altar on 'the mountain east of Bethel, having Bethel on the west and Ai on the east.' A few wretched hovels, the remains of an enormous cistern, and the ruins of a Greek church, are all that remain

Account of First Rank Hymns.

to indicate the position of ancient Bethel. After singing the hymn,

> Nearer, my God, to Thee,
> Nearer to Thee!

we pursued our journey northwards towards Central Palestine.

14. Hark, the glad sound! the Saviour comes,
    The Saviour promised long:
    Let every heart prepare a throne,
    And every voice a song.

This grand Advent hymn is one of rare excellence, and appeared in 1755. It is founded on the passage of Scripture which the Saviour read in the synagogue of Nazareth, out of the Book of the Prophet Isaiah: 'The Spirit of the Lord is upon Me; because He hath anointed Me to preach the gospel to the poor; He hath sent Me to heal the broken-hearted, to preach deliverance to the captives, and recovering of sight to the blind, to set at liberty them that are bruised, to preach the acceptable year of the Lord.'

The original hymn consists of seven stanzas, but the two following are seldom seen:—

> On Him the Spirit, largely poured,
>   Exerts its sacred fire;
> Wisdom and might, and zeal and love,
>   His holy breast inspire.
>
> His silver trumpets publish loud
>   The jubilee of the Lord;
> Our debts are all remitted now,
>   Our heritage restored.

Philip Doddridge, the well-known hymnist, was born in London in 1702. He lost both his parents in childhood, but the orphan was befriended by the Rev. Samuel Clarke and others. He received his education at Kibworth and Hinckley, and at the age of twenty his earnest piety induced him to become an Independent minister. For seven years he was pastor of the quiet village of Kibworth. At the urgent request of Dr. Watts, he opened an academy, first at Market Harborough, and the following year at Northampton, for the purpose of training young men for the ministry. He continued his collegiate duties for twenty years, and about 200 young students passed through his academy. Dr. Isaac Watts was his contemporary and steadfast friend. Both were Independent ministers, and writers of sacred song, and throughout life they continued to live in deep sympathy and brotherly love with each other. Dr. Watts was nearly thirty years his senior, but Doddridge, through enfeebled health, survived his more illustrious compeer three years only. Doddridge's literary works are both voluminous and valuable; the best known is *The Rise and Progress of Religion in the Soul*, written at the suggestion of Dr. Watts, whose declining strength did not permit him to carry out his own design. It is said that Baxter's *Saints' Rest* moved Watts and Doddridge to write *The Rise and Progress of Religion*. Further, this book was of great spiritual service to William Wilberforce, and prompted that illustrious benefactor of slaves to write his excellent treatise, *Practical View of Christianity*. Thus it

Account of First Rank Hymns. 83

happens that the three works alluded to form three consecutive links in the chain of the development of Christian doctrine.

The Family Expositor is considered to be Doddridge's greatest prose work, and was the fruit of many years' earnest study. It was published in 1739, when the author was only thirty-seven years old. He exercised great personal influence, and enjoyed the friendship of Bishop Warburton, the Countess of Huntingdon, the Wesleys, Whitefield, Hervey, Dr. Watts, and the other leaders of religious thought during the last century. His over-wrought life was brought to an early close by consumption, against the progress of which all efforts were of no avail. In 1751 he journeyed to Lisbon for the benefit of warmer air, but died soon after his arrival, in his fiftieth year.

Doddridge was undoubtedly a man of literary talent and distinguished piety, but it is chiefly as a hymn-writer that his name is known, and will continue to be handed down to posterity. His hymns were not printed during his life, but they were written, and most of them were sung from MSS. at the close of the author's sermons. They have accordingly been compared to 'spiritual amber fetched up and floated off from sermons long since lost in the depths of bygone time.' In 1740 Lady Gardiner called them 'charming hymns,' and urged the author to publish them. Robert Blair, author of *The Grave*, and a contemporary poet, expresses himself as delighted with Doddridge's hymns.

In 1755, four years after his death, Doddridge's

hymns, 364 in number, were published by Job Orton, his friend and faithful biographer; and James Montgomery passes the following high encomium upon them:—'They shine in the beauty of holiness; these offsprings of his mind are arrayed in the "fine linen, pure and white, which is the righteousness of saints," and like the saints they are lovely and acceptable, not for their human merit, for in poetry and eloquence they are frequently deficient, but for that fervent unaffected love to God, His service, and His people, which distinguishes them.'

15. How sweet the name of Jesus sounds
    In a believer's ear!

This favourite hymn by Newton first appeared in the *Olney Hymns* in 1779, entitled 'The Name of Jesus.' It is founded on a thought in Solomon's Song: 'Thy name is as ointment poured forth;' and it may also have been suggested by St. Bernard's 'Jesu, dulcis memoria,'—beautifully rendered by Edward Caswall in his 'Jesu, the very thought of Thee,' and by Neale in his 'Jesu, the very thought is sweet.' Both Doddridge and Charles Wesley have written similar hymns, and probably they all drew from the same ancient source, the 'Jesu, dulcis memoria' of St. Bernard, written about 1140 A.D.

John Newton, the well-known hymn-writer, was born in London in 1725. He lost his pious mother when only seven years old, and the boy's education was sadly

Account of First Rank Hymns. 85

neglected. He was 'much left to himself, to mingle with idle and wicked boys, and soon learnt their ways, and thus grew up to be a libertine and infidel. For many years he led a wild, profligate life : entered the navy, deserted, and was publicly whipped ; then became a slave-trader, and was for a while captain of a slave-ship. At the age of twenty-four, while on a voyage, he picked up a copy of Thomas à Kempis's *Imitation of Christ*, and after perusing the volume the thought struck him, 'What if these things should be true?' That very night a terrible storm arose, and the ship was nearly wrecked. This led him to solemn thought, and forthwith he experienced a religious change. In 1764, at the age of thirty-nine, he was ordained, and presented by the Earl of Dartmouth to the curacy of Olney, where he ministered with much earnestness for sixteen years. There he became very intimate with Cowper, and daily endeavoured to console the suffering poet. Newton was a man of considerable zeal, and vigorously propagated Calvinistic doctrines. Once a week he held a religious meeting at a vacant house in Olney, known as the 'Great House,' belonging to the Earl of Dartmouth. He persuaded Cowper to take a leading part in these meetings, and it is thought that the excitement intensified Cowper's dreadful malady. Both wrote hymns for these weekly assemblies. Newton in his diary for 1775 says, 'I usually make one hymn a week to expound at the Great House.' Together they composed the *Olney Hymns*, published in 1779, a collection of which Cowper composed sixty-eight, and Newton two hundred and eighty. In composing hymns for public worship, Newton tells us that his great object was to make them clear and simple, so that they might be readily understood by poor and unlearned, as well as by the rich and cultivated. 'Perspicuity, simplicity, and ease should be chiefly attended to; and the imagery and colouring of poetry, if admitted at all, should be indulged very sparingly, and with great judgment.' Newton subsequently became the well-known Rector of St. Mary's Woolnoth, London, and died in 1807 at the advanced age of eighty-two years.

16. Jerusalem, my happy home!
    Name ever dear to me!
  When shall my labours have an end,
    In joy, and peace, and thee?

In the British Museum is a thin quarto volume, numbered 15,225, with the name 'Queen Elizabeth' lettered on the back. It contains several pieces of sacred poetry, evidently written by Roman Catholics. One piece is headed, 'Here followeth the song Mr. Thewlis wrote;' another, 'Here followeth the song of the death of Mr. Thewlis.' It is known that John Thewlis was a Roman Catholic priest, barbarously murdered at Manchester in the year 1617. Then follows the above hymn, with the heading, 'A Song by F. B. P. to the tune of Diana.' Recent criticism tends to show that the initials stand for Francis Baker, Priest, a Roman Catholic who suffered persecution in

Account of First Rank Hymns. 87

the reign of Queen Elizabeth. The late Daniel Sedgwick, whose knowledge of English hymnology was unrivalled, thought the initials stood for Francis Baker Porter, a secular priest, the author of several devotional works, and for some time imprisoned in the Tower of London. The hymn by F. B. P. consists of twenty-six verses of four lines each, and begins :—

> Jerusalem, my happy home!
> When shall I come to thee?
> When shall my sorrows have an end?
> Thy joys when shall I see?

As the hymn is one of great beauty and simplicity, and as moreover it has proved a source of inspiration to many hymn-writers, who have reproduced its sublime sentiments in endless variety, it seems desirable to quote the whole of F. B. P.'s sacred ode :—

Hierusalem ! my happie home !
When shall I come to thee?
When shall my sorrows have an end ?
Thy joyes when shall I see ?

O happie harbor of the saints,
O sweete and pleasant soyle,
In thee no sorrow may be found,
Noe greefe, noe care, noe toyle!

In thee noe sicknesse may be seene,
Noe hurt, noe ache, noe sore ;
There is noe death, nor ugly dole,
But life for evermore.

Noe dampish mist is seene in thee,
Noe cold nor darksome night ;
There everie soul shines as the sun ;
There God Himselfe gives light.

There lust and lucre cannot dwell,
There envy bears no sway ;
There is noe hunger, heate, nor colde,
But pleasure everie way.

Hierusalem ! Hierusalem !
God grant I once may see
Thy endless joyes, and of the same
Partaker aye to bee !

Thy walls are made of pretious
  stones,
Thy bulwarkes diamondes
  square,
Thy gates are of right orient
  pearle,
Exceedinge riche and rare.

Thy turrettes and thy pinnacles
With carbuncles doe shine ;
Thy verrie streets are paved
  with gould,
Surpassinge cleare and fine.

Thy houses are of yvorie,
Thy windows crystal cleare ;
Thy tyles are made of beaten
  gould ;
O God, that I were there !

Within thy gates doth nothing
  come
That is not passing cleane ;
Noe spider's web, noe durt,
  noe dust,
Noe filthe may there be seene.

Ah ! my sweete Home, Hieru-
  salem,
Would God I were in thee !
Would God my woes were at
  an end,
Thy joyes that I might see !

Thy saints are crowned with
  glory great,
They see God face to face ;
They triumph still, they still
  rejoyce ;
Most happie is their case.

Wee that are heere in banish-
  ment
Continuallie doe moane ;
We sigh and sobbe, we weepe
  and waile,
Perpetuallie we groane.

Our sweete is mixed with
  bitter gaule,
Our pleasure is but paine ;
Our ioyes scarce last the looke-
  ing on,
Our sorrowes still remaine.

But there they live in such
  delight,
Such pleasure and such play,
As that to them a thousand
  yeares
Doth seeme as yesterday.

Thy vineyardes and thy or-
  chardes are
Most beautifull and faire,
Full furnishèd with trees and
  fruits,
Exceeding riche and rare.

Thy gardens and thy gallant
  walkes
Continually are greene ;
There growe such sweete and
  pleasant flowers
As noe where else are seene.

There nectar and ambrosia
  flow,
There muske and civette
  sweete,
There manie a faire and daintie
  drugge
Are trodden under feete.

There cinnamon, there sugar
  grow,
There nardeand balme abound;
What tounge can telle or harte
  containe
The ioyes that there are found?

Quyt through the streetes, with
  silver sound,
The Flood of Life doth flowe;
Upon whose bankes on everie
  syde,
The Wood of Life doth growe.

There trees for evermore beare
  fruite,
And evermore doe springe;
There evermore the Angels sit,
And evermore doe singe.

There David stands, with harpe
  in hands,
As master of the queere;
Tenne thousand times that man
  were blest,
That might this musicke heare!

Our Ladie singes Magnificat
With tones surpassinge
  sweete;
And all the Virginns beare their
  parte,
Sitting about her feete.

'Te Deum' doth Saint Ambrose singe,
Saint Austine doth the like;
Ould Simeon and Zacharie
Have not their songes to seeke.

There Magdalene hath left her
  mone,
And cheerfullie doth singe,
With blessed Saints whose
  harmonie
In everie street doth ringe.

Hierusalem! my happie Home!
Would God I were in thee!
Would God my woes were at
  an end,
Thy ioyes that I might see

The tone of the poem indicates that it is the work of a Roman Catholic, to wit, the stanza—

> Our Ladie singes Magnificat
> With tones surpassing sweete;
> And all the Virginns beare their parte,
> Sitting about her feete.

As Mr. Thewlis, mentioned in the quarto, is known to have been murdered in 1617, it follows that the book itself could not have been compiled before that year, although it contains poems of a much earlier date. It is now generally thought that the sacred song by

F. B. P. is a rendering of some old hymn, of which the original text and author are unknown. Probably it was drawn from several sources, and especially from an ancient Latin hymn of twenty-four long lines that appears in Daniel's *Thesaurus Hymnologicus*, and begins—

> Urbs beata Hierusalem, dicta pacis visio,
> Quae construitur in coelis vivis ex lapidibus.

This seems to have been designed primarily 'In Dedicatione Ecclesiae' ('For the dedication of a church'). The author and date of the original text are unknown, but it is believed to date from the eighth or ninth century. Unfortunately the Latin was tampered with in the seventeenth century, and in consequence the original lost much of its beauty and spirit. Dr. Neale says: 'This grand hymn of the eighth century was modernised in the reform of Pope Urban VIII. into the "Coelestis urbs Jerusalem," and lost half of its beauty in the process.' This opinion is amply confirmed by Archbishop Trench, who in his *Sacred Latin Poetry* says:—

'Of this rugged but fine old hymn the author is not known, but it probably dates from the eighth or ninth century. I have observed already upon the manner in which these grand old compositions were re-cast in the Romish Church at the revival of learning, which was, in Italy at least, to so large an extent a revival of heathenism. This is one of the few that have not utterly perished in the process; while yet, if we compare the first two rugged and somewhat uncouth stanzas, but withal so sweet, with the smooth iambics which in the Roman Breviary have taken their place, we shall feel how much of their beauty has disappeared.'

The original two stanzas are—

> Urbs beata Hierusalem, dicta pacis visio,
> Quae construitur in coelis vivis ex lapidibus,
> Et ab angelis ornata, velut sponsa nobilis
> Nova veniens e coelo, nuptiali thalamo
> Praeparata, ut sponsata copuletur Domino
> Plateae et muri ejus ex auro purissimo.

These stanzas, rendered into iambics in the Roman Breviary of the seventeenth century, are—

Coelestis urbs Jerusalem	O sorte nupta prosperâ,
Beata pacis visio,	Dotata Patris gloriâ,
Quae celsa de viventibus	Respersa Sponsi gratiâ,
Saxis ad astra tolleris	Regina formosissima,
Sponsaeque ritu congeris	Christo jugata Principi,
Mille angelorum millibus:	Coelo coruscas civitas.

The two concluding stanzas of the original hymn, Daniel, in his *Thesaurus Hymnologicus,* conceives not to have belonged to the hymn as first composed, but to have been added to it to adapt it to a Feast of Dedication. Not so. The hymn coheres intimately in all its parts, and in ceasing to be a hymn 'In Dedicatione Ecclesiae' it would lose its chiefest beauty. It is most truly a hymn of degrees, ascending from things earthly to things heavenly, and making those interpreters of these. The prevailing intention in the building and dedication of the church, with the rites thereto appertaining, was to carry up men's thoughts from that temple built with hands, which they saw, to that other, built of living stones, in heaven, of which this was but a shadow: compare two beautiful sermons by Hildebert. A

Sequence, 'De Dedicatione Ecclesiae,' which Daniel himself gives, should have preserved him from this error :—

> Blessed city, Heavenly Salem,
> Vision dear of peace and love.

This happy rendering by Dr. Neale, dated 1851, is a translation of the beautiful old Church Dedication Hymn, ' Urbs beata Hierusalem.'

Dr. Neale's translation of the second part of the old Latin hymn is the well-known version—

> Christ is made the sure foundation,
> Christ the Head and Corner-stone.
> Angulare fundamentum lapis Christus missus est.

The Most Reverend E. W. Benson, now Archbishop of Canterbury, has also translated the rugged eighth-century Latin hymn. His renderings appeared in the *Hymn-book for Wellington College*, and were written for the dedication of the College in 1863. These scholarly and elegant translations commence—

> Part I. Blessed city, Heavenly Salem,
> Peaceful vision dim-descried.

> Part II. Deeply laid a sure foundation,
> Christ the anointed Corner-stone.

The Rev. John Chandler in 1837 published an extremely spirited and deservedly popular translation of the second part, beginning—

> Christ is our Corner-stone,
> On Him alone we build.

At Karlsruhe exists a MS. of a long Latin hymn, thought to belong to the fifteenth century. The subject of the poem is ' The glory of the Heavenly Jeru-

Account of First Rank Hymns. 93

salem.' Although the author is unknown, yet the language and general ideas indicate that he belonged to the school of Thomas à Kempis. It is possible that the poem is a cento and expansion of the eighth-century Latin hymn. Dr. Neale made happy translations of the three portions of the hymn, the more striking stanzas having first appeared in the *Hymnal Noted*.

Part I. is 'Of the glory of the Heavenly Jerusalem in general,' and begins—

| If there be that skill to reckon | Quisquis valet numerare |
| All the number of the blest. | Beatorum numerum. |

Part II. is a great favourite, and is frequently employed as a dedication hymn. It consists of twelve stanzas of six lines each, and in the original is entitled 'Of the glory of the Heavenly Jerusalem as far as concerneth the Glorified Body:'—

| Light's abode, Celestial Salem, | Jerusalem luminosa |
| Vision whence true peace doth spring. | Verae pacis visio. |

It ought to be noticed that the opening Latin words appear to be a re-cast of the eighth-century hymn, 'Urbs beata Hierusalem, dicta pacis visio.'

The Third Part of the hymn, entitled 'Of the glory of the Heavenly Jerusalem, as concerning the endowments of the Glorified Soul,' commences—

| Eye hath never seen the glory, | Nec quisquam oculis vidit |
| Ear hath never heard the song. | Neque ullis sensibus. |

Not long after the date of this fifteenth-century hymn, was composed Francis Baker's English sacred song, 'Hierusalem! my happie Home,' and, judging from its general tone and language, it would appear that the author of this most beautiful song was acquainted with the Latin hymns of the eighth and fifteenth centuries.

Whether or not the beautiful hymn of Francis Baker is a translation, or rather cento, of the rugged old Latin hymn, it is certain that the English version has itself proved a source of inspiration to many hymn-writers, to wit—David Dickson, who was a distinguished Presbyterian minister of the seventeenth century, and became Professor of Divinity, first in Glasgow University, then in Edinburgh. He was deprived of his office at the restoration of Charles II., because he refused to take the Oath of Supremacy. Dickson had attained to manhood when F. B. P.'s hymn was discovered in the British Museum, and he died in 1663.

He was a good hymn-writer, and published about the year 1650 a volume of poems on pious and serious subjects. Amongst them is a long sacred poem, consisting of about 250 lines, on the Celestial Jerusalem. It is evidently a revision and enlargement of Francis Baker's hymn, although more than half appears to be original, inasmuch as Dickson's version is more than double that of Baker's. It begins with the well-known words—

> O mother dear Jerusalem!
> When shall I come to thee?

As might be expected, Dickson's poem expurgates sentiments thought to savour of Roman Catholicism.

Account of First Rank Hymns. 95

Thus 'Our Ladie singes Magnificat' becomes 'There Mary sings Magnificat.' Dickson himself has been severely condemned for appropriating to himself Baker's poem, and the expansion has been stigmatised as 'a quantity of his own rubbish.' This severity of language is not warranted, inasmuch as there exists no evidence to show that Dickson palmed off his enlarged cento as a poem entirely original, and many of his own stanzas, far from being rubbish, are pregnant with sublime thoughts.

Robert Wodrow wrote a Life of Dickson about fifty years after his death, and there the biographer states that he had 'seen in print some short poems published by Dickson in 1649, and among them, "O mother dear Jerusalem."' Founded on this testimony, the public concluded that the whole poem was original, and this misconception existed until the discovery of Baker's poem in the British Museum. It is, however, unfair to charge Dickson's memory with the error of posterity, unless there is proof that he was guilty of wilful plagiarism.

About two hundred years ago, and only thirty years after Dickson's death, appeared another version of Baker's hymn, by the Rev. W. Burkitt, Vicar of Dedham. The alterations made were not very happy, and in some places, indeed, destroyed both the spirit and sense of the original. Thus, where Baker had written

> Thy gardens and thy *gallant walkes*
> Continually are greene,

was rendered by Burkitt, 'Thy gardens and thy *pleasant*

fruits,' making it difficult to reconcile 'pleasant fruit' with the fact that it is continually green.

The present very beautiful version, found in almost all modern Hymnals,

> Jerusalem, my happy home,
> Name ever dear to me,

does not appear to be very old. It appeared in a Hymnal dated 1801, by Williams and Boden, entitled, *A Collection of* 600 *Hymns, designed as a New Supplement to Dr. Watts' Psalms and Hymns.* The hymn is there stated to be taken from the Eckington collection, but unfortunately nothing is said of the author of this favourite adaptation of Baker's hymn. The Rev. James Boden, one of the compilers of the hymnal, lived and died within a few miles of Eckington, a village in Yorkshire, and as he himself was a hymn-writer it is possible that he made this adaptation for the Eckington collection.

Fragments of Baker's sacred song are found in every Hymnal, and have gladdened the Christian Church for about three centuries. Truly has it been remarked that 'many versions of this prisoner's hymn have found their way into different parts of Europe, and many a home and many a prison it may have made the happier, by its simple soothing tones, and its tuneful alternations of plaintiveness and triumph. Snatches of it used to be heard among the hills and glens of Scotland. They lived in the memory and heart of many a Scotch mother, and seem to have been sung as devout and cheering accompaniments to the daily duties of cottage life. Nor was this without good fruit even in distant lands, fruit that sprang up far away from the spot where the seed first fell.'

'A young Scotchman who was on his deathbed at New Orleans,' says the American biographer of Whitefield, 'was visited by a Presbyterian minister, but continued for a time to shut himself up against all the good man's efforts to reach his heart. Somewhat discouraged, at last the visitor turned away, and scarcely knowing why, unless it were for his own comfort, began to sing "Jerusalem, my happy home." That was enough—a tender chord was touched. The young patient's heart was broken, and with bursting tears he said, "My dear mother used to sing that hymn." The prisoner, too, whose song went out from the Tower to fulfil such heavenly missions, now enjoys the city of his desire, and many have gathered around him there whose way thither had been brightened by the music of his hymn.'

> Jerusalem on high
> My song and city is,
> My home whene'er I die,
> The centre of my bliss.

This hymn on the 'New Jerusalem' is part of a poem, consisting of fourteen stanzas, on 'Heaven,' beginning—

> Sweet place, sweet place alone!
> The court of God most High.

It was written more than two centuries ago by Samuel Crossman, a Prebendary of Bristol Cathedral; born

1624, died 1683. The poem first appeared in a little book of nine poems entitled *The Young Man's Meditation, or some few Poems on Select Subjects.* The second piece, on 'Heaven,' is the best, but, beautiful as it is, the hymn was long forgotten. Its great popularity at present is partly owing to the fact that Lord Selborne specially commended it at the York Church Conference in 1866, and the York choir sang the hymn in the Minster on the occasion, to Dr. Croft's soul-stirring tune.

17. From Greenland's icy mountains,
    From India's coral strand.

This world-renowned hymn is generally regarded as the best missionary hymn ever written. It was written by Heber under peculiar circumstances. In 1819 a royal letter was issued requesting that collections should be made in all the churches of England on behalf of the Society for the Propagation of the Gospel. Heber, then Rector of Hodnet, went to Wrexham to hear the Dean of St. Asaph preach on the day appointed, and on the previous Saturday was requested by the Dean to compose a hymn for the missionary service of the next day. In a short time he composed the above hymn, which was sung on the morrow—Whitsunday 1819—in the parish church of Wrexham. Heber had always evinced great zeal for Christian missions, and his verses are an undying expression of his ruling missionary passion. Four years afterwards, 1823, he was induced to accept the

Bishopric of the vast diocese of Calcutta, which then included the whole of India, Ceylon, Mauritius, and Australia.

The hymn acquires additional interest from the fact that it is the work of one who was willing to leave his native land, his home, and much that is dear to a literary man, in order to undertake the vast responsibility of a far-reaching diocese. Before setting out for India in 1823 Bishop Heber met the Committee of the Society for the Propagation of the Gospel. One who was present on the occasion says: 'We shall long remember the sensation which he produced when he declared that his last hope would be to be the chief missionary of the Society in the East, and the emotion with which we all knelt down at the close— sorrowing most of all that we should see his face no more.'

A passage in his *Journal of a Voyage to India*, September 1823, throws light upon the lines, 'What though the spicy breezes blow soft o'er Ceylon's isle :' 'Though we were now too far off Ceylon to catch the odours of land, yet it is, we are assured, perfectly true that such odours are perceptible to a very considerable distance. In the Straits of Malacca a smell like that of a hawthorn hedge is commonly experienced; and from Ceylon, at thirty or forty miles, under certain circumstances, a yet more agreeable scent is inhaled.' For about three years Heber pursued the arduous duties of a missionary bishop with amazing zeal, but his constitution succumbed to the over-pressure of labour, and he died in April 1826—a missionary martyr in the prime of his life.

'The winds seem to have wafted Heber's song, and the rolling waters have borne it forth, till what was first sung in Wrexham Church in 1819 now rises from human hearts and lips over three parts of the world.'

Further particulars of the hymn, together with a facsimile of the original MS., were printed at Wrexham, and shown at the Great Exhibition of 1851. From this source we learn that on Whitsunday 1819 the late Dr. Shipley, Dean of St. Asaph and Vicar of Wrexham, preached a sermon in Wrexham Church in aid of the Society for the Propagation of the Gospel in Foreign Parts. That day was also fixed upon for the commencement of the Sunday evening lectures intended to be established in that church, and the late Bishop of Calcutta (Heber), then Rector of Hodnet, the Dean's son-in-law, undertook to deliver the first lecture. In the course of the Saturday previous, the Dean and his son-in-law being together at the Vicarage, the former requested Heber to write something for them to sing in the morning, and he retired for that purpose from the table, where the Dean and a few friends were sitting, to a distant part of the room. In a short time the Dean inquired, 'What have you written?' Heber, having then composed the first three verses, read them over. 'There, there; that will do very well,' said the Dean. 'No, no; the sense is not complete,' replied Heber. Accordingly he added the fourth verse, 'Waft, waft, ye winds, His story,' and the Dean being inexorable to his repeated request of 'Let me add another! O let me add another!' the hymn was thus completed which has since become so celebrated. It was sung the next morning in Wrexham Church for the first time.

18. Great God, what do I see and hear?
The end of things created.

This noble Advent hymn, generally known by the incorrect title of 'Luther's Hymn,' has a peculiar history. The tune to which it is almost invariably sung is from a German air of the sixteenth century, and is called 'Luther,' which may, in part at least, account for the popular misnomer, viz., 'Luther's Hymn.'

The original German hymn, from which the above is drawn, was the work of Bartholomew Ringwaldt, a Lutheran village pastor, born in 1530, died in 1598 at the age of sixty-eight years. Ringwaldt's German hymn first appeared in 1585, and consisted of seven stanzas. It was, in style at least, written in imitation of an ancient Latin hymn—'Dies irae, dies illa,' composed three centuries before Ringwaldt's day by Thomas of Celano, a Franciscan monk.

In 1722 an English translation of Ringwaldt's hymn was made by Jacobi, and appeared in his *Psalmodia Germanica*. The first stanza commences thus—'' Tis sure that awful time will come.'

In the course of the year 1598, in a little place in Prussia called Langfeldt, the Lutheran pastor, a man of cheerful courage and genial spirit, came to the end of

his earthly course, after a life in which he had done his best to cheer the spirits of his flock by dint of spiritual song-singing. Famine, pestilence, fire, and flood had kept him and his neighbours in continued suffering; and the times seemed favourable to no hymns but those of penitence and anticipation of judgment. But Bartholomew Ringwaldt brought out hymn after hymn on these subjects, all simple, vigorous, Luther-like hymns, and among the rest the stanza beginning—
'Great God, what do I see and hear?'

It is not known by whom this stanza was rendered into English as given above; but in 1812 it caught the attention of the then well-known Dr. Collyer, who during the first half of this nineteenth century was the most popular dissenting minister in London. In 1812 Dr. Collyer compiled, chiefly for the use of his own congregation, a Hymnal, in which were 57 original hymns by himself. Among them was the above well-known stanza, which he erroneously thought to be a translation of part of a German hymn written by Luther.

Dr. Collyer had added to it three stanzas of his own, and these, with a few slight alterations, make up the well-known hymn as it appears in our present Hymnals. In a note to his Hymnal that appeared in 1812 Dr. Collyer says: 'This hymn, which is adapted to Luther's celebrated tune, is universally ascribed to that great man. As I never saw more than this first verse, I was obliged to lengthen it for the completion of the subject, and am responsible for the verses that follow.'

Account of First Rank Hymns.

19. Our God, our help in ages past,
    Our hope for years to come,
    Our shelter from the stormy blast,
    And our eternal home!

This noble metrical version of the earlier part of the 90th Psalm is by Isaac Watts, and appeared in 1719. It received several corrections at the hands of John Wesley; amongst others, the opening words 'Our God' were changed to 'O God.' In its altered form the hymn appears in 1738 in Wesley's first Hymn-book. The original consists of nine stanzas, but the following three are seldom seen :—

> Thy word commands our flesh to dust—
> Return, ye sons of men :
> All nations rose from earth at first,
> And turn to earth again.
>
> The busy tribes of flesh and blood,
> With all their loves and cares,
> Are carried downwards by the flood,
> And lost in following years.
>
> Like flowery fields the nations stand,
> Pleased with the morning light ;
> The flowers beneath the mower's hand
> Lie withering ere 'tis night.

This hymn is generally considered to be the best rendering of the 90th Psalm, and a writer of the *Oxford Essays* in 1858 regards it as Watts's best paraphrase.

20. Saviour, when in dust to Thee,
    Low we bow the adoring knee;
    When repentant to the skies
    Scarce we lift our weeping eyes.

Sir Robert Grant, author of this plaintive Litany hymn, was born in 1785 of an ancient Scotch family. He graduated at Cambridge with high honours in 1806, and became successively barrister, Member of Parliament, Privy Councillor, and, in 1834, Governor of Bombay. He held this exalted position for four years, and died in India in 1838. At various periods of his life he wrote several hymns of a high order of merit; twelve of them were published in 1839 by his brother, Lord Glenelg, in a small volume entitled *Sacred Poems*. These hymns show considerable poetic genius and rich spiritual life. The above appears as No. 2 in the collection, but it had already appeared a quarter of a century before in the *Christian Observer*, entitled 'A Litany.' It is indeed a hymn-prayer, and as such must be accounted as one of the best of its kind. The original has been often and widely varied, but with questionable taste.

21. All people that on earth do dwell,
    Sing to the Lord with cheerful voice.

This grand metrical version of the 100th Psalm is supposed to be the work of William Kethe, a native of

Scotland, and an exile with Knox at Geneva in 1555. He was one of the translators of the Geneva Bible, and twenty-five of his Psalms were published in the old Psalter of 1561. In 1563 we find Kethe chaplain to the English forces at Havre, and afterwards Rector of Okeford in Dorset. A sermon still exists, printed in black-letter, preached at Blandford at the Sessions held there in 1571, by 'William Kethe, minister and preacher of God's Word.' This Psalm is sometimes assigned to Hopkins, joint-editor with Sternhold of the first Metrical Psalter attached to the Prayer-Book, but not on any good ground. Of the sixty-two Psalms composed by Hopkins, the 100th is amongst them, but Hopkins's version is much inferior to the above, and shows him to be incapable of such a high-class production. This truly grand version, which takes rank with the foremost of our hymns, is a universal favourite. The cause of its popularity is in a great measure due to the fact that it is free from sectarian doctrine and party feeling. It appeals directly to those fundamental doctrines of our common religion, doctrines which soothe the deep religious cravings of the soul,—namely, that God is the great universal Father of the human race, and that He watches over His offspring with the loving care that an Eastern shepherd shows for his flock. The purity of rhythm, the simplicity of language, and the dignified music to which it is sung, have doubtless combined to increase its popularity.

The tune, commonly known as the 'Old Hundredth,' takes rank in the highest class of music, and is therefore a fitting accompaniment to Kethe's grand version.

The melody is thought to have been composed by Guillaume Franc, a native of Rouen, who for about a quarter of a century took a leading part in the cathedral of Lausanne, and died in 1570. Franc is said to have taken the chief share in setting to music the Psalms for the Reformed Church at Geneva; and the melody, set originally to the 134th Psalm, appeared then in connection with Franc's work. The majesty of the strains have induced some musicians to imagine that it is made up of fragments of Gregorian melodies, but this is doubtful. The tune soon appeared in England, for it is found in Daye's Metrical Psalter of 1563. The melody is said to have been harmonised in 1565 by Claude Goudimel, a musician of considerable ability. Goudimel established a school of music at Rome, and the celebrated Palestrina is thought to have been one of his pupils.

He joined the Reformed Church, and was killed in 1572 in the massacre of the Huguenots. This tune, originally called 'The Hundredth,' now familiarly known as 'The Old Hundredth,' was also in former times named ' Savoy,' from the fact that it was sung by a Huguenot congregation that worshipped at the Savoy, London, in the reign of Elizabeth.

22. Brief life is here our portion ;
 Brief sorrow, short-lived care ;
 The life that knows no ending,
 The tearless life, is there.

<small>Hic breve vivitur, hic breve plangitur, hic breve fletur ;
Non breve vivere, non breve plangere retribuetur.</small>

This lovely and well-known hymn is an extract from 'De Contemptu Mundi,' commonly called 'The Rhythm of Bernard de Morlaix, Monk of Cluny, on the Celestial Country.' Our English rendering of the Latin verses is the work of the Rev. Dr. John Mason Neale, and first appeared in 1858.

John Mason Neale, the learned and voluminous hymn-writer, and ardent promoter of the modern High Church movement, was born in London in 1818. He was the only son of the Rev. Cornelius Neale, who died when his boy was only five years old. John however received a pious training from his mother, and gave early promise of his great ability. He graduated at Cambridge in 1840, and between 1845 and 1861 he ten times obtained the Seatonian prize for an English sacred poem, a feat without parallel in the annals of the University. In 1846 he was appointed Warden of Sackville College, East Grinstead, a post he retained for more than twenty years, till his death in 1866. Neale was a man of extraordinary literary toil, abounding also in labours of piety and benevolence. Both as a sacred poet and scholar, he showed remarkable ability, and possessed a marvellous power of translating hymns from the Latin and Greek, retaining the beauty, vigour, and often the rhythm of the original. His beautiful translations are very numerous, and they are steadily increasing in public favour from year to year. It may truly be affirmed that Neale has exerted a greater influence upon English Hymnody than any other hymnist of the nineteenth century. During the last days of his life it was a source of comfort and delight to him to listen to his children singing his own sacred songs. He died in 1866, at the comparatively early age of forty-eight, and was buried at East Grinstead, the scene of his labours, with great ritualistic splendour. It has justly been observed, that amid all his mediæval research, and erudite knowledge of the Eastern Church, he remained steadfast in the pure, simple faith of the Saviour. The following high tribute of praise has been paid to his memory:—'Of all his teachings and all his elevating of the spiritual intellect, the most edifying to my own soul was when I saw him in his last illness, laying in the dust all his works and all his talents, and casting himself as a little child only on the atoning work of Jesus Christ.'

Neale's literary works are voluminous, and amongst them his chief contributions to Hymnology are—

'Mediæval Hymns and Sequences,' published in 1851.
'Hymni Ecclesiae,' ,, 1851.
'Hymns for Children,' ,, 1854.
'The Rhythm of Bernard of Cluny,' ,, 1858.
'Hymns of the Eastern Church,' ,, 1863.
'Joys and Glories of Paradise,' ,, 1865.

The following hymns are Neale's best known trans-

Account of First Rank Hymns.

lations, arranged according to the chronology of the originals:—

Renderings from St. Ambrose: fourth century—
'O God of truth, O Lord of might.'
'Now that the daylight fills the sky.'
'Jesu, the virgins' Crown, do Thou.'
'O Trinity, most blessed light.'
'Light's glittering morn bedecks the sky.'
'O God, Thy soldiers' great reward.'
'O Lord, most high, eternal King.'

From Prudentius: fourth century—
'Of the Father's love begotten.'

From St. Anatolius: fifth century—
'The day is past and over.'
'Fierce was the wild billow.'

From Sedulius: fifth century—
'Why doth that impious Herod fear.'

Venantius Fortunatus: sixth century—
'The royal banners forward go.'
'The God whom earth and sea and sky.'
'Sing, my tongue, the glorious battle.'

Gregory the Great: sixth century—
'Father of mercies, hear.'

St. Andrew of Crete: eighth century—
'O the mystery, passing wonder.'
'Christians, dost thou see them.'

Venerable Bede: eighth century—
'A hymn for martyrs sweetly sing.'
'The great forerunner of the morn.'

St. Cosmas: eighth century—
'Christ is born, tell forth His fame.'

St. John Damascene: eighth century—
    ''Tis the day of Resurrection.'
    'Those eternal bowers.'

St. Stephen the Sabaite: eighth century—
    'Art thou weary, art thou languid.'

St. Theodulph: ninth century—
    'All glory, laud, and honour.'

St. Joseph of the Studium: ninth century—
    'Let our choir new anthems raise.'
    'And wilt Thou pardon, Lord?'
    'Stars of the morning, so gloriously bright.'
    'O happy band of pilgrims.'
    'Jesus, Lord of life eternal.'
    'Safe home, safe home in port.'

Theoctistus of the Studium: ninth century—
    'Jesu! name all names above.'

Godescalcus: ninth century—
    'The strain upraise of joy and praise. Alleluia.'

Metrophanes of Smyrna: tenth century—
    'O Unity of threefold light.'

Peter Damiani: eleventh century—
    'O what terror in thy forethought.'
    'O Cross, whereby the earth is blessed.'

St. Bernard of Clairvaux: twelfth century—
    'Jesu! the very thought is sweet.'

Bernard of Cluny: twelfth century—
    'Brief life is here our portion.'
    'For thee, O dear, dear country.'
    'Jerusalem the golden.'
    'Jerusalem the glorious.'
    'Jerusalem exulting.'

Account of First Rank Hymns.

Adam of St. Victor: twelfth century—
  'The church on earth, with answering love.'
  'The praises that the blessed know.'

St. Thomas Aquinas: thirteenth century—
  'Sing, my tongue, the Saviour's glory.'
  'Humbly I adore Thee, hidden Deity.'

23. Come, Holy Ghost, our souls inspire,
And lighten with celestial fire.

This celebrated hymn, found in the Ordination Service, is a translation made by Bishop Cosin from an ancient Latin hymn commencing 'Veni, Creator Spiritus.' John Cosin was born at Norwich in 1594. He became Chaplain to Charles, and shortly after the Restoration in 1660 he was made Bishop of Durham. He continued Bishop for twelve years, and died at Westminster in 1672.

As early as 1627 Cosin published a *Collection of Private Devotions*, and among the collection is found 'Prayers for the Third Hour.' In the latter appears the above beautiful rendering of 'Veni, Creator Spiritus,' the translation being by Cosin himself. The Anglican Church has recognised in this hymn deep spirituality and extraordinary dignity. It has therefore been signally distinguished as the only metrical hymn retained in the Book of Common Prayer. It is used in the Offices for the Ordering of Priests and Consecration of Bishops, as well as at the coronation of our English monarchs. In the Romish Church the original Latin hymn is used at the creation of the Pope, and on other occasions of peculiar solemnity. The original probably dates from the Ambrosian era, which is the second half of the fourth century, and its majestic dignity tends to prove that there is a calm and steady glow in these early Latin hymns, a straightforward plainness of speech and an unconscious force which grows on the mind. They have a Roman majesty of their own, the majesty of a national anthem, the subdued fire of the battle-song of a disciplined army. They are grand national anthems of the Church militant, and their practical plainness, their healthy objective life, are bracing as mountain air.

Some assign the authorship of the 'Veni, Creator Spiritus,' to Gregory the Great, who died in 604, and others erroneously assign it to the Emperor Charlemagne.

The hymn found a place in the ancient Ordinal, and its first recorded use in public was in 898 A.D., at the translation of some saint's relics, as recorded in the Annals of the Benedictine monks. In the Sarum Breviary it is directed to be used at the hour of Tierce, that is, 9 o'clock A.M., on the three days after the Festival of Whitsunday.

The Latin contains eight stanzas short metre; while Cosin's celebrated translation contains four stanzas of long metre.

The second and longer rendering in the Ordination Service first appeared in the Second Edwardian Prayer-Book in 1552, and was the work of an early Reformer.

24. My God, my Father, while I stray
    Far from my home on life's rough way,
    O teach me from my heart to say,
       'Thy will be done.'

Miss Charlotte Elliott, the authoress of this favourite hymn, was the daughter of Mr. Charles Elliott, and granddaughter of the Rev. Henry Venn, a celebrated preacher of the last century. Her two brothers, the Rev. Henry Venn Elliott, and the Rev. E. B. Elliott, were well-known Brighton clergymen. She was born in 1789, and for many years resided at Torquay, where she was distinguished for her piety and benevolence. She always manifested great sympathy for those in sorrow and sickness. As a hymn-writer her efforts have been highly appreciated, and many of them are deservedly popular. Several of the hymns were written in an arbour overlooking the beautiful bay at Torquay.

Her later years were spent at Brighton, where she died in 1871 at the advanced age of eighty-two.

The above hymn, with the familiar refrain, 'Thy will be done,' at the end of each stanza, first appeared in 1835 in her well-known collection, *The Invalid's Hymn-book*. Two different forms of this hymn afterwards appeared under the authoress's own sanction, and the three texts differ considerably from each other.

This comforting hymn, provoking to Christian resignation, gains additional beauty from a consideration of Miss Elliott's own experience. In a letter to her sister she writes: 'Even in the vale of suffering there are blessed companions to associate with, sweet consolations to partake of, heavenly privileges to enjoy. For myself, I am well content to tread it, and to remain in it till my weary feet stand on the brink of Jordan. But I have been many years learning this difficult lesson, and even now am but little skilled in this blessed alchemy. How many hard struggles, and apparently fruitless ones, has it cost me to become resigned to this appointment of my Heavenly Father! But the struggle is now over.' The death of her dear brother Henry in 1865 was to her a heavy affliction, for 'she had always hoped and expected that he would minister to her in her dying hours.' Her meek submission under the severe chastisement is well set forth in the language of her own well-known hymn:—

> What though in lonely grief I sigh
> For friends beloved no longer nigh?
> Submissive still, would I reply,
>   ' Thy will be done.'
>
> Though Thou hast called me to resign
> What most I prized,—it ne'er was mine;
> I have but yielded what was Thine,
>   ' Thy will be done.'

25. Hail the day that sees Him rise   Alleluia!
    To His throne above the skies.   Alleluia!

This hymn was written by Charles Wesley for Ascension Day. It glows with a fine elevated strain, and is the most popular of our English Ascension-tide hymns. The original appeared in 1739 in *Hymns and Sacred*

Poems, and consisted of ten stanzas, four of which are usually omitted in modern Hymnals. 'Hallelujah' is generally sung at the end of each line. The hymn appeared, with some slight alterations, in Madan's collection in 1760. The original line, 'There the pompous triumph waits,' was changed to 'There for Him high triumph waits.' Wesley was fond of the words 'pomp' and 'pompous,' judging from their frequent use in his hymns,—thus, 'And lead the pompous triumph on,' 'By the pomp of Thine ascending.' These words somewhat grate upon our ears, but it ought to be noticed that Wesley uses the terms in the sense of the Greek original,—πομπή among the Greeks being a religious word, meaning a 'religious procession.' The four stanzas of the original usually omitted are as follows :—

> Circled round with angel powers,
> Their triumphant Lord and ours,
> Conqueror over death and sin,
> Take the King of Glory in.
>
> Master, will we ever say,
> Taken from our heart to-day,
> See Thy faithful servants, see,
> Ever gazing up to Thee.
>
> Ever upward let us move,
> Wafted on the wings of love,
> Looking when our Lord shall come,
> Longing, grasping after home.
>
> There we shall with Thee remain,
> Partners of Thy endless reign ;
> There Thy face unclouded see,
> Find our Heaven of heavens in Thee.

26. Hail to the Lord's Anointed,
   Great David's greater Son!
Hail, in the time appointed,
   His reign on earth begun!

This grand missionary hymn was written by James Montgomery, Christmas 1821, and was first printed privately on a leaflet for the use of the congregation at Fulneck, Yorkshire, of which congregation the author was a member. It is an admirable paraphrase of the 72d Psalm, full of the spirit of David's inspired words. Four months after it was written the poet repeated it at the close of a speech which he delivered at a missionary meeting held in a Wesleyan school-room, Liverpool, in 1822. Dr. Adam Clarke occupied the chair, and being much struck with the beauty of the piece, begged the MS. of the author, and inserted it in his 'Commentaries' in connection with the 72d Psalm. The rendering of 'The mountains shall bring peace to the people, and the little hills, by righteousness' is exquisitely beautiful—

   Before Him, on the mountains,
   Shall peace, the herald, go;
   And righteousness, in fountains,
   From hill to valley flow.

James Montgomery, sometimes called 'the Cowper of the nineteenth century,' was born at Irvine, Ayrshire, in 1771. His father was a Moravian minister, and James, when only seven years old, was sent to school to the Moravian seminary of Fulneck, Yorkshire. Here for nine years he enjoyed a liberal and religious education. When only a young man, twenty-three years old, he undertook the editorship of *The Sheffield Iris*, and continued to edit that newspaper for above thirty years. In early manhood the poet was subject to fits of despondency, as Cowper was, but his Christian faith increased with his age. When forty-three years old he became a professed member of the Moravian Church, and in all his subsequent writings he approved himself a strong advocate of Christianity as the fruitful source of 'things pure, lovely, and of good report.' None of his hymns were published until 1822, when the poet was over fifty years old. His works have enriched our poetry and general literature, and his literary labours were publicly rewarded in 1833 by a Government pension of £200 a year. He enjoyed this pension for twenty years, and died at Sheffield in 1854 at the venerable age of eighty-two.

'His poetry appeals to universal principles, imperishable affections, and to the elements of our common nature.' He wrote a great number of hymns, and few hymn-writers have attained as great popularity. His flashes of genius and flights of fancy show him to be a poet of a high order, while 'his hymns illustrate the close connection there is between a pure heart and a fine fancy.'

27. Hosanna to the living Lord!
    Hosanna to the Incarnate Word!

This grand hymn, consisting of five stanzas in the original, is by Bishop Heber, and first appeared in the

Christian Observer for October 1811. In his collection published in 1827, called *Hymns Written and Adapted to the Weekly Church Service of the Year*, the above is assigned to the First Sunday in Advent. It forms a fitting welcome to the coming Saviour, and is founded on the Gospel for this Sunday, which describes the triumphal entry of Christ into Jerusalem : ' And the multitudes that went before, and that followed, cried, saying, Hosanna to the Son of David : Blessed is He that cometh in the name of the Lord ; Hosanna in the highest.'

As the triumphal procession occurred on Palm Sunday, the hymn is suitable for that day also.

28. Oft in danger, oft in woe,
    Onward, Christians, onward go !
    Fight the fight, maintain the strife,
    Strengthened with the bread of life.

Henry Kirke White, author of the above, was born of humble parents at Nottingham in 1785. In boyhood he gave indications of poetic genius, for when only fifteen years old he gained a silver medal for a translation from Horace, and at nineteen published a volume of his poems. He became anxious to prepare himself for the Church, and some generous friends, seeing that he was a young man of great promise, enabled him to enter Cambridge in 1804. There he was known as a diligent student, and for two successive years he was placed at the examinations as first man of

Account of First Rank Hymns. 119

his year. Excessive study undermined his frail constitution, and in his third College year the tight-strung cord snapped, and in October 1806 he sank into an early grave at the age of twenty-two. Like a beam of light Henry Kirke White appeared upon the earth, and thus suddenly passed away.

Truly has it been said: 'This poet of promise, who has been named "the Crichton of Nottingham," averts the arrows of criticism by the melancholy brevity of his career. We think more of what he would have accomplished than of the works he had actually produced. Before the critic with searching eye had had time to find spots in the sun, he weeps because that sun has set to rise no more.' As a hymnist he is known by his 'Christiad,' an epic poem, and ten hymns published in 1812, many years after his death.

The above hymn was found after his decease, scribbled on the back of a mathematical paper, and seems to have been written by the young man while pursuing his mathematical studies by the light of the midnight lamp. The original consisted of only ten lines, and ran thus—

> Much in sorrow, oft in woe,
> Onward, Christians, onward go !
> Fight the fight, and worn with strife,
> Steep with tears the Bread of Life.
>
> Onward, Christians, onward go !
> Join the war and face the foe ;
> Faint not ; much doth yet remain ;
> Dreary is the long campaign.
>
> Shrink not, Christians ! will ye yield ?
> Will ye quit the painful field ?

This unfinished hymn was completed in 1827 by Frances Fuller Maitland, and then appeared substantially in the same form in which it is now usually sung.

    29. Thou, whose almighty word
        Chaos and darkness heard.

The Rev. John Marriott, M.A., author of the above hymn, was born in Leicestershire in 1780. He was educated at Oxford, and after taking holy orders became a private tutor in the family of the Duke of Buccleuch. He was subsequently presented with a living in Warwickshire, where he laboured for many years, but on account of his wife's delicate health he was obliged to resign his charge in order to remove to the more genial clime of Devonshire. He died near Exeter in 1825, aged forty-five years. The above was composed in 1813, but such was the humility of the author that he declined to permit this beautiful hymn to appear in print. For twelve years it remained almost unknown, until at length some of the author's private friends, conscious of its high merits, obtained permission to print it in a small religious magazine called the *Family Visitor*. It was speedily copied into many collections, and is now a general favourite.

    30. Come, let us join our cheerful songs
        With angels round the throne.

This grand hymn of praise was composed by Watts, and appeared in 1709.

Account of First Rank Hymns.

It is founded on Rev. v. 11, 12: 'I beheld, and I heard the voice of many angels round about the throne, and the beasts, and the elders: and the number of them was ten thousand times ten thousand, and thousands of thousands; saying with a loud voice, Worthy is the Lamb that was slain to receive power, and riches, and wisdom, and strength, and honour, and glory, and blessing.' The original consists of five stanzas, all of which are usually retained in our modern Hymnals. It is one of the most popular hymns of invitation to the Church Militant to join in the praises of the Church Triumphant.

Keble's well-known hymn, 'Behold the glories of the Lamb,' is simply a variation from Watts's 'Come, let us join our cheerful songs.'

31. Glorious things of thee are spoken,
    Zion, city of our God.

This noble hymn by Newton appeared in the *Olney Hymns* in 1779, entitled, 'Zion, or the City of God.'

It is a paraphrase of the 87th Psalm, 'His foundation is in the holy mountains. The Lord loveth the gates of Zion more than all the dwellings of Jacob. Glorious things are spoken of thee, O city of God.'

This Psalm always had a great charm for the author. Rahab and Babylon represented his former profligate life, while Zion was the emblem of his renewed state.

32. O worship the King all-glorious above !
    O gratefully sing His power and His love !
    Our Shield and Defender, the Ancient of Days,
    Pavilioned in splendour, and girded with praise.

This spirited hymn of praise was written by Sir Robert Grant, and first appeared in 1839, a year after the author's death. It is a free metrical version of a portion of the 104th Psalm, beginning, 'O my God, Thou art very great; Thou art clothed with honour and majesty.'

33. The Son of God goes forth to war,
    A kingly crown to gain,
    His blood-red banner streams afar ;
    Who follows in His train ?

This well-known hymn by Bishop Reginald Heber is a glorious triumph-song suitable for the Festivals of Martyrs. It was written for St. Stephen's Day, the proto-martyr, and appeared in the collection of Heber's hymns published in 1827, the year after the author's death.

'Heber's hymns are dear to every section of the Christian Church, elegant in structure, flowing in rhythm, and charged with Christian sentiment.' He wrote most of his hymns during the tranquil years he spent as pastor of Hodnet, from 1807 to 1823. Here in peaceful retirement he cherished the desire to improve our devotional poetry and introduce a Hymnal into the Church of England. Accordingly he composed a number of hymns, which first appeared in the *Chris-*

tian Observer in 1811. Amongst these were the well-known hymns commencing 'Brightest and best of the sons of the morning,' 'Hosanna to the living God,' 'Lord of mercy and of might,' 'O Saviour, is Thy promise fled,' 'O Saviour, whom the holy morn,' etc.

The Bishop of London for a time dissuaded him from publishing a general Church Hymn-book, but in 1812 Heber published a small volume entitled *Poems and Translations for Weekly Church Service*. The work went through several editions.

After Heber's death, his widow, Mrs. Amelia Heber, published, in 1827, *Hymns Written and Adapted to the Weekly Church Service of the Year*. This volume was arranged on the same principle as the subsequently published volume, Keble's *Christian Year*, and, besides Heber's own compositions, contained hymns by Jeremy Taylor, Addison, Sir Walter Scott, Dean Milman, and others.

In Heber's Poetical Works, published in 1842, there appear forty-nine hymns written for Sundays and Festivals of the Christian year, and eight additional ones for special occasions, making a total of fifty-seven hymns composed by this sacred poet. Heber was amongst the first to suggest the idea of introducing a Hymnal into the public service of the Church. Since Heber's death, half a century ago, thousands of Hymnals have been compiled, some for local, some for general use; but, on the principle of 'the survival of the fittest,' a few excellent Hymnals have forced the great majority into comparative obscurity.

34. Christ, whose glory fills the skies,
 Christ, the true, the only Light.

This beautiful morning hymn by Charles Wesley is founded on Mal. iv. 2: 'Unto you that fear My name shall the Sun of Righteousness arise with healing in His wings.'

It was written in 1740, and appeared in 1743 in *Hymns and Sacred Poems*.

Speaking of the above, James Montgomery, no mean judge, says 'it is one of Charles Wesley's loveliest progeny.' The original consists of three stanzas, and they are usually quoted without alteration in modern Hymnals; but, strangely enough, in the Methodist Hymn-book the first stanza is omitted altogether, and one of a nature entirely different is substituted. It runs thus—

> O disclose Thy lovely face,
> Quicken all my drooping powers.
> Gasps my fainting soul for grace,
> As a thirsty land for showers;
> Haste, my Lord, no more delay;
> Come, my Saviour, come away.

35. Lord, when we bend before Thy throne,
 And our confessions pour.

Joseph Dacre Carlyle, B.D., the author of the above, was born at Carlisle in 1759. From the Cathedral School of that city he went to Cambridge, and gained a fellowship at Queen's College. He studied Oriental literature, and became an eminent Oriental scholar. He

Account of First Rank Hymns.

was appointed Professor of Arabic in the University of Cambridge in 1794, and the next year he succeeded Paley as Chancellor of the Diocese of Carlisle. In 1799 this learned and accomplished divine accompanied the Earl of Elgin to Constantinople, when that nobleman was appointed ambassador to the Porte, that he might examine the literary treasures of the East. The Professor visited also Asia Minor and the Isles of Greece. On his return to England he was made Vicar of Newcastle-on-Tyne and Chaplain to the Bishop of Durham. When in residence at Carlisle he regularly attended St. Cuthbert's Church. John Fawcett, the Vicar, was a very intimate friend of the Professor, and on the occasion of his compiling a Hymn-book for Public Worship, Carlyle sent him the above hymn. It appeared first in the collection published 1802, and is headed 'Introductory to Public Worship.' The Professor died in 1804, and the year after his poems were published in a volume entitled *Poems suggested chiefly by Scenes in Asia Minor and Syria*. The above hymn, with two others, appears at the end of the volume.

36. Sweet the moments, rich in blessing,
    Which before the Cross I spend;
   Life and health and peace possessing
    From the sinner's dying Friend.

The above in its present form is from the pen of the Honourable and Rev. Walter Shirley, and first appeared in 1770. It is really a re-cast of a hymn beginning,

'While my Saviour I'm possessing.' The original was written by James Allen, a native of Gayle, Wensleydale, Yorkshire, born in 1734. In 1757 he edited a collection of hymns known as *The Kendal Hymn-book*. Allen connected himself with Benjamin Ingham, an erratic preacher of the Wesleyan revival, and afterwards became successively a member of the Church of England, a Wesleyan, a Moravian, and an adherent of Lady Huntingdon's sect. He ultimately built a chapel on his own estate in Wensleydale, where he preached till his death in 1804.

Allen's hymn is poor, but Shirley's alterations are so many and important that the re-cast is virtually a new hymn, and as such the above has deservedly gained its present popularity.

37. 'Christ the Lord is risen to-day,' Hallelujah!
    Sons of men and angels say. Hallelujah!

This hymn for Easter Day was written by Charles Wesley in 1739, and appears in his *Hymns and Sacred Poems*. The original consists of eleven stanzas, but seldom more than six are used. When this hymn is set to the old noble tune known as 'Easter Hymn,' each line requires 'Hallelujah' at the end of it.

The hymn must be distinguished from two resembling it. First, from one ascribed to Jane Leeson, which is really a translation from a twelfth-century 'Prose,' and begins the same as the above :—

> Christ the Lord is risen to-day ;
> Christians, haste your vows to pay.

Account of First Rank Hymns.

Secondly, from the more popular Easter hymn commencing—

> Jesus Christ is risen to-day, Hallelujah!
> Our triumphant holy-day,

which appeared first at Northampton, ten years after the publication of Wesley's, and is supposed to be the composition of one of Doddridge's pupils.

> 38. For thee, O dear, dear country,
> Mine eyes their vigils keep.
>
> O bona Patria, lumina sobria te speculantur.

This lovely hymn, consisting of ten stanzas of four lines each, is from the 'Rhythm of Bernard of Cluny on the Heavenly Country,' translated from the Latin by Dr. Neale in 1858. It sets forth the heavenly homesickness of the Cluniac monk, and indeed that deep yearning of souls in all ages who 'declare plainly that they seek a country, and desire a better country, that is, an heavenly.'

> 39. God, that madest earth and heaven,
> Darkness and light;
> Who the day for toil hast given,
> For rest the night.

The first stanza of this hymn, consisting of eight lines, is by Bishop Heber, and appeared in 1827, the year after the author's death.

He had spent sixteen years of his ministerial life at Hodnet, Shropshire, on the borders of the Principality of Wales, and this hymn was probably written to be sung to a well-known popular Welsh air. This may also account for the peculiar metre in which it is written. There is a German morning hymn by Heinrich Albert, rendered into English in the *Lyra Germanica*, with a similar beginning, but Heber's hymn is not a translation of this. The second stanza, beginning 'Guard us waking, guard us sleeping,' was composed by Richard Whately, Archbishop of Dublin, born 1787, died 1863. It appeared in 1855, and was appended to his *Lectures on Prayer* in 1860. The verse seems to be a free translation of an ancient antiphon used at the service of Compline :—' Salva nos Domine vigilantes, custodi nos dormientes, ut vigilemus in Christo, et requiescamus in pace.' (Preserve us, O Lord, waking, guard us sleeping, that we may wake in Christ, and rest in peace.)

40. Jesus shall reign where'er the sun
    Does his successive journeys run.

This deservedly popular hymn is a rendering by Watts of the 72d Psalm. It is entitled 'Christ's Kingdom among the Gentiles,' and it gives prominence to the thoughts contained in 'He shall have dominion also from sea to sea, and from the river unto the ends of the earth. In His days shall the righteous flourish, and abundance of peace so long as the moon endureth. All kings shall fall down before Him; all nations shall serve Him.' Watts laboured at his Metrical Psalter from 1712 till 1716, during the period that he was unable to pursue his public duties through bodily infirmity. The whole Psalter was published in 1719, and soon the above became a favourite missionary hymn. The original consists of eight stanzas, of which the second and third are almost invariably omitted. They run thus:—

> Behold the islands with their kings,
> And Europe her best tribute brings;
> From north to south the princes meet,
> And pay their homage at His feet.
>
> There Persia, glorious to behold,
> There India shines in Eastern gold,
> And barbarous nations at His word
> Submit and bow, and own their Lord.'

'Perhaps one of the most interesting occasions on which this hymn was used is that on which King George the Sable, of blessed memory, gave a new Constitution to his people, exchanging a heathen for a Christian form of government. Under the spreading branches of the banyan-trees sat some five thousand natives from Tonga, Fiji, and Samoa, on Whitsunday 1862, assembled for divine worship. Foremost among them all sat King George himself. Around him were seated old chiefs and warriors who had shared with him the dangers and fortunes of many a battle,—men whose eyes were dim, and whose powerful frames were bowed down with the weight of years. But old and young rejoiced alike together in the joys of that day, their faces most of them radiant with Christian joy, love, and hope. It would be impossible to describe the deep feeling manifested when the solemn service began by the entire audience singing Dr. Watts's hymn, "Jesus shall reign where'er the sun." Who as much as they could realise the full meaning of the poet's words?—for they had been rescued from the darkness of heathenism and cannibalism, and they were that day met for the first time under a Christian king, and with Christ Himself reigning in the hearts of most of those present. That was indeed Christ's kingdom set up in the earth.'

41. My God, and is Thy table spread?
    And doth Thy cup with love o'erflow?
Thither be all Thy children led,
    And let them all Thy sweetness know.

This very beautiful hymn by Philip Doddridge is the most popular of our Communion hymns. It was inserted at the end of the Prayer-Book about the beginning of this century under the following circumstances: The University printer was a dissenter, and he filled up the blank leaves at the end of the Supplement to the 'New Version' with such hymns as he thought would be acceptable to the public. Amongst them was 'My God, and is Thy table spread?' This was done without authority, but as no one interfered, the hymns were allowed to remain. Although the above is the work of a Nonconformist preacher, the sacramental doctrine is very pronounced; and it is curious to notice how this has offended some compilers of Church of England Hymnals. Thus, in the beautiful lines—

    Hail, sacred feast, which Jesus makes,
      Rich banquet of His flesh and blood,

'memorial' is sometimes substituted for 'rich banquet.'

Account of First Rank Hymns.

42. O Thou from whom all goodness flows,
  I lift my soul to Thee;
In all my sorrows, conflicts, woes,
  Good Lord, remember me.

Thomas Haweis, author of this hymn, was born at Truro in 1732. He was educated at Cambridge, became a physician, subsequently took holy orders, was appointed Chaplain to the Countess of Huntingdon, and rector of a parish in Northamptonshire. Haweis was a distinguished popular preacher, and one of the founders of the Church Missionary Society. The above hymn first appeared in 1792, in his *Carmina Christo, or Hymns to the Saviour*, a collection containing about 250 original hymns by the author. The original consisted of six stanzas, and the words 'remember me' at the end of each stanza were probably suggested by the words of the dying thief on the cross, 'Lord, remember me.'

43. When our heads are bowed with woe,
When our bitter tears o'erflow,
When we mourn the lost, the dear,
Jesu, Son of Mary, hear!

Henry Hart Milman, author of this hymn, was the youngest son of Sir Francis Milman, physician to George III., and was born in London in 1791. He was educated at Eton and Oxford, and shortly after, being ordained in 1817, he was appointed Vicar of St. Mary's, Reading. For ten years, from 1821 till 1831, he was Professor of Poetry in Oxford. Subsequently he was appointed Canon of Westminster, and in 1849 promoted to be Dean of St. Paul's. He died in 1868, much regretted. 'The charm of his conversation was missed from the social circle, and the Church felt that a prince and a great man had fallen in Israel.'

His talents and writings were of a high order. His chief prose works are: *Christianity from the Birth of Christ to the Abolition of Paganism in the Roman Empire;* a *History of Latin Christianity;* and a *History of the Jews.* His poetical works also enjoy a high reputation, and his hymns are of great excellence. The above beautiful and affecting hymn first appeared in 1827 in the hymn-book published by Heber's widow after his death. In this collection it is appointed for the sixteenth Sunday after Trinity; the Gospel for that day—being an account of the funeral procession of the son of the widow of Nain, 'When the Lord saw her He had compassion on her, and said unto her, Weep not'—strikes the key-note to the spirit of the hymn. Of all hymns it is the most appropriate to introduce into the Funeral Service, and often has it proved to be a comfort to sorrowing mourners.

44. Where high the heavenly temple stands,
    The house of God not made with hands,
    A great High Priest our nature wears,
    The Guardian of mankind appears.

Michael Bruce, author of this hymn, was born of humble pious parents at Kinnesswood, Kinross-shire, in 1746. In youth he was distinguished for his piety and abilities; and some friends, recognising his talents, supplied him with the works of the great poets, and encouraged him in literary pursuits. His parents' means being very limited, Bruce had to contend with hardship and poverty.

He conducted a small school for some time, and by practising much self-denial succeeded in spending four sessions in Edinburgh University as a Divinity student. Self-denial, poor fare, and mental exertions, proved too much for his frail constitution, and brought on a rapid consumption. Thus in 1766, when only twenty years old, he returned to his native village to die. In the spring of 1767, conscious that his end was approaching, he wrote the pathetic 'Elegy on Spring,' and very affecting is the sixteenth stanza, where, referring to his own declining health, he writes—

> Now, Spring returns; but not to me returns
> The vernal joy my better years have known;
> Dim in my breast life's dying taper burns,
> And all the joys of life with health are flown.

In July 1767, at the early age of twenty-one, the youthful sacred poet with calm resignation passed to his eternal rest.

'The life of this poet was almost a counterpart of that of Henry Kirke White, who flourished a generation later. In both instances the light of genius shone forth for a time, and then was all too suddenly put out.'

The above much-prized hymn was added to the Scottish Paraphrases in 1781. Sometimes it is attributed to John Logan, who ignobly published it under his own name sixteen years after Bruce's death. Recent investigations have established Bruce's claim to its authorship beyond all reasonable doubt.

Other hymns found in the Scottish Paraphrases by the same author are those beginning, 'Few are thy days and full of woe,' 'O happy is the man who hears,' 'Behold, the mountain of the Lord,' and 'The hour of my departure's come.'

45. While shepherds watched their flocks by night,
    All seated on the ground.

The Metrical Psalter known as the 'New Version' is the joint work of two Irishmen—Nahum Tate and Nicholas Brady. Three of the hymns of the New Version have found a place among 'First Rank Hymns,' viz., 'While shepherds watched their flocks by night,' 'Through all the changing scenes of life,' and 'As pants the hart for cooling streams.'

Nahum Tate was born in Dublin in 1652, and educated at Trinity College of that city. His father was a clergyman, distinguished as one of the chief writers on sacred poetry of the Elizabethan era. Nahum made his way to London, where he soon became known as a literary man and writer of poems, sacred and profane. In 1690 he was made Poet-Laureate to King William III., and held this position for a quarter of a century till his death in 1715.

Nicholas Brady, born in 1659 at Bandon, Cork, was educated at Westminster, Oxford, and Dublin. He was a zealous partisan of the Prince of Orange, and

Account of First Rank Hymns.　135

was made Chaplain to King William. He held a living at Richmond, Surrey, and 'here, in one of the pleasant retreats of that charming neighbourhood, he translated some of the Psalms.'

Tate and Brady, Poet-Laureate and Royal Chaplain respectively, were co-workers and fellow-Psalmists in the production of the 'New Version.' This Metrical Psalter was authorised by King William in 1696, and for nearly two centuries it has been annexed to the Book of Common Prayer as the authorised Psalter of the Church of England.

The two Irish poets worked in such harmony that it is not known which Psalms are by Tate and which by Brady. The poetry of the New Version is not of a high order for the most part, but the rendering is literal, simple, and suitable for public worship. The following Psalms are general favourites, and will always occupy a place in our Hymnals :—

Through all the changing scenes of life,	Ps. 34.
As pants the hart for cooling streams,	Ps. 42.
Have mercy, Lord, on me,	Ps. 51.
To bless Thy chosen race,	Ps. 67.
O God of Hosts, the mighty Lord,	Ps. 84.
With one consent let all the earth,	Ps. 100.
Ye boundless realms of joy,	Ps. 148.

In 1703, that is, seven years after the publication of the New Version, appeared a Supplement, called 'The Appendix, with Hymns.' The hymns are by Tate, and the best-known hymn in the collection is the familiar Christmas one—

　　While shepherds watched their flocks by night.

46. All hail the power of Jesus' name!
　　Let angels prostrate fall;
　　Bring forth the royal diadem,
　　And crown him Lord of all.

This hymn was written a hundred years ago by Edward Perronet. In Charles Wesley's diary, about 1750, are found frequent references to one in whom he took a deep interest, and whom he familiarly calls 'Ned.' This was Edward Perronet, son of the Rev. Vincent Perronet, Vicar of Shoreham, Kent, for half a century. Edward became a preacher, first in Wesley's Connexion, then under the direction of Lady Huntingdon, and ultimately was appointed minister to a small Nonconformist congregation at Canterbury. He died in 1792, and his dying words were: 'Glory to God in the height of His divinity; glory to God in the depth of His humanity; glory to God in His all-sufficiency: and into His hands I commend my spirit.' The above hymn was first published anonymously in the *Gospel Magazine* in 1780. It was entitled 'On the Resurrection,' and contained eight stanzas. The stanza beginning 'O that with yonder sacred throng' does not appear in the original, and is an addition of some later hymnist. Perronet's well-known hymn is founded on the latter part of Revelation xix.: 'On His head were many crowns, and on His vesture and on His thigh a name written, King of kings, and Lord of lords.'

The familiar tune 'Miles Lane' was composed for this hymn by Shrubsole, organist at Spafields Chapel,

Account of First Rank Hymns. 137

and it is said that Perronet at his death left a large sum of money for Shrubsole.

47. Come, ye thankful people, come,
    Raise the song of Harvest-home!
    All is safely gathered in
    Ere the winter storms begin.

Henry Alford, author of this jubilant harvest hymn, was born in London in 1810. He graduated at Cambridge, and became a Fellow of Trinity College. Having taken holy orders, he soon distinguished himself both as an eloquent preacher and profound scholar. His great work, by which he will be best known to posterity, is *The Greek Testament, with Notes*, a scholarly production of great value. The first volume was issued in 1849, and the whole work was completed in 1861. Alford has attained to some celebrity as a hymn-writer. In 1831 he published a volume entitled *Poems and Poetical Fragments*. Again in 1844 appeared a small collection called *Psalms and Hymns adapted to the Sundays and Holydays throughout the Year*. In 1867 he published *The Year of Praise*, a hymnal containing 326 hymns, of which 55 were written by himself at various intervals of his laborious life. In 1857 he was made Dean of Canterbury, an office he held till his death in 1871.

The harvest hymn, consisting of four double stanzas, appeared in 1844, and, in a revised form, appeared in his *Year of Praise*.

It is founded on the passage, 'He shall come again

with rejoicing, bringing his sheaves with him' (Ps. cxxvi. 6).

48. Father of Heaven, whose love profound
    A ransom for our souls hath found.

This hymn appeared in Cotterill's Selection of Psalms and Hymns in 1810. In some of the copies the name J. Cooper is appended, and therefore the hymn is ascribed to him. Cooper was rector of a small parish in Staffordshire, and died in 1833, about a quarter of a century after the appearance of the hymn.

The original consists of four stanzas, respectively addressed to 'Father of Heaven,' 'Almighty Son,' 'Eternal Spirit,' 'Mysterious Godhead,' and is therefore a hymn suitable for Trinity Sunday.

49. God moves in a mysterious way
    His wonders to perform.

Composed by William Cowper in 1773, when fifty years of age, during a solitary walk in the fields around Olney. Ten years before, the poet had been afflicted with madness, and for eight months had been confined in a lunatic asylum. While sauntering alone in a meditative mood, he had a presentiment of another attack of his awful malady. Trusting in God to guide him through the gloom, he wrote this matchless hymn, assured that

> Behind a frowning providence
> He hides a smiling face.

During the six years he resided at Olney he composed

Account of First Rank Hymns. 139

sixty-seven hymns for the Olney collection, of which the above was the last. Shortly afterwards he was bereft of reason, and compelled to give up all literary pursuits for seven years.

Of this hymn Montgomery says, 'It is a lyric of high tone and character, and rendered awfully interesting by the circumstances under which it was written, in the twilight of departing reason.'

50. How bright these glorious spirits shine!
    Whence all their white array?

This well-known hymn is the composition of William Cameron, founded on a hymn of Dr. Watts. William Cameron was born in 1751, and studied at Aberdeen University. In 1745, a few years before his birth, there had been appended, without authority, to the Scotch Psalter a collection of hymns known as the 'Paraphrases.' In 1775 the General Assembly commissioned William Cameron, John Logan, and others, to revise the collection. This they did, and in 1781 appeared the revised and enlarged edition of the Paraphrases, consisting of sixty-seven hymns. The above, from the pen of Cameron, appeared in the collection. In 1785 he was ordained minister to the parish of Kirknewton, and there he ministered until his death in 1811. The first stanza is only slightly varied from Watts, which runs thus—

> These glorious minds, how bright they shine!
>   Whence all their white array?
> How came they to the happy seats
>   Of everlasting day?

In the other stanzas the wording is wholly Cameron's, and the hymn, as a re-cast, is a great improvement on Watts. Other Paraphrases by Cameron are, 'While others crowd the house of mirth,' and 'Ho! ye that thirst, approach the spring.'

51. Jesus lives! no longer now
    Can thy terrors, death, appal us;
Jesus lives! by this we know
    Thou, O grave, canst not enthrall us.
               Alleluia!

This hymn is a translation from the German by Miss F. E. Cox, and first appeared in 1841 in *Sacred Hymns from the German*. Miss Cox's first translation consisted of six stanzas of six lines each, but as early as 1852 the hymn was re-cast, the two last lines of each stanza being omitted, and 'Alleluia' added after each stanza. The original German was composed by Christian F. Gellert, son of a Lutheran pastor, born in Saxony in 1697. He became Professor of Moral Philosophy in the University of Leipzig, where he died in 1769. Gellert was a man of deep piety and unfeigned humility, but unfortunately, like his English contemporary William Cowper, was subject to constant attacks of melancholy. He was justly regarded as an eloquent lecturer and tender hymnist. That his life was a constant struggle against poverty and ill-health must add to the interest we feel in his works. Before composing a hymn he always prayed that his soul might

Account of First Rank Hymns. 141

be prepared aright for the subject. On one occasion he writes: 'I will for a time lay aside this work; perhaps God of His grace will inspire my mind with new vigour, and improve my present dispositions.'

> 52. O Lord, turn not Thy face from me,
>   Who lie in woeful state,
> Lamenting all my sinful life,
>   Before Thy mercy-gate.

This favourite hymn, entitled 'The Lamentation or a Sinner,' first appeared in 1562, appended to the first complete edition of the Old Version of the Psalter by Sternhold and Hopkins. The initial M. was attached to the hymn in the earlier editions of the Psalter, as well as to several Psalms. It was therefore thought to be written by Mardley, a contemporary hymnist; but in a copy of the Old Version found in the British Museum, dated 1563, the name Markant appears instead of the initial M. Markant, therefore, and not Mardley, is probably the author of the hymn. John Markant, or Marchant, is known also as the compiler of a volume of poems, published in 1580, entitled *Verses to Divers Good Purposes*. The present form of the hymn is a cento by Bishop Heber, founded on the original eleven stanzas, which, although somewhat bald and prosaic, yet possess a vigorous ruggedness. The last verse of the quaint original ought to be better known—

> Mercy, good Lord, mercy I ask,   For mercy, Lord, is all my suit,
>   This is the total sum: Lord, let Thy mercy come.

53. Our blest Redeemer, ere He breathed
His tender last farewell.

'This most beautiful hymn, the very rhythm of which is peace,' was composed by Miss Harriet Auber, born in London 1773. This talented lady lived in quietude and seclusion, and spent the greater part of her long life at Hoddesdon, near London, where her memory is still cherished with affection. In 1829 she published *The Spirit of the Psalms*, a metrical version of select portions of the Psalms of David. The work contains, besides her own translations, a number of hymns by various authors, as Heber's hymn for Easter Day, and pieces selected for the leading Church seasons. Miss Auber wrote much lyric poetry, as well as devotional, and both kinds are distinguished for high merit and beauty. Her rendering of the 75th Psalm, beginning, 'That Thou, O Lord, art ever near,' is an admirable translation, retaining the grandeur and simplicity of the original. Miss Mackenzie, the authoress of a beautiful tale called *Private Life*, and other literary contributions, was a much valued friend of Miss Auber. They lived together during the latter years of life, and were buried side by side in the quiet cemetery of Hoddesdon. Truly they were 'lovely and pleasant in their lives, and in their death they were not divided.' Miss Auber died in 1862, having attained to the venerable age of nearly fourscore and ten.

54. Through the day Thy love hath spared us;
   Now we lay us down to rest;
Through the silent watches guard us,
   Let no foe our peace molest!
      Jesus, Thou our Guardian be!
      Sweet it is to trust in Thee.

Thomas Kelly, author of this beautiful evening hymn, was the son of an Irish judge, and was born in Dublin in 1769. He graduated with honours in Trinity College, Dublin, and being designed for the bar, he entered the Temple. While in London he enjoyed the friendship of Edmund Burke. He began to entertain very serious religious views, and consequently, renouncing the law as a profession, he took holy orders in 1792, when twenty-three years of age. His doctrines were somewhat extreme, and his opinions, publicly proclaimed against the Church of England, were so strong, that the Archbishop of Dublin deemed it expedient to inhibit Kelly from preaching in the Dublin churches. He consequently left the Church, and became a Nonconformist minister. Possessed of an ample fortune, and filled with godly zeal, he built several chapels, and gradually rallied around him a strong Evangelical party. Kelly died in Dublin in 1855, at the advanced age of eighty-six. His dying words were, 'Not my will, but Thine, be done.'

Kelly will be remembered chiefly as a hymn-writer. His hymns first appeared in 1804, in a volume entitled *Hymns on Various Passages*. In the first edition there were only 96 hymns, but in each subsequent issue the number greatly increased, until in the seventh edition, published in 1853, when the author was eighty-four years of age, there appeared 767 hymns. A few written in his earlier days were omitted; but in the Preface to this edition the aged hymnist writes: 'It will be perceived by those who read these hymns that though there is an interval between the first and last of nearly sixty years, both speak of the same great truths, and in the same way. In the course of that long period the author has seen much and heard much, but nothing that he has seen or heard has made the least change in his mind that he is conscious of as to the grand truths of the Gospel.' The above evening hymn is perhaps the best known of all Kelly's hymns. It consists of two stanzas of six lines each, and first appeared in 1806. The hymn is very popular, and has found its way into most Hymnals; but the line ' Now we lay us down to rest' seems to indicate that it was designed rather for private use than for public worship.

55. Children of the Heavenly King,
　　As ye journey, sweetly sing;
　　Sing your Saviour's worthy praise,
　　Glorious in His works and ways!

John Cennick, author of the above, was born of a Quaker family in 1717, at Reading, where for some years he was a land-surveyor. He suffered much spiritual distress, but, through the preaching of George

Account of First Rank Hymns. 145

Whitefield, obtained light and peace. He then devoted his energies to the service of God, and became a preacher among the Wesleyans. After a while he left the Wesleyans, and, together with his friend William Hammond, joined the Moravians. John Wesley spoke of him as 'that weak man, John Cennick, who confounded the poor people with strange doctrines.' He died in 1755, when thirty-eight years of age. He is favourably known as a hymn-writer. The above appeared in 1742 in his *Sacred Hymns for the Children of God in the Day of their Pilgrimage*. The original consists of twelve stanzas, but these have been subjected to many variations.

> 56. Glory be to Jesus,
>   Who, in bitter pains,
>   Poured for me the Life-blood
>   From His sacred veins.

This plaintive hymn on the Passion of Christ is a translation by Edward Caswall of an Italian Indulgence hymn, beginning 'Viva! Viva! Gesu.' The original probably dates from the eighteenth century, and is found in *Aspirazioni Divote*. The English version first appeared in the *Masque of Mary and other Poems*, a work by Caswall, published in 1858.

> 57. Go to dark Gethsemane,
>   Ye that feel the tempter's power,
>   Your Redeemer's conflict see;
>   Watch with Him one bitter hour:

> Turn not from His griefs away;
> Learn of Jesus Christ to pray.

This favourite Passion hymn, appropriate to Holy Week, was written by James Montgomery in 1820, and first appeared in the *Christian Psalmist* in 1825, headed 'Christ our Example in Suffering.' The original has undergone many alterations, which have considerably improved the hymn.

A few years ago, while making a sojourn in Jerusalem, we set out for the Mount of Olives on the evening of Holy Thursday, that we might visit the Garden of Gethsemane by moonlight, and tread the scene of the Saviour's Agony on the very night, and at the very hour, when His 'soul was exceeding sorrowful, even unto death.' Gethsemane means an olive and wine-press, and here were fulfilled the dark words of the prophet, 'I have trodden the wine-press alone, the great wine-press of the wrath of God, the wine-press trodden without the city.' Passing Gethsemane, we walked a few paces up the Mount of Olives, and sat down on a rock overlooking the Garden. The moon was still bright, and the venerable olive-trees were casting dark shadows across the sacred ground. The silence of night increased the solemnity. No human voice was heard, and the stillness was only broken by the occasional barking of dogs in the city. We read by the light passages bearing on the Agony, and James Montgomery's solemn hymn,

> Go to dark Gethsemane,
> Ye that feel the tempter's power.

Account of First Rank Hymns. 147

58. Guide me, O Thou great Jehovah!
    Pilgrim through this barren land.

William Williams, author of the above, called the Watts of Wales, was born in 1717, near Llandovery, Carmarthenshire. He received a good education, and underwent a course of study for the medical profession, but on hearing an eloquent sermon preached in a village churchyard, his soul was stirred within him, and he forthwith resolved to devote his life to the work of the ministry. He was accordingly ordained a deacon of the Established Church, but shortly afterwards became an itinerant preacher amongst the Welsh Calvinistic Methodists. 'In this capacity he laboured perseveringly for nearly half a century, incessantly hastening from place to place in every part of the Principality to preach the Gospel to listening thousands. His sermons, warm with his own fervour, bright with the vivid picturing of his lively imagination, and always radiant with the presence of his Divine Master, produced a most powerful effect upon his impressible fellow-countrymen, and Williams, working with such men as Rowlands and Harris, was felt as a power in the association meetings of the Connexion to which he belonged. He was as much celebrated for his poetry in his native tongue as he was for his talent and usefulness in preaching the Gospel. The popularity of the preacher opened the way for the reception of his poems, and the excellence of the pieces themselves made them retain their place when once received. They are now generally used by all denominations of Christians in the Principality, and held in the highest veneration by the people.' Williams wrote several works on Theology, and published in Welsh four series of hymn-books consisting of his own pieces. He also published two English hymn-books entitled respectively *Hosannah to the Son of David* and *Gloria in Excelsis*. After enduring much suffering, this excellent hymn-writer and preacher departed to his rest in 1791, aged seventy-four.

His best-known hymn, 'Guide me, O Thou great Jehovah,' was originally written in Welsh about the year 1760. In 1771 it was translated into English by the Rev. Peter Williams, and the next year appeared another rendering by the author himself. Shortly afterwards it was printed by Lady Huntingdon on a leaflet, with the heading, 'A favourite hymn sung by Lady Huntingdon's young collegians. Printed by the desire of many Christian friends. Lord, give it Thy blessing!'

The hymn also appeared in Whitefield's collection, dated 1774.

Another favourite hymn by Williams is that commencing

> O'er the gloomy hills of darkness,
> Look, my soul, be still and gaze.

It appeared in his *Gloria in Excelsis*, 1772; and as this noble hymn was composed before our great Missionary Societies were called into existence it may justly be regarded as the ancestor of many excellent missionary hymns written since Williams's time.

Account of First Rank Hymns.

59. Jesu, the very thought of Thee
    With sweetness fills the breast,
    But sweeter far Thy face to see,
    And in Thy presence rest.

Jesu, dulcis memoria	Sed super mel, et omnia,
Dans vera cordi gaudia,	Ejus dulcis praesentia.

Seven Latin poems are ascribed to St. Bernard of Clairvaux, the best known being 'Jubilus rhythmicus de nomine Jesu' (Jubilee rhythm on the name of Jesus). The original poem consists of forty-eight stanzas of four lines each, that is, about 200 lines (verses), and is distinguished for its deep spirituality, ardent love, and poetic beauty. The above, with Parts II. and III. of Hymn 178, *Hymns Ancient and Modern*, is a portion of St. Bernard's Latin poem beautifully rendered in English by Edward Caswall, M.A., and first appeared in his *Lyra Catholica* in 1849. The original was composed by St. Bernard about 1140 A.D., so that this ancient hymn is seven and a half centuries old.

St. Bernard of Clairvaux, known as the great Bernard, was born at Fontaine in Burgundy in 1091. His father was a nobleman, and his mother was the well-known Lady Aletta, distinguished alike for piety and benevolence. Bernard's childhood was spent in company with several brothers amidst the vineyards and corn-fields of his father, and his early training was conducted by his pious mother. In early youth he was sent to the Cathedral School of Chatillon, where he acquired a sufficient knowledge of Latin to preach extempore in that language, and write Latin hymns with grace and fluency. Lady Aletta died while Bernard was still a boy, and the mother's death-chamber made a serious impression on the youth's mind. Feeling that her strength was almost exhausted, she requested some priests to recite the 'Litany of the Dying.' With feeble voice she lisped after them the petition, 'By Thy Cross and Passion, good Lord, deliver us,' and suddenly falling back, expired. At the age of twenty-two Bernard became a monk in the Convent of Citeaux, near Dijon, where for three years he practised much austerity. At the age of twenty-five he was sent as the leader of twelve monks to found a new monastery. They journeyed northward, and at length settled in a lonely valley surrounded by pathless forests, known as the 'Valley of Wormwood.' By dint of hard manual labour the monks soon transformed the desolate untilled land into a smiling garden, and the 'Valley of Wormwood' was named 'Clairvaux'—the bright valley.

Of the labours of these pious men it may truly be said, 'The wilderness and the solitary place shall be glad for them; and the desert shall rejoice, and blossom as the rose. It shall blossom abundantly, and rejoice even with joy and singing.'

The Abbey of Clairvaux rose to the sound of sacred song, and Bernard became first Abbot of the new monastery. By the monks he was beloved as a father; his influence was extraordinary, and his reputation spread over all Christendom. Popes and kings sought his counsel, monasteries after the Clairvaux model were founded in every part of Europe, while the Catholic Church began to regard Bernard as the champion of orthodoxy. Five of his brothers became monks of Clairvaux, and Bernard's lamentation on the death of his much-beloved brother Gerard is a touching outpouring of affection and resignation :—' Who could ever have loved me as he did ? He was a brother by blood, but far more by religion. Thou, Gerard, art in the eternal presence of the Lord Jesus, and hast angels for thy companions; but what have I to fill up the void thou hast left? Fain would I know thy feelings towards me, my brother, my beloved, if indeed it is permitted to one bathing in the Divine radiance to call to mind our misery, to be occupied with our grief. Thou hast laid aside thy infirmities, but not thy love, for love abideth, and through eternity thou wilt not forget me. He hath given, He hath taken away, and while we deplore the loss of Gerard, let us not forget that he was given. God grant, Gerard, I may not have lost thee, but that thou hast preceded me, and I may be with thee where thou art. For of a surety thou hast rejoined those whom on thy last night below thou didst invite to praise God, when suddenly, to the great surprise of all, thou with a serene countenance and a cheerful voice didst commence chanting " Praise ye the Lord from the heavens; praise Him, all ye angels." At that moment, O my brother, the day dawned on thee, though it was night to us; the night to thee was all brightness. And so he died, and so dying he wellnigh changed my grief into rejoicing, so completely did the sight of his happiness overpower the recollection of my own misery. O Lord, Thou hast but called for Thine own. Thou hast but taken what belonged to Thee. And now my tears put an end to my words. I pray Thee, teach me to put an end to my tears.'

Bernard moved much about in the world, and his life was a very busy one, but the tranquil monastery of Clairvaux was his home for the long period of thirty-eight years. When on his deathbed the monks stood weeping around him, and Bernard with tears in his eyes murmured, 'I am in a strait betwixt two, having a desire to depart and be with Christ, which is far better; nevertheless the love of my children urgeth me to remain here below.' 'These were his last words. Then fixing his dove-like eyes on heaven, his spirit passed away from earth to be where Gerard and his mother were for ever with the Lord.' He died in 1153 A.D., aged 62.

Earnest, self-denying, spiritually-minded, St. Bernard is regarded as one of the chief saints of the Romish Church, and Luther called him 'the best monk that ever lived.'

60. O God of Bethel! by whose hand
    Thy people still are fed;
Who through this weary pilgrimage
    Hast all our fathers led.

This beautiful hymn, founded on Jacob's vow at Bethel (Gen. xxviii. 20, 21), is from the pen of Philip Doddridge, although some think it was composed by Darracott, one of his pupils. It has also been erroneously attributed to John Logan, appointed a minister at Leith in 1770. In Doddridge's own manuscript the hymn bears date 1736-7, so that it was

Account of First Rank Hymns.

written before Logan was born. It appears however that Logan in 1775 altered and improved the original, but unfortunately in 1781 he adopted it as his own without any acknowledgment.

At an early period it found a place in the Scotch Paraphrases, and in its present form the hymn has been generally accepted for a hundred years. It was an especial favourite with David Livingstone, who as a Scotch boy had become familiar with the Paraphrases in the days of youth. Often did the great African traveller, when wandering o'er the desert wastes, far from human habitations, and fearful lest his scant provisions should fail him in his pilgrimage, take from his pocket a small copy of the Paraphrases, and amid the solitude read aloud—

> O God of Bethel! by whose hand
>   Thy people still are fed;
> Who through this weary pilgrimage
>   Hast all our fathers led.
>
> Through each perplexing path of life
>   Our wand'ring footsteps guide;
> Give us each day our daily bread,
>   And raiment fit provide.

61. Ride on, ride on in majesty!
   In lowly pomp ride on to die!
   O Christ, Thy triumphs now begin
   O'er captive death and conquered sin.

This hymn, by Dean Milman, first appeared in 1827 in the hymn-book projected by Bishop Heber, and published by his widow the year after Heber's death. In this collection it is appointed as the hymn for the Sunday before Easter, usually called Palm Sunday, and it is a fitting introduction to the account of the Saviour's suffering during Passion Week. The original consists of five stanzas, of which the first is almost invariably omitted in modern Hymnals. It is—

> Ride on, ride on in majesty !
> Hark ! all the tribes Hosanna cry !
> Thine humble beast pursues his road,
> With palms and scattered garments strewed.

Milman wrote this and his other well-known hymns between 1820 and 1830, while he was Professor of Poetry in Oxford, at a period when he reached the zenith of his fame as a poetical writer.

62. Songs of praise the angels sang,
    Heaven with Hallelujahs rang,
    When Jehovah's work begun,
    When He spake, and it was done.

This joyous hymn, consisting of six stanzas, was written by James Montgomery, and first appeared in 1819 in Cotterill's Selection of Hymns. It appears that Montgomery was associated with Cotterill in the compilation of this Hymnal.

The hymn is founded on Job xxxviii. 7, 'The morning stars sang together, and all the sons of God shouted for joy,' and is full of exhortation to provoke an expression of gratitude to God for all His mercies.

63. Through all the changing scenes of life,
    In trouble and in joy.

This hymn occurs in the New Version by Tate and Brady, and is their rendering of the 34th Psalm. It bears date 1696.

64. Just as I am, without one plea,
    But that Thy blood was shed for me,
    And that Thou bidst me come to Thee,
    O Lamb of God, I come!

This immortal hymn was written by Charlotte Elliott in 1836, and appeared in the first edition of her *Hours of Sorrow cheered and comforted.*

'With its rich evangelical doctrine, its candour and simplicity, its personal confession of sin, and expressions of trust, it has taken a great hold on the public mind.' The Rev. Henry Venn Elliott, brother of the gifted authoress, said of this hymn: 'In the course of a long ministry I hope I have been permitted to see some fruit of my labours, but I feel that far more has been done by a single hymn of my sister's.' It has been translated into almost every language of Europe, as well as into Arabic, and it is said to be used in Southern Europe as in England. In 1822 Charlotte Elliott, when thirty-three years of age, was introduced, at her father's house in Clapham, to Dr. Malan, a pastor of

Geneva. The conversation of this spiritually-minded clergyman made a deep religious impression on her mind. She had been much troubled with religious doubts and fears. So in one of Dr. Malan's letters to her he writes, 'Dear Charlotte, cut the cable; it will take too long to unloose it; cut it, it is a small loss; the wind blows, and the ocean is before you—the Spirit of God and eternity.' Her state of mind is reflected in her own touching words—

> Just as I am, though tossed about
> With many a conflict, many a doubt,
> Fightings and fears within, without,
> O Lamb of God, I come!

65. New every morning is the love
    Our wakening and uprising prove;
    Through sleep and darkness safely brought,
    Restored to life, and power, and thought.

This admirable morning hymn is the opening poem of *The Christian Year*, and is deservedly very popular. The original consists of sixteen stanzas, beginning—

> Hues of the rich unfolding morn,
> That, ere the glorious sun be born . . .

The whole piece is an admirable exposition of the words, 'His compassions fail not; they are new every morning.' One writer truly remarks: 'For the understanding of those verses, which are sung in church, it will be found very useful to become thoroughly familiar with the rest, especially the introductory verses, which raise the soul to the realisation of the feelings expressed in the hymn. The true difficulty of actually feeling and entering into the spirit of the morning hymn is that so few persons are really familiar with sunrise in summer, and that for so many the "hues of the rich unfolding morn," the "rustling breeze," the "fragrant clouds of dewy steam," are indeed but wasted treasures of delight. If only we had more experience of these things, if they greeted us hastening early to the sanctuary of God, we should gain much more from our daily lives. But evening hymns are much more real to us, because they refer to a time when we are more frequently alive to the beauties of nature.'

66. Praise, my soul, the King of Heaven,
    To His feet thy tribute bring.

This jubilant hymn by Lyte first appeared in 1834, in his *Spirit of the Psalms*, and is a paraphrase on the 103d psalm.

On visiting the land of Lyte in Devon, one writer says: 'It was evening when we arrived at Brixham, and I sauntered to enjoy a look at the waters of Torbay, the sea which the parish psalmist used to look upon so lovingly. I stood gazing until the moon arose and flung her train of light over the waves. Then the stars came out, and as I watched them brightening, voices of children arose from the village. While the charm was still upon me, a clear mature voice from near the shore commenced singing one of Lyte's hymns. It seemed as if the poet had imbued that shore with his *Spirit of the Psalms*.'

67. Praise the Lord! ye heavens, adore Him,
    Praise Him, angels, in the height;
Sun and moon, rejoice before Him,
    Praise Him, all ye stars of light.

This hymn is a paraphrase of the 148th Psalm, which begins: 'Praise ye the Lord. Praise ye the Lord from the heavens: praise Him in the heights.' It has been traced to a collection of *Psalms, Hymns, and Anthems for the Foundling Chapel*. The collection bears date 1796, but the hymn seems to have been printed on a sheet of paper, and inserted in the Hymnal, as has been proved not later than 1806. It has sometimes been attributed to the Rev. John Kempthorne, a clergyman of Gloucester; sometimes to Bishop Mant, but not on any good authority. Nothing is really known of its author.

68. Soldiers of Christ, arise,
    And put your armour on.

This hymn, suitable for Confirmation, is by Charles Wesley. It is founded on Eph. vi. 11-18, 'Put on the whole armour of God,' etc., and is indeed a spirited paraphrase of that passage, descriptive of the Christian soldier.

The original first appeared in 1749, in *Hymns and Sacred Poems*, and consisted of sixteen stanzas of eight lines each. The hymn, as it appears in modern Hymnals, is a selection of a few of the original stanzas.

69. The strain upraise of joy and praise.
Alleluia !

Cantemus cuncti melodum. Alleluia !

This famous hymn is a translation by Dr. Neale, and first appeared in the *Hymnal Noted* in 1858. The original Latin is generally thought to be the work of Godescalcus, although Mone contends that it is a Sequence of the eleventh century.

Godescalcus, or Gottschalk, was a monk of the famous Abbey of St. Gall, near Constance. His sacred songs show that he had deep sympathy with Nature and accurate Scriptural knowledge. Few particulars are known of his life, but he died in 868 A.D.

The above is called the Alleluiatic Sequence, a name that requires some little explanation. In the Western Church, an anthem called the Gradual was sung between the Epistle and Gospel, and at the end of this anthem was sung 'Alleluia,' which was often prolonged to a great extent, somewhat after the 'Amen' in the Hallelujah Chorus of 'The Messiah.' Notker, a monk of St. Gall, the monastery of Godescalcus, about the year 900 A.D., caused a species of anthem to take the place of this Alleluia. The words of the anthem were rhythmical but not metrical, and they were called a Sequence, literally, 'following,' because they followed the Gradual, and they are also named a Prose, because they were not metrical.

The above is named Alleluiatic Sequence, because each verse is followed by Alleluia.

The celebrated Sequence by Notker begins ' Media vita in morte sunt,' etc. From this Sequence were taken the impressive words of our Burial Service : ' In the midst of life we are in death : of whom may we seek for succour, but of Thee, O Lord, who for our sins art justly displeased ? ' and the sentences following. The words are said to have been suggested to Notker by his seeing persons climb the dangerous cliffs near the monastery in search of the samphire.

> 70. There is a land of pure delight,
> Where saints immortal reign.

This favourite hymn was written by Isaac Watts when he was only twenty-two years old. The original consists of six stanzas, and is entitled 'A Prospect of Heaven makes Death easy.' It is founded on one of the last scenes in the life of Moses. Not being permitted to enter the Promised Land with the hosts of Israel, God allowed His servant to behold a distant prospect of Canaan from the top of Mount Pisgah. So ' Moses went up from the plains of Moab unto the mountain of Nebo, to the top of Pisgah.' There on the summit stood the veteran leader of Israel. 'His eye was not dim, nor his natural force abated,' as, looking across the swellings of Jordan, he gazed upon the land promised to Abraham and his seed for ever.

> Sweet fields, beyond the swelling flood,
> Stand dressed in living green ;
> So to the Jews old Canaan stood,
> While Jordan rolled between.

Account of First Rank Hymns.

According to a local tradition, this hymn is intimately connected with the scenery around Southampton. It appears that the author, seated in his home, could see the arm of the sea known as Southampton Water, and 'beyond the swelling flood' stood the green glades of the New Forest. According to another account, Watts could see the waters of the river Itchen, with the rich landscape of the Isle of Wight in the far-distant view. The varied beauties of the noble prospect suggested to the poet thoughts of the river Jordan, 'the narrow stream of death,' and the glories of the Heavenly Canaan 'beyond the swelling flood.'

> Could we but climb where Moses stood,
>   And view the landscape o'er,
> Not Jordan's stream, nor death's cold flood,
>   Should fright us from the shore.

71. Thou art gone up on high
    To mansions in the skies,
    And round Thy throne unceasingly
    The songs of praise arise.

Emma Toke, author of the above, wrote several hymns at the request of a friend who was collecting suitable hymns for the Committee of the Society for Promoting Christian Knowledge when they were compiling their Hymn-book. The compositions were sent anonymously, but were considered sufficiently good to be published in the Society's Hymnal in 1851. The late Dr. Dykes composed for the above Ascension-tide hymn the noble tune called 'Olivet,' from the scene of the Ascension, and when sung to this tune 'few hymns touch a deeper chord.' Mrs. Toke is the wife of the Rev. Nicholas Toke, Rector of Godington, Ashford, Kent.

> 72. Ye servants of the Lord,
> Each in his office wait,
> Observant of His heavenly word,
> And watchful at His gate.

This Advent hymn, by Philip Doddridge, was published in 1755, shortly after the author's death. It contains good admonitions to Christian hope and watchfulness.

> 73. As with gladness men of old
> Did the guiding star behold;
> As with joy they hailed its light,
> Leading onward, beaming bright,—
> So, most gracious God, may we
> Evermore be led to Thee.

William Chatterton Dix, author of this favourite hymn, was the son of John Dix, a surgeon at Bristol, and was born in that city in 1837. He was educated at Bristol Grammar School, and trained for mercantile pursuits. The above hymn, consisting of five stanzas, has received special commendation from Lord Selborne, who quotes it as a proof that the power of writing good hymns is not wanting in our own day. It is an Epiphany hymn, founded on the passage in St. Matthew ii. 1, 2 :

'Now when Jesus was born in Bethlehem of Judæa in the days of Herod the king, behold, there came wise men from the east to Jerusalem, saying, Where is He that is born King of the Jews? for we have seen His star in the east, and are come to worship Him.'

74. Love Divine, all love excelling,
    Joy of heaven, to earth come down!

This well-known hymn by Charles Wesley is founded on Col. i. 27, 'Christ in you, the hope of glory.' The original consists of three double stanzas, and these appear without alteration, except that 'loves' is made singular. The original ran, 'Love divine, all loves excelling.' The hymn was written in 1743, and appeared in one of Wesley's collections in 1747.

75. O come, all ye faithful,
    Joyful and triumphant,
  O come ye, O come ye to Bethlehem;
    Come and behold Him, etc.

This favourite Christmas hymn is a translation by Canon Oakeley from a Latin hymn beginning 'Adeste fideles, Laeti triumphantes,' said to have been taken from a 'Graduale' of the Cistercian monks.

The author, the Rev. Frederick Oakeley, graduated at Oxford about fifty years ago, and took a lively interest in the 'Tractarian Movement' of that time. He took holy orders, and was promoted to be a Prebendary of Lichfield Cathedral, but in 1845 seceded to the Church of Rome.

He translated the above hymn in 1841 while he was incumbent of St. Margaret's, London. The original Latin is by some attributed to Bonaventura, an Italian saint of the thirteenth century.

76. O help us, Lord, each hour of need,
    Thy heavenly succour give;
  Help us in thought, and word, and deed,
    Each hour on earth we live!

This hymn, by Dean Milman, was written, with many others, for a hymn-book compiled by Bishop Heber, entitled *Hymns Adapted to the Weekly Church Service of the Year*, and published by Heber's widow in 1827.

The above hymn is appointed for the second Sunday in Lent, and the first words of each stanza, 'O help us,' are evidently taken from the Gospel for that Sunday, wherein the poor Syro-Phœnician woman with great earnestness says to Christ, 'Lord, help me.' The original consists of six stanzas, but two of them are usually omitted in modern Hymnals.

77. Thou art the Way; to Thee alone
    From sin and death we flee;
  And he who would the Father seek,
    Must seek Him, Lord, by Thee.

Bishop Doane, author of this hymn, was born in the United States in 1799. He distinguished himself in youth during his College career, and having entered the

Account of First Rank Hymns. 165

ministry he was soon after appointed to be Rector of Holy Trinity, Boston. In 1832 he was consecrated Bishop of New Jersey, an office he filled with much efficiency. He died in 1859. As a hymn-writer he is known by several hymns composed for the festivals. The above appeared in 1824 in *Songs by the Way*, although from the Preface it appears to have been written some years previously. The hymn is founded on St. John xiv. 6 : 'I am the way, the truth, and the life : no man cometh unto the Father but by Me.'

> 78. Forth in Thy name, O Lord, I go,
>   My daily labour to pursue.

This hymn, by Charles Wesley, appeared in *Hymns and Sacred Poems*, 1749.

In the Methodist Hymn-book it is entitled 'A Hymn before Work,' and it is indeed a good practical hymn, which might be used with advantage in the morning before beginning the labours of the day.

> 79. Lord, dismiss us with Thy blessing,
>   Fill our hearts with joy and peace :
>   Let us each, Thy love possessing,
>   Triumph in redeeming grace.

The Hon. and Rev. Walter Shirley, author of the above, belonged to the Earl Ferrers family, and was born in 1725. His three elder brothers were successively Earls, and he was cousin to the celebrated Countess of Huntingdon. Having taken holy orders, he manifested great interest in the Evangelical movement of the last century, and was the intimate friend of Whitefield and the Wesleys. He obtained the living of Loughrea, in the county of Galway, Ireland, where, after suffering much bodily affliction, he died in 1786. As a hymnist he compiled Lady Huntingdon's Hymn-book in 1764, and is best known as the author of two favourite hymns, 'Sweet the moments, rich in blessing,' and 'Lord, dismiss us with Thy blessing.' The latter is sometimes ascribed to Rev. George Burder and others, but Shirley's son, the Rev. Walter Shirley, asserted that his father was author, and this opinion is universal among his offspring. It first appeared in *A Collection of Hymns*, published in 1774, and afterwards in Lady Huntingdon's Hymn-book.

About ninety years ago a venerable man, who had passed his threescore years, and was evidently so great a sufferer as not to be able to take a pulpit, or even to lie down, used to be found sitting in his chair preaching with his latest breath in a crowded drawing-room, and to those who filled the lobby and staircase of a spacious dwelling, in order to catch his last earnest tones. He was a hymnist, and composed a hymn for the use of those who then gathered to hear him, that they might sing on parting from under the sound of his loved voice. It has become a part of the Christian service of song, and is the well-known dismissal hymn, "Lord, dismiss us with Thy blessing." The author was the Honourable and Rev. Walter Shirley, the friend of

Whitefield and the Wesleys, a lover of missions, and co-worker of his relative, Lady Huntingdon.'

80. Lord of mercy and of might,
   Of mankind the life and light.

This beautiful Lenten hymn, by Heber, first appeared in the *Christian Observer* for November 1811. In his collection of 1827 it is assigned to Quinquagesima. The hymn is indeed a short touching Litany, each stanza ending with the supplication, 'Jesus, hear and save!' The Gospel for Quinquagesima gives an account of the healing of the blind man who sat by the wayside begging, and who, on hearing that Jesus of Nazareth passed by, earnestly and importunately called out, 'Jesus, thou Son of David, have mercy on me.'

81. When gathering clouds around I view,
   And days are dark, and friends are few.

This affecting hymn is from the pen of Sir Robert Grant, and first appeared in the *Christian Observer* in 1806. As Sir Robert was born in 1785, he could not have been more than twenty-one years of age when he composed the hymn. It is perhaps better suited for private use than public worship.

82. Brightest and best of the sons of the morning!
   Dawn on our darkness, and lend us Thine
      aid!

This well-known and favourite Christmas hymn is by Bishop Heber, and first appeared in the *Christian*

Observer in 1811. In his collection of hymns published in 1827 the above is assigned to 'Epiphany,' or Manifestation of Christ to the Gentiles. It is founded on the Gospel narrative for that day: 'Behold, there came wise men from the east to Jerusalem, saying, Where is He that is born King of the Jews? for we have seen His star in the east, and are come to worship Him.' It is sometimes urged against the hymn that it contains an apostrophe to the Star of Bethlehem to be our guide; but the poetic fancy of addressing inanimate nature is not without sanction in the Inspired Word, *e.g.* in Psalm 148: 'Praise Him, ye waters that be above the heavens; fire and hail; snow and vapour; stormy wind fulfilling His word.' When in 1824 Bishop Heber was making a missionary tour through the northern provinces of India, he spent Christmas-tide at Meerut, where on 19th December he consecrated a large church. On the occasion he writes: 'I had the gratification of hearing my own hymns, "Brightest and best of the sons of the morning," and that for St. Stephen's Day, sung better than I ever heard them sung in a church before.'

83. Christians, awake! salute the happy morn
    Whereon the Saviour of the world was born;
    Rise to adore the mystery of love
    Which hosts of angels chanted from above.

John Byrom, author of this Nativity hymn, was born at Manchester in 1691. He graduated at Cambridge,

Account of First Rank Hymns.

and became Fellow of Trinity College in 1714. His ancestors held a good position in Lancashire; and on the death of his brother he succeeded to the family estates. Byrom was a scientific and religious layman, and a man of mark in his day. He was a friend of the Wesleys; and John Wesley says of him: 'In my journey from Liverpool to Birmingham I read Dr. Byrom's Poems. He has all the wit and humour of Dr. Swift, together with much more learning, a deep and strong understanding, and above all, a serious vein of piety. We have some of the finest sentiments that ever appeared in the English tongue; some of the noblest truths expressed with the utmost energy of language and the strongest colours of poetry.' The original of the above, consisting of forty-eight lines, was published in 1773, after the author's death. The hymn attained great popularity in Lancashire—the author's native county—and for upwards of a century has held its high position in our hymn-books. Byrom died in 1763, in his seventy-second year.

> 84. Lord of the worlds above,
> How pleasant and how fair
> The dwellings of Thy love,
> Thy earthly temples are!

This hymn, by Dr. Isaac Watts, is his third metrical version of the first portion of the 84th Psalm: 'How amiable are Thy tabernacles, O Lord of hosts! My soul longeth, yea, even fainteth for the courts of the Lord; my heart and my flesh crieth out for the living

God.' The original consists of four long stanzas, and first appeared in 1719 under the heading, 'Longing for the house of God.'

> 85. O for a closer walk with God!
>   A calm and heavenly frame;
>   A light to shine upon the road
>   That leads me to the Lamb.

This affecting hymn, consisting of six stanzas, was written by William Cowper in 1772, and gives expression to his own inward fears and conflicts. Its pathetic words bear indication of the impending melancholy which shortly afterwards fell upon him. The above hymn, and 'God moves in a mysterious way,' were written in the 'twilight of departing reason;' for in 1773 Cowper sank into a state of despondency, and continued so for five years. Under these circumstances how affecting it is to ponder the last verse—

>   So shall my walk be close with God,
>   Calm and serene my frame;
>   So purer light shall mark the road
>   That leads me to the Lamb.

> 86. Rejoice, the Lord is King!
>   Your Lord and King adore.

This hymn was written by Charles Wesley in 1743, and appeared in 1746 in *Hymns for our Lord's Resurrection*, a tract containing sixteen hymns.

The original consists of six stanzas; the two last, usually omitted in modern Hymnals, are—

> He all His foes shall quell,
>   Shall all our sins destroy,
> And every bosom swell
>   With pure seraphic joy;
> Lift up your heart, lift up your voice;
> Rejoice, again I say, Rejoice.
>
> Rejoice in glorious hope!
>   Jesus, the Judge, shall come,
> And take His servants up
>   To their eternal home;
> We soon shall hear the archangel's voice,
> The trump of God shall sound, Rejoice!

87. The Lord will come, the earth shall quake,
    The hills their fixèd seat forsake.

This Advent hymn was one of four sent by Heber to the *Christian Observer* in October 1811, with the initials D. R., the extreme letters of his Christian name Reginald with D reversed. 'They were accompanied by a letter complaining of the defects in existing Church hymns, such as the too familiar epithets applied to the Divine Being, and similar blemishes, and asking suggestions for improvement.' In Heber's collection of 1827 the above is assigned to the Second Sunday in Advent, and is founded on the Gospel for this Sunday, which describes the second coming of Christ: 'Men's hearts failing them for fear, and for looking after those things which are coming on the earth: for the powers of heaven shall be shaken. And then shall they see the Son of Man coming in a cloud with power and great glory.'

88. Angels, from the realms of glory,
  Wing your flight o'er all the earth.

This magnificent Christmas hymn, by James Montgomery, appeared in 1819. One writer says: 'For comprehensiveness, appropriateness of expression, force, and elevation of sentiment, this hymn may challenge comparison with any hymn that was ever written in any language or country.'

89. As pants the hart for cooling streams,
  When heated in the chase.

This is a beautiful rendering of the 142d Psalm, taken from the New Version by Tate and Brady. It appeared in 1696, and is therefore about two centuries old. The hymn is deservedly a favourite, and its popularity has been increased by means of the music of Spohr's glorious anthem.

90. Come, gracious Spirit, Heavenly Dove,
  With light and comfort from above;
  Be Thou our Guardian, Thou our Guide,
  O'er every thought and step preside.

Simon Browne, author of the above, was born at Shepton Mallet, Somerset, in 1680, and was thus a contemporary of Dr. Watts. In 1716 he became pastor of the Independent Chapel in Old Jewry, London. During the last years of his life he suffered from a peculiar species of aberration, and died in 1732. His hymns

Account of First Rank Hymns.

were published in a small volume entitled *Hymns and Spiritual Songs*, in three books, designed as a supplement to Dr. Watts'. The Preface is interesting in the history of hymnology, as it gives an account of the earlier hymn-writers. The above is the best known in the collection. It was written about 1720, and is headed, 'The soul giving itself up to the conduct and influence of the Holy Ghost.' The original, which has been much altered, began—

> Come, Holy Spirit, Heavenly Dove,
> My sinful maladies remove.

The hymn must be distinguished from one by Dr. Watts beginning—

> Come, Holy Spirit, Heavenly Dove,
> With all Thy quickening powers.

91. For Thy mercy and Thy grace,
    Faithful through another year,
    Hear our song of thankfulness;
    Father, and Redeemer, hear.

The Rev. Henry Downton, author of this hymn, graduated at Cambridge in 1840, and was ordained in 1843. For many years he was incumbent of St. John's, Chatham, and subsequently British Chaplain at Geneva. He is now Rector of Hopton, Suffolk. The above beautiful hymn for New Year's Eve first appeared in 1843 in the *Church of England Magazine*. It originally consisted of seven stanzas, but many of these have been considerably altered.

92. Lead us, Heavenly Father, lead us
   O'er the world's tempestuous sea;
Guide us, guard us, keep us, feed us,
   For we have no help but Thee:
Yet possessing every blessing,
   If our God our Father be.

James Edmeston, author of this hymn, was born in 1791. He was educated at Hackney, where his parents lived. His grandfather by the mother's side was the Rev. Samuel Brewer, for fifty years an Independent minister in Stepney: and the young poet was brought up an Independent. He afterwards joined the Church of England, and in a letter dated 1866, shortly before his death, he writes, 'From early years I had a strong leaning towards the Church of England, the service of which I always found more congenial to my own feelings.'

He wrote a very great number of hymns, and thus largely contributed to our modern hymnology. He died in 1867, in the seventy-sixth year of his age. The above favourite hymn appeared in his *Sacred Lyrics* in 1821. Another well-known hymn of Edmeston's is—

   Saviour, breathe an evening blessing,
   Ere repose our spirits seal.

93. Lord, as to Thy dear Cross we flee,
   And plead to be forgiven,
So let Thy life our pattern be,
   And form our souls for heaven.

John Hampden Gurney, author of the above, was the

son of John Gurney, a Baron of the Exchequer, and was born in London in 1802. After graduating at Cambridge, he took holy orders in 1827. For seventeen years he was Curate of Lutterworth, and in 1847 he was appointed Rector of St. Mary's, Marylebone, an appointment he held till his death in 1862.

In 1850 he compiled, together with Thomas Garnier and Charles Baring, late Bishop of Durham, a collection of hymns for use in some of the Marylebone churches The above hymn, on the imitation of Christ, bears date 1838, and appeared in the Marylebone collection in 1851.

> 94. Lord, in this Thy mercy's day,
> Ere it pass for aye away,
> On our knees we fall and pray.

This striking penitential hymn is the composition of the Rev. Isaac Williams, B.D., born in 1802. He graduated at Oxford, and became a Fellow of Trinity College, and subsequently Rector of Bisley, Gloucestershire. With Keble and Newman he contributed several sacred odes to the *Lyra Apostolica*, and wrote several of the *Tracts for the Times*.

In 1839 appeared his *Hymns translated from the Parisian Breviary*, a collection from which many beautiful hymns have found their way into our modern Hymnals. Among them are the following:—

O Heavenly Jerusalem, Of everlasting halls.	Coelestis, O Jerusalem.
Great mover of all hearts, whose hand.	Supreme motor cordium.

The original found in the Paris Breviary is by Charles Coffin.

Lo! from the desert homes.   Nunc suis tandem novus e latebris.

The original Latin is also by Charles Coffin.

'Morn of morns, and day of days,' founded on a Latin hymn in the Paris Breviary.

In 1842 Mr. Williams published *The Baptistery, or the Way of Eternal Life, in Verse*, a long poem, consisting of 105 stanzas, and among them the plaintive hymn, 'Lord, in this Thy mercy's day.'

95. O God, unseen yet ever near,
    Thy Presence may we feel ;
And, thus inspired with holy fear,
    Before Thy footstool kneel.

Edward Osler, author of this favourite Communion hymn, was born at Falmouth in 1798. His parents were dissenters, but soon he became devotedly attached to the Church of England. He possessed considerable talent, and so retentive was his memory that he could repeat the whole of the New Testament in the original Greek. Osler entered the medical profession, but much of his time was devoted to literary and religious pursuits. He died at Truro in 1863, much beloved by a wide circle of friends.

The above hymn was written in 1837, and first appeared in a monthly magazine called *Church and King*, a work to which Osler contributed about seventy original psalms and hymns.

96. That day of wrath, that dreadful day.

Dies irae, dies illa.

All the great mediæval hymn-writers, with one exception, were cowled monks, and their sacred songs were composed within the convent walls. Their hymns on the Celestial Country will gladden the Christian Church as long as the sun and moon endureth; but the lives of the cloistered writers are for the most part hidden from our knowledge, inasmuch as they pursued the noiseless tenor of their ways in the cells of tranquil monasteries. We have already noticed that the first half of the twelfth century—the era of the Crusades—was the great harvest season of mediæval hymns. Sweet singers preceded and sweet singers followed this period; but their songs were only the first-fruits and after-gleanings of the great harvest of sacred song. Hildebert, Archbishop of Tours; Bernard, monk of Cluny; St. Bernard, Abbot of Clairvaux; Adam of St. Victor, a member of the renowned religious house of St. Victor of Paris; and Peter the Venerable, the gentle Abbot of Cluny, united to chant the grand chorus, and filled the Church with songs of gladness throughout the twelfth century. After this chorus comes a subdued silence; but scarcely had the echoes of the loud burst of song died away, until they blend and are lost in the rising tones of the magnificent mediæval chant, the 'Dies Irae.'

Thomas of Celano, called by his countrymen Tommaso da Celano, is named from his birthplace, Celano, a small town near Lake Fucino, in the further Abruzzi, a province in the northern part of the kingdom of Naples. Thomas was the scholar and intimate friend of St. Francis of Assisi, the founder of the Franciscan Order of monks, and was one of the eleven disciples who formed the nucleus of that religious body in 1208 A.D. The members of the order were named Fratres Minores, 'Lesser Brethren,' to remind them that humility was their cardinal virtue. In England they were called Minorites and Grey Friars, from the grey colour of their habit. The Order spread rapidly, and it is said that within fifty years the members numbered 200,000, and possessed at least a thousand monasteries. St. Francis himself died in 1226 A.D., and the splendid memorial church erected on the site of the chapel where he worshipped at Assisi is considered to be one of the very finest specimens of Gothic architecture of the Middle Ages.

Thomas of Celano enjoyed the implicit confidence of his master, and was therefore appointed custos or guardian of those branches of the Order in the Rhenish provinces. On the death of the saint, Thomas returned to Rome, and by command of Pope Gregory wrote an account of his master's life, a biography which is still regarded as the most authentic record of the times and labours of St. Francis. It is, however, as a hymn-writer, and especially as the author of that sublime and awful judgment hymn, the 'Dies Irae,' that the name of Thomas of Celano is of world-wide renown. This precious hymn lay neglected for above half a century, and any writer might then have appropriated it as his own. Even at the present day its authorship is some-

Account of First Rank Hymns. 179

times ascribed to Gregory the Great, but without any good authority. The Latin rhythm is much superior to that of such an early age; and as Gregory flourished about 600 A.D., it is highly improbable that any hymn of his would lie neglected for about seven hundred years. It has also been ascribed to St. Bernard of Clairvaux, but those who are acquainted with the subjective loveliness of this hymnist will readily perceive that the 'Dies Irae' is too austere in tone, and too masculine in character, to be the work of the tender-hearted Abbot of Clairvaux. Moreover, so high was the reputation of the saint, both in life and after death, that no composition of his would remain unnoticed for a hundred years. Other names have been claimed as authors, but on so slight authority that their claims are scarcely worthy of investigation. In former ages a bitter rivalry existed between the two religious Orders, the Dominicans and Franciscans, and it is well known that members of the former have actually stigmatised the noble hymn as a 'rhythmus inconditus,' 'an uncouth poem.' This fact alone is a strong presumption that the 'Dies Irae' was the work of a Franciscan. The question of authorship has been thoroughly investigated of late years by Mohnike, and the results are stated in Daniel's *Thesaurus Hymnologicus*. The evidence is overwhelming in favour of Thomas of Celano, so that it may be regarded as a moral certainty that he is the author of this, the greatest and noblest of Latin hymns.

Of all hymns of the Western Church the 'Dies Irae' has obtained the widest fame, and not only has this unapproachable Sequence distanced other hymns, but its popularity has increased from generation to generation. Several causes have contributed to this. First, the Latin is happily written in triple rhyme, or triplets, and the three verses of each stanza have fitly been compared to three successive blows of a hammer upon an anvil. Secondly, the theme is expressed with such sublimity and unadorned simplicity that it can readily be understood by both the young and the aged. Thirdly, the subject-matter is of individual interest to every member of the human race. 'It is appointed unto men once to die, and after that the judgment.' As all must appear at the tribunal of final doom, so each soul feels a personal concern in the awful picture here drawn of the scene of the Last Judgment. These merits and many others have conspired to form a unanimous verdict that the 'Dies Irae' is the great mediæval masterpiece of sacred song. Its influence upon European literature has been greater than that of any other hymn, and it has been translated into all the languages of civilised countries. It was introduced into the Liturgy of the Roman Church in the fourteenth century, previous to the year 1385 A.D., and it has ever since formed a solemn requiem or mass for the souls of the departed. It is known to be one of the highest and most difficult tasks of musicians to compose music worthy of the awful solemnity of the 'Dies Irae,' and yet this task has been successfully accomplished by Cherubini, Mozart, Palestrina, and other musical celebrities.

The grandeur of the Latin original has induced many

Account of First Rank Hymns.   181

English hymnists to render it into our own language. Jeremy Taylor, in a letter to his friend John Evelyn, writes: 'I was thinking to have begged of you a translation of that well-known hymn, "Dies irae, dies illa," which, if it were a little changed, would make an excellent divine song.' It does not appear that Evelyn complied with his friend's request. We have, however, several English renderings at an early period. One of the first now extant is that of Sylvester, a hymnist of the reign of James I., published in 1621. About thirty years after we find a very good translation by Richard Crashaw, son of an eminent London divine, and a hymnist of Charles the First's reign. This translation of the 'Dies Irae' is pronounced by Pope to be the best of Crashaw's compositions. The first stanza runs thus:—

>Hear'st thou, my soul, what serious things
>Both the Psalm and Sibyl sings,
>Of a sure Judge, from whose sharp ray
>The world in flames shall fly away?

The above appeared in 1648 in Crashaw's *Steps to the Temple*.

Another English rendering that ought to be noticed is that by Wentworth Dillon, Earl of Roscommon, a hymnist of the reign of Charles II. Although living in a corrupt age his writings are singularly pure; so that Pope says of him—

>In all Charles's days,
>Roscommon only boasts unspotted lays.

Some stanzas from his translation are still to be found in our modern Hymnals, to wit:—

> The last loud trumpet's wondrous sound
> Shall wake the nations under ground ;
> Where then, my God, shall I be found,
> When all shall stand before Thy throne ;
> When Thou shalt make their sentence known ;
> And all Thy righteous judgment own ?

Dr. Johnson, in his Life of Roscommon, says : 'At the moment in which he expired he uttered, with an energy of voice that expressed the most fervent devotion, two lines of his own version of " Dies Irae "'—

> My God, my Father, and my Friend,
> Do not forsake me in my end.'

The poet died in 1684, and was buried with great pomp in Westminster Abbey.

Dr. Johnson, his biographer, always wept when he attempted to repeat the old hymn of Thomas of Celano.

About the middle of last century appeared a hymn founded on the 'Dies Irae,' commencing, 'Lo! He cometh, countless trumpets.' This hymn was by a Moravian minister named John Cennick. In 1758, eight years after its publication, Charles Wesley published a cento founded on Cennick's hymn. This is now the popular hymn beginning with Wesley's stanza, 'Lo! He comes with clouds descending.' The third and fourth stanzas, commencing respectively, 'Every island, sea, and mountain,' and ' Now redemption, long expected,' are from Cennick's hymn. In 1805, embodied in *The Lay of the Last Minstrel*, appeared a translation of a few stanzas of the 'Dies Irae.' It is happily introduced as sung in Melrose Abbey by the holy fathers as a solemn requiem or hymn for the dead. The stanzas are a free translation of the original Latin, but they are generally considered to possess more of the spirit and tone of an English hymn than the more literal translations of the same. It is well known that Sir Walter was very fond of the 'Dies Irae,' and speaking of it on one occasion he said, 'To my Gothic ear this old hymn is more solemn and affecting than fine classical poetry; it has the gloomy dignity of the Gothic Church.'

'The awful burthen of the song,'

>   Dies irae, dies illa
>   Solvet saeclum in favillâ,

represented as sung by the monks of Melrose Abbey in their solemn requiem for the dead, is—

>   That day of wrath, that dreadful day,
>   When heaven and earth shall pass away,
>   What power shall be the sinner's stay?
>   How shall he meet that dreadful day?
>
>   When, shrivelling like a parchèd scroll,
>   The flaming heavens together roll;
>   When louder yet, and yet more dread,
>   Swells the high trump that wakes the dead;
>
>   O! on that day, that dreadful day,
>   When man to judgment wakes from clay,
>   Be Thou the trembling sinner's stay,
>   Though heaven and earth shall pass away.

Throughout life this hymn was an especial favourite with the illustrious novelist, and his biographer relates a most affecting incident of his last days, how that in his last moments he frequently repeated portions of the 'Dies Irae:'—

'He seemed to suffer no bodily pain, and his mind, though hopelessly obscured, appeared, when there was any symptom of consciousness, to be dwelling, with rare exceptions, on serious and solemn things. . . . Whatever we could follow him in was a fragment of the Bible, especially the prophecies of Isaiah and the Book of Job, or some petition in the Litany, or a verse of some Psalm in the old Scotch metrical version, or of some of the magnificent hymns of the Romish ritual, in which he had always delighted, but which probably hung on his memory now in connection with the church services which he had attended while in Italy. We very often heard distinctly the cadence of the " Dies Irae." '

Of all the translations of the 'Dies Irae' the most effective English rendering is that of the Rev. William Josiah Irons, D.D., published in 1848. The translator was the son of an eminent dissenting minister, and rose to be Vicar of Brompton, and a Prebendary of St. Paul's, London. His version is now regarded as the accepted rendering for church use of the grandest mediæval hymn, and justly so, for his version embodies all those features that constitute a perfect translation. The original Latin consists of seventeen triplets and two couplets, making in all fifty-five lines, and Dr. Irons has preserved this form of rhythm, and rendered the poem in nineteen triplets, or fifty-seven lines. As our remarks are rather suggestive than exhaustive, it would be beyond the province of this brief notice to criticise the whole poem; but since the first triplet suggests

Account of First Rank Hymns. 185

many interesting questions, it seems desirable to make a few remarks on the opening stanza—

Dies irae, dies illa	Day of wrath ! O day of mourning !
Solvet saeclum in favillâ,	See fulfilled the prophets' warning !
Teste David cum Sibyllâ.	Heaven and earth in ashes burning.

It has been truly observed that the opening words, 'Dies irae,' 'Day of wrath !' strike the key-note to the whole poem. This expression is borrowed from the Vulgate version of Zephaniah i. 15, and many thoughts in the poem are suggested by that passage : 'That day is a day of wrath, a day of trouble and distress, a day of wasteness and desolation, a day of darkness and gloominess, a day of clouds and thick darkness.' In mediæval sacred verse it was usual to speak of the Day of Judgment as the ' Dies irae,' or ' Day of wrath.'

The third line, ' Teste David cum Sibyllâ,' literally, ' David being a witness, together with the Sibyl,' that is, to the reality of the Day of Judgment, has been objected to. It has been urged that a Sibyl, who in Pagan mythology was accounted a prophetess, but who in fact was little better than a fortune-teller, ought not to be called upon as a witness to Christian truth, and spoken of in terms of equality with David, the Psalmist of Israel. It ought, however, to be remembered that in the Middle Ages the Sibylline verses were regarded as second only to the Holy Scriptures in prophetic authority, and therefore the fact that the coming judgment was attested by the Sibyl would exercise considerable influence with those who regarded the Sibylline verses as inspired. Consequent, however, upon this objection, we find that in the Paris Breviary and elsewhere the line is omitted, and in its stead are inserted, 'Crucis expandens vexilla,' 'Unfurling the banners of the Cross,' in accordance with a prevailing expectation that a banner with an inscribed Cross would appear in the sky on the Day of Judgment. This expectation was founded upon St. Matthew xxiv. 30, 'Then shall appear the sign of the Son of Man in heaven.'

Sometimes we find the reading 'Teste Petro,' instead of 'Teste David,' probably from the fact that St. Peter bears special witness to the final conflagration, saying, ''The heavens shall pass away with a great noise, and the elements shall melt with fervent heat.'

Although it has been said that the 'Dies Irae' is too austere, and too full of awful solemnity, there is yet, in the tenth stanza, a most touching allusion to the Saviour's wondrous tenderness—

Quaerens me sedisti lassus,	Faint and weary Thou hast sought me,
Redemisti crucem passus,	On the cross of suffering bought me;
Tantus labor non sit cassus.	Shall such grace be vainly brought me?

This stanza seems to be founded on St. John iv. 6: 'Now Jacob's well was there. Jesus therefore, being wearied with His journey, sat thus on the well.' How affecting it is to think of the Saviour, weary and tired with the labour of a toilsome journey, urging upon an abandoned Samaritan woman the need of drinking that living water springing up into everlasting life!

Of more recent English translations the best known

Account of First Rank Hymns.

are the following: Dean Alford's version, beginning 'Day of anger, that dread day;' Isaac Williams's version, beginning 'Day of wrath, that awful day;' Archbishop Trench's version, beginning 'O that day, that day of ire.'

The translations in the German are even more numerous than those in English. In a volume by Lisco, published in 1843, appear fifty-five versions in German; and since translations have been made in all languages of civilised nations, it may with truth be asserted that throughout the whole range of hymnology no single hymn has exercised so great an influence on the literature of the world as the great masterpiece of the Middle Ages, the 'Dies Irae' of Thomas of Celano.

> 97. The day is past and over,
>   All thanks, O Lord, to Thee;
> I pray Thee that offenceless
>   The hours of dark may be.

Τὴν ἡμέραν διελθὼν.

This is a translation by Dr. Neale of a beautiful Greek hymn, supposed to have been written by St. Anatolius about the middle of the fifth century. Anatolius was raised to be Patriarch of Constantinople in 450 A.D., and after governing the Eastern Church for eight years with firmness and wisdom, he departed to his rest in 458 A.D. The Monophysite controversy continued to rage during his Patriarchate, and the East was torn with discord and persecution, but the personal influence of Anatolius tended to advance piety and peace. His hymns are full of life and beauty, and it is matter of deep regret that they are not more numerous. Before his time Christian poets imitated the style of classical writers, but Anatolius, with great success, struck out a new path of harmonious prose, so that his sacred songs mark a new era in the Greek hymnology.

The original of the above Greek evening hymn is still sung throughout the Isles of Greece. Dr. Neale's account is full of interest: 'This little hymn, which I believe is not used in the public service of the Church, is a great favourite in the Greek Isles. Its peculiar style and evident antiquity may well lead to the belief that it is the work of our present author. It is to the scattered hamlets of Chios and Mitylene what Bishop Ken's evening hymn is to the villages of our own land, and its melody singularly plaintive and soothing.' The first epoch of Greek hymnology continued for about three centuries after the time of Anatolius, but although there were several writers of pretty hymns during this period, yet our present Church song is not much indebted to their compositions.

98. The roseate hues of early dawn,
The brightness of the day.

Cecil Frances Alexander, the accomplished authoress of the above, is an Irish lady, daughter of Major Humphreys. In 1848 she published *Hymns for Little*

Account of First Rank Hymns. 189

Children, a collection which contains many beautiful hymns for young people. Among them are the well-known sacred songs, 'There is a green hill far away,' and 'Once in royal David's city.' In 1850 she was married to the Rev. William Alexander, M.A., now Bishop of Derry.

Other well-known hymns by Mrs. Alexander are—

> 'We are but little children weak,' published in 1850.
> 'Jesus calls us; o'er the tumult,'   ,,   1853.
> 'When wounded sore, the stricken deer,' ,,   1858.
> 'When Christ came down on earth of old.'
> 'He is risen! He is risen!'

The above hymn first appeared in 1853 in *Psalms and Hymns for Public Worship*, issued by the S.P.C.K. The original was, however, re-cast, and appeared as an evening hymn in 1858. The first four lines were—

> The crimson of the sunset sky,
> The last gold lines of day,
> Along the mountains' rosy verge,
> How fast they fade away!

In its present form the hymn was published in 1859, in her *Legend of the Golden Prayer*.

99. When all Thy mercies, O my God,
    My rising soul surveys.

This hymn, by Addison, was originally appended to one of his essays on 'Praise to God' in the *Spectator* of August 1712. The hymn is called 'An Act of Thanksgiving.'

'How gracefully this hymn embodies the thoughts of a thankful soul, and with what musical ease it gives expression to the feelings of one who has reached the point of happy retrospect in mature life! The hymnist appears to sing under the influence of the inspired verse, "Surely goodness and mercy follow me all the days of my life, and my dwelling shall be in the house of the Lord for ever." Addison is not excelled even by the saintly Doddridge.'

Joseph Addison, the master of English prose, was born in Wiltshire in 1672. His father rose from humble circumstances to be Dean of Lichfield. Addison studied at Salisbury, and became a graduate of Oxford, where he lived for ten years. There is still pointed out 'his favourite walk under the elms which fringe the meadow on the banks of the Cherwell.'

The elegance of his Latin verse while an undergraduate attracted attention, and gained him honour. While still a young man he wrote a laudatory poem on the campaign of King William III. This, together with a Latin poem on the Treaty of Ryswick, secured for him a public pension of £300 a year. With this annuity he was enabled to gratify his travelling desires, and accordingly in 1700 he started on a prolonged Continental tour. After some stay in Paris he embarked at Marseilles, and while sailing along the coast of Italy encountered a great storm, somewhat common in this part of the Mediterranean. 'The captain of the ship gave up all for lost, and confessed himself to a Capuchin who happened to be on board. The English heretic, in the meantime, fortified himself against the perils of death with devotions of a different kind.' To this storm we are indebted, probably, for a beautiful hymn called the 'Traveller's Hymn,' and published in the *Spectator* in 1712—

> How are Thy servants blest, O Lord,
> How sure is their defence!

The hymn is deservedly a favourite with travellers in foreign lands, and with those in peril on the ocean.

On his return to England he celebrated the victory of Blenheim in 1704 in a poem called ' The Campaign,' in which the Duke of Marlborough, leading the battle, is compared to an angel directing a storm. This and other poems raised Addison very high in the estimation of the nation, and he was promoted from one public office to another until, in 1717, he attained to the responsible situation of Secretary of State. In 1716 he married the Countess Dowager of Warwick, but unfortunately the union was an unhappy one. He died in 1719. On his deathbed he sent for his stepson, the Earl of Warwick, a gay young man, hoping that his dying counsel might be the means of reforming the young man's character. On arriving Lord Warwick said, 'I believe and hope you have some commands for me. I shall hold them most sacred.' Whereupon the dying poet, grasping the youth's hand, said earnestly, 'See in what peace a Christian can die,' and shortly after passed to his rest.

Addison's fame as a literary man rests, to a great extent, upon the accomplished essays he contributed to the *Spectator* from 1711 to 1714. These are exquisite devout papers of the highest excellence, written in the maturity of his mind, and regarded by many literary men as the masterpiece of English prose. To many of these essays was appended a hymn, and these sacred songs have become permanent favourites, and found their way into many modern Hymnals.

> 100. All glory, laud, and honour,
> To Thee, Redeemer, King.
> *Gloria, laus, et honor.*

This hymn is a translation from the Latin stanzas of Theodulph by Dr. J. M. Neale, and first appeared in 1851. Theodulph is said to have been of Gothic descent, and was born in Italy in the eighth century. He became Abbot of a Benedictine monastery at Florence, and afterwards Bishop of Orleans. The Bishop was imprisoned for some time at Metz on a false accusation, and it is said that the above processional hymn for Palm Sunday was composed in his cell. As the Emperor Lewis and his court were passing the prison on their way to the cathedral, Theodulph, seated at the little dungeon window, sang this hymn, which arrested the Emperor's attention, and caused the good Bishop to be forthwith liberated. He died in 821 A.D., just a quarter of a century after the death of St. Stephen the Sabaite.

> 101. Art thou weary, art thou languid?
> *Κόπον τε καὶ κάματον.*

This touching hymn is a translation from the Greek of St. Stephen the Sabaite, an Eastern monk of the

Account of First Rank Hymns. 193

eighth century. The rendering was the work of Dr. John Mason Neale, and first appeared in 1862 in his *Hymns of the Eastern Church*. It differs considerably from the Greek text, but it does justice to the sweetness and simplicity of the original stanzas, which are called by the translator, 'Idiomela in the week of the oblique tone.' The Greek name 'Idiomela,' literally '*peculiar strains*,' refers to the peculiar rhythm of the original and the chanted strains appointed to be sung to this piece in the Eastern Church service. Stephen was born in 725 A.D., and when only ten years old was placed in the Greek monastery of Mar Saba, situated in the wildest part of the wilderness of Judæa. In this solitary retreat he spent the whole of his life, and after being a monk for about sixty years, died in the monastery in his seventieth year. Stephen is therefore called the 'Sabaite,' a name applied to every monk of Mar Saba. St. John Damascene, or St. John of Damascus, the last of the Greek Fathers, was Stephen's uncle; and he was also for many years a monk of the same place. St. Cosmas of Jerusalem, the friend of St. John of Damascus, and the most learned of the Greek poets, was also a Sabaite. Those three monks were contemporaries, and were all distinguished as writers of sacred poetry. Stephen was the youngest of the three, and his love of religious song was doubtless in some measure due to the influence of his two elder brethren of the monastery. Of his sacred poems, one of the best is that on 'The Martyrs of Mar Saba,' which gives an account of the monks slain while defending their monastery against the attacks of lawless marauders. Eleven centuries ago Stephen sang his sweet hymns amid the sterile wastes of Judæa, so that of his sacred songs it is literally true that 'the wilderness and the solitary place shall be glad for them.'

The well-known tune to which the above hymn is usually sung was written by Rev. Sir Henry Baker, Bart., and named 'Stephanos,' after the Syrian monk.

We visited Mar Saba a short time ago, while making a journey through Palestine, and found that the monastery stands nobly on a lofty cliff overhanging the valley of the Kedron, which here forms a deep chasm. It was founded in the beginning of the sixth century, and this secluded convent has therefore stood in the midst of savage desolation for fourteen centuries. Several times in the course of ages it has been plundered and the inmates put to death by Persians, Moslems, and Bedouin Arabs; and therefore for the sake of safety the monastery is surrounded by massive walls, and further guarded by two strong towers near the entrance, which tend to give the edifice the appearance of a fortress in a commanding position. On being admitted inside the gate we found chapels, chambers, and cells innumerable, for the most part cut out of the rock, perched one above the other, and connected by rocky steps and intricate passages. The huge building seems as if it were clinging to the face of a steep precipice, so that it is difficult to distinguish man's masonry from the natural rock. Many of the monks of this tranquil convent are well-known historical persons. St. Sabas, the founder, died

Account of First Rank Hymns. 195

and was buried here in 532. The three sacred poets above mentioned were monks of Mar Saba in the eighth century.

The Sabaites at present number about forty, and their rule is very severe, being under a vow never to eat animal food. They have seven religious services in twenty-four hours—five by day and two by night. Although they seemed severe in their habits, they received us kindly, and we were carefully conducted by a monk through the whole monastery. We were shown their gaily-decorated chapel, the tomb of St. Sabas, the tomb of John of Damascus, and a cave chapel containing thousands of skulls of martyred monks. We were led to the belfry on the roof of their little sanctuary, and saw the bells which send forth their beautiful chimes, and gladden the hearts of pilgrims, who, 'weary and languid,' pursue their journey through the desolate wilderness. The bells of Mar Saba recalled to mind the soothing words—

>   Far, far away, like bells at evening pealing,
>   The voice of Jesus sounds o'er land and sea.

We were then conducted to a terrace, from the dizzy height of which we looked down into the deep gorge of the Kedron, 500 feet below. Every morning wolves and jackals assemble at the bottom of the rocks, and are fed by the monks, who cast down food to the ravenous animals. Viewed from this terrace, the scene around and below is one of stern desolation, and a sight so impressive as never to be forgotten. Mar Saba was much more endeared to us when we remembered that here Stephanos, eleven centuries ago, wrote the touching hymn :

> Art thou weary, art thou languid,
> Art thou sore distressed?
> 'Come to me,' saith One, 'and, coming,
> Be at rest.'

102. Before Jehovah's awful throne,
    Ye nations, bow with sacred joy.

The above lines form the commencement of an excellent rendering of the 100th Psalm, written by Dr. Watts in 1719. The original consisted of six stanzas, of which the first and fourth are generally omitted in modern Hymnals. The second, as written by Watts, ran thus—

> Nations attend before His throne,
>   With solemn fear, with sacred joy,
> Know that the Lord is God alone,
>   He can create, and He destroy.

John Wesley in 1741 dropped the first two lines, and substituted his own majestic words—

> Before Jehovah's awful throne,
>   Ye nations, bow with sacred joy,

thus 'giving a noble completeness to the hymn, opening it with a majesty suitable to its continued swell, and preparing us for that sublime close which leaves the devout multitude rapt before God in solemn joy—

> Wide as the world is Thy command,
>   Vast as eternity Thy love;
> Firm as a rock Thy truth shall stand,
>   When rolling years shall cease to move.

'The Christian Church will never cease to enjoy the grand swell of this Psalm as given by Watts, but thanks will ever be due to John Wesley for making the first verse worthy of the last.'

Watts's version of the 100th Psalm has been pronounced to be one of the noblest, as it is also one of the best-known, versions of all thanksgiving Psalms.

103. God of our life, to Thee we call,
 Afflicted at Thy feet we fall;
 When the great water-floods prevail,
 Leave not our trembling hearts to fail!

This hymn for times of trouble was composed by William Cowper, and appeared in *Olney Hymns* in 1779. It is entitled, 'Looking upwards in a Storm,' and is founded on the 42d Psalm, 'All Thy waves and Thy billows are gone over me.'

104. In token that thou shalt not fear
 Christ crucified to own,
 We print the cross upon thee here,
 And stamp thee His alone.

This noble hymn for the Office of Baptism was written by Dean Alford in 1832, and is therefore one of the earliest of his hymns. It was first sung in the same year at the baptism of the author's first-born child. The hymn is thought to have been suggested by the following passage in Hooker's *Ecclesiastical Polity* :—' Seeing therefore that to fear shame, which doth worthily follow sin, and to bear undeserved reproach constantly, is the general duty of all men professing Christianity, . . . we are in that respect to acknowledge the good and profitable use of this ceremony, and not to think it superfluous that Christ hath His mark applied unto that part where bashfulness appeareth, in token that they that are Christians should be at no time ashamed of His ignominy.'

105. Now thank we all our God,
    With heart and hands and voices,
  Who wondrous works hath done,
    In whom His world rejoices.

Martin Rinkart, author of this hymn, was a German poet and pastor born in Saxony in 1586. He was of humble parentage, but by dint of energy supported himself as a student in theology at Leipzig, and afterwards became pastor of Eilenberg, his native place. During the pestilence of 1637 Rinkart was indefatigable in ministering to the wants of his suffering people, and though subjected to the persecution of bitter enemies, he persevered through evil report and good report in living a most pious and useful life. He died in 1649 at the age of fifty-five.

Rinkart's original begins in the well-known words, 'Nun danket alle Gott,' and the above is an excellent rendering made in 1858 by Miss Winkworth. The first two stanzas are a metrical version of the following passage in the Apocryphal Book of Ecclesiasticus :—

Account of First Rank Hymns.

'Now therefore bless ye the God of all, who only doeth wondrous things everywhere, which exalteth our days from the womb, and dealeth with us according to His mercy. He granteth us joyfulness of heart, and that peace may be in our days in Israel for ever; that He would confirm His mercy with us, and deliver us at His time.'

CHAPTER III.

Second Rank Hymns:
INDEX, SUMMARY, AND ACCOUNT OF EACH.

INDEX OF SECOND RANK HYMNS.

List of the 110 Second Rank Hymns, arranged in order of merit, with names of Authors, Dates, and Marks of Approval.

Order.	Hymns.	Authors.		Marks.
106.	Come, Holy Spirit, come,	Hart,	1759.	29
107.	Creator Spirit, by whose aid,	Dryden,	died 1700.	29
108.	Day of wrath, O day of mourning,	Irons, 1853, *from* Thomas of Celano, 13th cent.		29
109.	God of mercy, God of grace,	Lyte,	1834.	29
110.	Jesu, Thou joy of loving hearts,	Ray Palmer, 1833, *from* St. Bernard,	1150.	29
111.	O for a heart to praise my God,	Wesley,	1743.	29
112.	Spirit of mercy, truth, and love,	Anon.,	1775.	29
113.	The Lord my pasture shall prepare,	Addison,	1712.	29
114.	The voice that breathed o'er Eden,	Keble,	1857.	29
115.	Thy way, not mine, O Lord,	Bonar,	1856.	29
116.	We sing the praise of Him who died,	Kelly,	1804.	29
117.	A few more years shall roll,	Bonar,	1844.	28
118.	Awake and sing the song,	Hammond,	1745.	28
119.	Father of mercies, in Thy Word,	Steele,	circa 1760.	28
120.	How beauteous are their feet,	Watts,	1709.	28
121.	Praise to God, immortal praise,	Barbauld,	1773.	28
122.	The spacious firmament on high,	Addison,	1712.	28
123.	For ever with the Lord,	Montgomery,	1825.	27
124.	From all that dwell below the skies,	Watts,	1709.	27
125.	Have mercy, Lord, on me,	Tate and Brady,	1703.	27
126.	In the hour of trial,	Montgomery,	1825.	27

Index of Second Rank Hymns.

Order.	Hymns.	Authors.		Marks.
127.	Jesus, where'er Thy people meet,	Cowper,	1779.	27
128.	O day of rest and gladness,	Bp. Wordsworth,	1865.	27
129.	O for a thousand tongues, to sing,	Wesley,	1743.	27
130.	On Jordan's bank the Baptist's cry,	Chandler, 1837,	*from*	
		C. Coffin,	1755.	27
131.	Pleasant are Thy courts above,	Lyte,	1847.	27
132.	Saviour, breathe an evening blessing,	Edmeston,	1820.	27
133.	There is a fountain filled with blood,	Cowper,	1779.	27
134.	Ye boundless realms of joy,	Tate and Brady,	1703.	27
135.	According to Thy gracious word,	Montgomery,	1825.	26
136.	Come, Holy Spirit, Heavenly Dove,	Watts,	1709.	26
137.	I heard the voice of Jesus say,	Bonar,	1856.	26
138.	Jesu, meek and gentle,	Prynne.	1856.	26
139.	Jesus calls us; o'er the tumult,	Alexander,	1853.	26
140.	Not all the blood of beasts,	Watts,	1709.	26
141.	Sweet is the work, my God, my King,	Watts,	1709.	26
142.	The head that once was crowned with thorns,	Kelly,	1804.	26
143.	There is a book who runs may read,	Keble,	1827.	26
144.	Who are these like stars appearing,	Cox, 1841,	*from*	
		Schenk,	1727.	26
145.	Blest are the pure in heart,	Keble,	1827.	25
146.	Hark! the song of Jubilee,	Montgomery,	1825.	25
147.	O God of hosts, the mighty Lord,	Tate and Brady,	1703.	25
148.	O Jesu, Lord of heavenly grace,	Chandler, 1837, *from* St.		
		Ambrose, 4th century.		25
149.	O Spirit of the Living God,	Montgomery,	1825.	25
150.	The Lord of might from Sinai's brow,	Heber,	1827.	25
151.	To bless Thy chosen race,	Tate and Brady,	1703.	25
152.	When God of old came down from heaven,	Keble,	1827.	25
153.	Ye servants of God, your Master proclaim,	Wesley,	1743.	25
154.	Christ is our corner-stone,	Chandler, 1837,	*from*	
		Latin of 8th century.		24
155.	Far from my heavenly home,	Lyte,	1847.	24
156.	Father, whate'er of earthly bliss,	Steele,	1780.	24
157.	Hark! my soul, it is the Lord,	Cowper,	1779.	24
158.	Hark! the sound of holy voices,	Wordsworth,	1863.	24
159.	Lord, it belongs not to our care,	Baxter,	1681.	24
160.	Lord, teach us how to pray aright,	Montgomery,	1825.	24
161.	May the grace of Christ our Saviour,	Newton,	1779.	24
162.	Sweet Saviour, bless us ere we go,	Faber,	1852.	24
163.	The happy morn is come,	Haweis,	1792.	24
164.	There is a blessed home,	Sir H. W. Baker,	1852.	24
165.	Three in One, and One in Three,	Rorison,	1850.	24

Index of Second Rank Hymns.

Order.	Hymns.	Authors.		Marks.
166.	Alleluia! song of sweetness,	Neale, 1851, *from* Latin of 13th century.		23
167.	Almighty God, Thy Word is cast,	Cawood,	1825.	23
168.	Bread of Heaven, on Thee we feed,	Conder,	1824.	23
169.	Come, let us to the Lord our God,	Morrison,	1770.	23
170.	Come, Thou long-expected Jesus,	Wesley,	1743.	23
171.	Eternal Father, strong to save,	Whiting,	1860.	23
172.	Hark, the voice of love and mercy,	Evans,	1787.	23
173.	Light of those whose dreary dwelling,	Wesley,	1745.	23
174.	Lo! round the throne at God's right hand,	M. L. Duncan, *from* R. Hill, died in 1833.		23
175.	O Thou, to whose all-searching sight,	J. Wesley, 1748, *from* Tersteegen,		23
176.	Onward, Christian soldiers,	Baring-Gould,	1865	23
177.	Salvation! O the joyful sound,	Watts,	1709.	23
178.	See the destined day arise,	Mant,	1837.	23
179.	The sun is sinking fast,	Caswall,	1858.	23
180.	Thine for ever, God of love,	Maude,	1848.	23
181.	Thou hidden love of God,	J. Wesley, 1743, *from* Tersteegen.		23
182.	Come, let us join our friends above,	Wesley,	1743.	22
183.	Come, my soul, thy suit prepare,	Newton,	1779.	22
184.	Jerusalem on high,	Crossman,	1664.	22
185.	Lead, kindly Light,	Newman,	1833.	22
186.	Lord, pour Thy Spirit from on high,	Montgomery,	1825.	22
187.	O where shall rest be found,	Montgomery,	1825.	22
188.	The Church's one foundation,	Stone,	1865.	22
189.	The God of Abraham praise,	Olivers,	1772.	22
190.	The strife is o'er, the battle done,	Potts, 1860, *from* a Latin hymn, 12th cent.		22
191.	We love the place, O Lord,	Bullock,	1854.	22
192.	Approach, my soul, the mercy-seat,	Newton,	1779.	21
193.	Arm of the Lord, awake, awake,	Shrubsole,	1795.	21
194.	As now the sun's declining ray,	Chandler, 1837, *from* Paris Breviary.		21
195.	Blow ye the trumpet, blow,	Wesley,	1743.	21
196.	Bread of the world, in mercy broken,	Heber,	1827.	21
197.	Day of judgment, day of wonders,	Newton,	1779.	21
198.	Hail! Thou once despisèd Jesus,	Bakewell,	1760.	21
199.	Hark! what mean those holy voices,	Cawood,	1775-1852.	21
200.	Lord of the harvest, once again,	Anstice,	1836.	21
201.	My faith looks up to Thee,	Ray Palmer,	1830.	21
202.	O holy Saviour, Friend unseen,	Elliott,	1834.	21

Summary of Second Rank Hymns.

Order.	Hymns.	Authors.		Marks.
203.	This is the day the Lord hath made,	Watts,	1709.	21
204.	At the Lamb's high feast we sing,	Campbell, 1850, *from* Roman Breviary.		20
205.	Christian, dost thou see them,	Neale, 1862, *from* St. Andrew of Crete, 7th century.		20
206.	Ere another Sabbath's close,	Anon.,	1832.	20
207.	O Christ, Thou hast prepared a place,	Chandler, 1837, *from* Paris Breviary.		20
208.	O happy band of pilgrims,	Neale, 1862, *from* St. Joseph of the Studium, 9th century.		20
209.	O Lord of heaven and earth and sea,	Wordsworth,	1863.	20
210.	O Love divine, how sweet Thou art,	Wesley,	1743.	20
211.	O Thou, the contrite sinner's Friend,	Elliott,	1837.	20
212.	Saviour, blessed Saviour,	Thring,	1862.	20
213.	Thee we adore, O hidden Saviour,	Woodford,	1863.	20
214.	To the Name that speaks salvation,	Neale, 1851, *from* Aquinas.		20
215.	When Christ the Lord would come on earth,	Alford,	1835.	20

SUMMARY OF SECOND RANK HYMNS.

All hymns found in twenty Hymnals and upwards, and in fewer than thirty, have been classified as hymns of the *second* rank.

Of these there are 110, composed by 57 hymn-writers, of whom—

36 authors contribute	1 hymn each	=	36 hymns.
9	,,	2	,,	18	,,
4	,,	3	,,	12	,,
4	,,	4	,,	16	,,
1	,,	5	,,	5	,,
1	,,	7	,,	7	,,
2	,,	8	,,	16	,,
57 authors.				110 hymns.	

Summary of Second Rank Hymns.

Arranging the hymn-writers according to the number of hymns contributed, they stand thus—

Montgomery,	8	Steele,	2	Faber,	1
Chas. Wesley,	8	Wesley, J.,	2	Hammond,	1
Dr. Watts,	7	Alexander, C. F.,	1	Hart,	1
Chandler,	5	Alford,	1	Haweis,	1
Keble,	4	Anstice,	1	Hill,	1
Neale,	4	Sir H. Baker,	1	Irons,	1
Newton,	4	Bakewell,	1	Mant,	1
Tate and Brady,	4	Barbauld,	1	Maude,	1
Bonar,	3	Baring-Gould,	1	Morrison,	1
Cowper,	3	Baxter,	1	Newman,	1
Lyte,	3	Bullock,	1	Olivers,	1
Bp. Wordsworth,	3	Campbell, Robt.,	1	Potts,	1
Addison,	2	Caswall,	1	Prynne,	1
Anon.,	2	Conder,	1	Rorison,	1
Cawood,	2	Cox,	1	Shrubsole,	1
C. Elliott,	2	Crossman,	1	Stone,	1
Heber,	2	Dryden,	1	Thring,	1
Kelly,	2	Edmeston,	1	Whiting,	1
Ray Palmer,	2	Evans,	1	Woodford,	1

☞ There are thus twenty-one authors who have contributed two or more hymns.

Nineteen of the above hymn-writers contribute also to First Rank hymns. They are Addison, Alexander, Alford, Caswall, Cowper, Cox, Edmeston, Elliott, Haweis, Heber, Keble, Kelly, Lyte, Montgomery, Neale, Newton, Tate and Brady, Watts, C. Wesley.

Number of Second Rank Hymns found in the chief Hymnals.

Of the 110 hymns included in the Second Rank—

1. The Hymnal Companion . contains 96 and omits 14
2. Church Hymnal (Irish) . ,, 85 ,, 25

Summary of Second Rank Hymns. 205

3. The Church of England
   Hymn-Book . . contains 73 and omits 37
4. The Westminster Abbey
   Hymn-Book . . ,, 66 ,, 44
5. Church Hymns (S.P.C.K.) ,, 62 ,, 48
6. Hymns Ancient and Modern ,, 54 ,, 56

Of the 110 hymns of the Second Rank—

1. The *Hymnal Companion* omits the following 14 hymns—

> 109. God of mercy, God of grace.
> 125. Have mercy, Lord, on me.
> 130. On Jordan's bank the Baptist's cry.
> 147. O God of hosts, the mighty Lord.
> 167. Almighty God, Thy Word is cast.
> 173. Light of those whose dreary dwelling.
> 194. As now the sun's declining ray.
> 199. Hark! what mean those holy voices.
> 200. Lord of the harvest, once again.
> 204. At the Lamb's high feast we sing.
> 205. Christian, dost thou see them.
> 207. O Christ, Thou hast prepared a place.
> 213. Thee we adore, O hidden Saviour.
> 215. When Christ the Lord would come on earth.

2. The *Church Hymnal* omits 25 hymns of the Second Rank, viz.—

108	138	158	174	200
109	143	160	191	204
112	149	166	193	206
121	152	168	194	211
122	153	169	197	215

3. The *Church of England Hymn-Book* omits 37 hymns of the Second Rank, viz.—

| 113 | 119 | 122 | 129 | 133 | 137 |
| 114 | 120 | 124 | 131 | 136 | 140 |

206 Summary of Second Rank Hymns.

141	156	164	172	183	197
149	157	165	173	184	198
151	161	166	177	193	205
155	162	170, 171	182	195	214

4. The *Westminster Abbey Hymn-Book* omits 44 of the Second Rank, viz.—

107	128	154	178	194	203
108	131	159	183	196	205
116	134	160	184	197	206
118	135	161	189	198	208
119	136	163	190	199	210
121	140	166	191	201	212
126	153	172	192	202	214
		177	193		

5. *Church Hymns* omits 48 hymns of the Second Rank, viz.—

106	129	150	170	182	199
107	133	151	172	183	200
111	134	156	173	184	201
113	135	157	174	187	202
119	136	161	177	192	206
120	140	163	178	193	208
122	142	167	179	195	211
125	146	169	181	197	212

6. *Hymns Ancient and Modern* omits 56 hymns of the Second Rank, viz.—

106	126	141	161	182	198
107	127	146	163	183	199
111	129	148	167	187	201
113	132	149	169	189	202
118	133	150	170	192	203
119	134	151	172	193	206
120	135	153	173	195	207
121	136	156	175	196	211
122, 124	140	159	177, 181	197	215

Account of Second Rank Hymns.

106. Come, Holy Spirit, come,
   Let Thy bright beams arise;
   Dispel the sorrow from our minds,
   The darkness from our eyes.

Joseph Hart, author of this hymn, was born of pious parents in London in 1712. In youth he displayed considerable ability, but for many years he led a loose, dissipated life. A sermon preached in the Moravian Chapel, Fetter Lane, seems to have been the means of bringing peace to his soul, and his subsequent career was marked by great devotion to the cause of Christianity. In 1759 he distinguished himself by preaching and hymn-writing, and soon afterwards he became an Independent minister. Hart died in 1768. The above originally consisted of nine stanzas, and first appeared in 1759 in his *Hymns composed on various Subjects*. It was probably suggested by the well-known Latin hymn 'Veni, Sancte Spiritus.'

107. Creator Spirit, by whose aid
   The world's foundations first were laid,
   Come, visit every humble mind,
   Come, pour thy joys on humankind;
   From sin and sorrow set us free,
   And make Thy temples worthy Thee.

John Dryden, author of the above, is accounted one of the greatest of British poets. He was born at Aldwinkle, Northamptonshire, in 1631, and received his education at Westminster School and Cambridge. His poems, plays, and prose works are very numerous, and were edited by Sir Walter Scott in eighteen octavo volumes. He died in 1700, and was interred in Westminster Abbey.

The above is his best-known hymn, and is a successful rendering of the grand old Latin hymn, 'Veni, Creator Spiritus,' commonly attributed to St. Ambrose, Archbishop of Milan. Dryden's translation is a somewhat free paraphrase, consisting of thirty-nine lines. The well-known rendering of the 'Veni, Creator Spiritus' beginning ' Come, Holy Ghost, our souls inspire,' is the work of Bishop Cosin.

108. Day of wrath, O day of mourning,
  See fulfilled the prophets' warning,
  Heaven and earth in ashes burning.

This grand translation from the Latin of Thomas of Celano is by the late Dr. W. J. Irons, Prebendary of St. Paul's. It was made in 1853. (See Hymn 96.)

109. God of mercy, God of grace,
  Show the brightness of Thy face;
  Shine upon us, Saviour, shine,
  Fill Thy Church with light divine.

This happy rendering of the 67th Psalm is from the pen of the sweet Christian hymnist, Henry Francis

Lyte. It first appeared in his *Metrical Version of the Psalms*, published in 1834. (See Hymn 5.)

110. Jesu, Thou joy of loving hearts!
Thou fount of life! Thou light of men!

(Jesu, dulcedo cordium,
Fons vivus, lumen mentium)

is a portion of St. Bernard's 'Jubilee rhythm' rendered by Dr. Ray Palmer in 1833. Dr. Ray Palmer is an American sacred poet, born in 1808, whose hymns are justly admired in England and America. It ought to be noted that six well-known hymns are translations of St. Bernard's 'Jubilee rhythm.' Two have already been noticed. The other four are as follows :—

'O Jesu, King most wonderful!'
'Jesu! the very thought is sweet.'
'O Jesu! Thou the beauty art.'
'Jesu! Thy mercies are untold.'

111. O for a heart to praise my God,
A heart from sin set free.

This hymn was written by Charles Wesley in 1742, and appeared in the second edition of *Hymns and Sacred Poems* in 1743. It expresses in glowing strains the spiritual hunger and thirst after righteousness felt by the poet, and is founded on the words from the 51st Psalm, 'Create in me a clean heart, O God, and renew a right spirit within me.'

The original consists of eight stanzas, all of which appear in the Methodist Hymn-book. It has been said of this hymn, 'Here is undoubtedly an evangelical prayer for the love which restores the soul to a state of sinless rest and Scriptural perfection.'

112. Spirit of mercy, truth, and love,
    O shed Thine influence from above;
    And still from age to age convey
    The wonders of this sacred day.

This excellent Whitsuntide hymn has been traced to a collection of hymns used in the Foundling Chapel, London, as early as 1774. It is commonly attributed to a Shropshire clergyman by name of Kyle, but this is a mistake, inasmuch as his collection of hymns did not appear for many years after the above date. The original consists of three short stanzas, and is founded on the words, 'I will pour out My Spirit upon all flesh,' descriptive of the outpouring of the Holy Ghost on the Feast of Pentecost. It must not be confounded with a Whitsuntide hymn by Kelly beginning 'Spirit of truth, on this Thy day.'

113. The Lord my pasture shall prepare,
    And feed me with a shepherd's care.

This favourite hymn by Addison was first appended as a sequel to one of his essays, in the *Spectator* of July 1712, on 'Trust in God.' The essay contained the following memorable words: 'The person who has a firm trust on the Supreme Being is powerful in His

Account of Second Rank Hymns.

power, wise by His wisdom, happy by His happiness. He reaps the benefit of every Divine attribute, and loses his own insufficiency in the fulness of Infinite perfection.' The hymn is an excellent paraphrase of the 23d Psalm, a great favourite with Addison: 'The Lord is my shepherd, I shall not want,' etc.

114. The voice that breathed o'er Eden,
  That earliest wedding day,
The primal marriage blessing,
  It hath not passed away.

This beautiful marriage hymn was written in 1857 for the Salisbury Hymnal, where it appears with the heading, 'Holy Matrimony. To be sung at the commencement of the service.' It is indeed the noblest hymn we possess for the celebration of holy wedlock, and for comprehensiveness cannot be surpassed, stretching back as it does to the union of our first parents, and reaching forward to the Marriage Supper of the Lamb.

115. Thy way, not mine, O Lord,
  However dark it be;
Lead me by Thine own hand,
  Choose out the path for me.

This favourite hymn was written by Dr. Horatius Bonar while he was minister at Kelso, and appeared first in 1856. (See Hymn 117.)

116. We sing the praise of Him who died,
    Of Him who died upon the cross;
    The sinner's hope let men deride,
    For this we count the world but loss.

This exquisite hymn is from the pen of Thomas Kelly, and appeared in 1815. Before it was prefixed the text Gal. vi. 14, on which it is founded: 'God forbid that I should glory, save in the cross of our Lord Jesus Christ.'

In his *English Church Hymnody* Lord Selborne says of this hymn: 'It is distinguished by a calm subdued power, rising gradually from a rather low to a very high key. I doubt whether Montgomery ever wrote anything quite equal to this.'

117. A few more years shall roll,
    A few more seasons come,
    And we shall be with those that rest
    Asleep within the tomb.

Horatius Bonar, D.D., the author of this favourite hymn, was born in Edinburgh in 1808. He was ordained to the ministry at Kelso in 1837, and continued his labours there for about thirty years. He was then called to a ministerial charge in Edinburgh, where he still labours. His religious works are both voluminous and popular. He is also favourably known as a hymn-writer, and his sacred poems are a valuable contribution to our hymnology. In 1857 was published his *Hymns of Faith and Hope*, and in this collection appeared 'A few more years shall roll.' This universal favourite was composed in 1844, and was entitled 'A Pilgrim's Song.' The first four lines of the fourth stanza, viz.

> A few more Sabbaths here
> Shall cheer us on our way,
> And we shall reach the endless rest,
> The eternal Sabbath day,

is a translation of an old Latin hymn which runs thus—

> Illic nec sabbato
> Succedit sabbatum
> Perpes laetitia,
> Sabbatizantium.

The frequent repetition of the phrase 'A few more,' followed in each succeeding verse respectively by 'years, suns, storms, struggles, Sabbaths,' the vivid contrasts in every stanza between the fleeting things of earth and the abiding joys of heaven, and the varied epithets applied to the day of resurrection, have tended to increase the popularity of this much-esteemed hymn.

> 118. Awake and sing the song
>   Of glory to the Lamb,
> Wake every heart and every tongue
>   To praise the Saviour's name.

William Hammond, author of this hymn, was born in 1719. He graduated at Cambridge, and became an accomplished scholar. He was much impressed by the Wesleyan revival, became a Calvinistic Methodist

Account of Second Rank Hymns.

preacher, and subsequently, with his friend Cennick, joined the Moravian Brethren. Hammond died in 1783, and was interred at Chelsea, London. His hymns are full of Scripture truth and Christian experience. In 1745 was published his *Psalms, Hymns, Spiritual Songs, and Discourses*, containing several translations of Breviary hymns as well as original hymns. In the Preface he writes: 'In the following pages are a number of hymns suited to the various states and capacities of the children of God.' The above hymn appears in the book, consisting of sixteen stanzas, and founded on Rev. xv. 3: 'They sing the song of Moses and the song of the Lamb, saying, Great and marvellous are Thy works, Lord God Almighty, just and true are Thy ways, thou King of saints.'

119. Father of mercies, in Thy Word
    What endless glory shines;
    For ever be Thy name adored
    For these celestial lines.

Anne Steele, the author of the above, was the daughter of a Baptist minister at Broughton in Hampshire, and was born in 1716. She was throughout her life distinguished for piety and benevolence, and although an invalid, owing to an accident in childhood, she yet bore her sufferings with Christian resignation. She died in 1778, aged sixty-one, and immediately before her peaceful departure exclaimed, 'I know that my Redeemer liveth.'

Miss Steele's poetical works include 144 hymns and 34 metrical versions of the chief of David's Psalms.

The above hymn on the excellence of Holy Scripture is one of the few hymns out of very many on the same subject that has met with general approval. The original consisted of twelve stanzas, and was written about 1760.

> 120. How beauteous are their feet,
> Who stand on Zion's hill.

This sweet hymn by Watts is founded on Isaiah lii. 7 : 'How beautiful upon the mountains are the feet of him that bringeth good tidings, that publisheth peace ; that bringeth good tidings of good, that publisheth salvation ; that saith unto Zion, Thy God reigneth !' The original consists of six stanzas, and is entitled, 'The blessedness of Gospel times.' It is considered to be one of Watts's best paraphrases.

> 121. Praise to God, immortal praise,
> For the love that crowns our days ;
> Bounteous Source of every joy,
> Let Thy praise our tongues employ ;
> All to Thee, our God, we owe,
> Source whence all our blessings flow.

Mrs. Barbauld, author of this hymn, was daughter of Dr. John Aikin, and was born at Kibworth Harcourt, Leicestershire, in 1743. She soon distinguished herself as an accomplished writer. In 1774, when thirty-one years old, she married the Rev. R. Barbauld, a Unitarian minister, who was ultimately stationed at Stoke-Newington, London. She wrote twelve hymns, of which the above is the best known, and appeared in a volume of *Miscellaneous Poems* in 1773, while the gifted writer was still Miss Aikin.

Mrs. Barbauld died in 1825.

122. The spacious firmament on high,
  With all the blue ethereal sky,
  And spangled heavens, a shining frame,
  Their great Original proclaim.

This renowned hymn first appeared at the end of one of Addison's essays, in the *Spectator* of August 1712, on 'The right means to strengthen Faith.' It is an inimitable rendering of the first part of the 19th Psalm: 'The heavens declare the glory of God, and the firmament showeth His handiwork,' etc. It is thought that Addison when writing this had in his mind a passage in Shakespeare's *Merchant of Venice*:

  'There's not the smallest orb which thou behold'st
    But in his motion like an angel sings,
    Still quiring to the young-eyed cherubins.'

The idea here certainly seems to be reproduced in Addison's words—

    For ever singing, as they shine,
    ' The hand that made us is divine.'

Although it is perhaps better adapted for reading as a poem than for singing as a hymn, yet it is found in

Account of Second Rank Hymns.

many of our Hymnals, and Sir Roundell Palmer says: 'For my own part, I fervently hope it will always remain there. Praise to God as glorified in His works is the substance and essence of every part of that hymn, as it is of the beautiful verses of the 19th Psalm on which it is founded. If it be not poetry, I do not know what is; and to prove that it is song, and soul-stirring song too, it is only necessary to hear it, as I often have, heartily sung to an appropriate tune.'

> 123. For ever with the Lord!
> Amen, so let it be:
> Life from the dead is in that word,
> 'Tis immortality.

This noble hymn, of world-wide popularity, is from the pen of James Montgomery, and was taken from the *Poet's Portfolio* in 1835. The original consists of twenty-two stanzas, of which twenty-one are printed in Montgomery's *Original Hymns*, 1835. This sublime poem is full of ardent aspirations for the Better Land, akin to the earnest longings of Bernard of Cluny for the Celestial Country. The following lines are frequently used as a refrain after each stanza—

> Here in the body pent,
> Absent from Him I roam;
> Yet nightly pitch my moving tent
> A day's march nearer home.

This refrain has become familiar as household words, and the two last lines have been spoken of as a 'watchword of the Church militant.'

124. From all that dwell below the skies
   Let the Creator's praise arise.

This grand hymn of praise is Watts's metrical rendering of the 117th Psalm. It appeared in his Psalter, published in 1719, and is entitled 'Praise to God from all Nations.' It is rendered more familiar to us from the fact that it is set to Walmsley's anthem.

The original consisted of two stanzas, but some unknown author has added a third, which sometimes appears in Hymnals :—

>Your lofty themes, ye mortals, bring,
>In songs of praise divinely sing;
>The great salvation loud proclaim,
>And shout for joy the Saviour's name.

125. Have mercy, Lord, on me,
   As Thou wert ever kind,
Let me, opprest with loads of guilt,
   Thy wonted mercy find.

This penitential hymn is a metrical version of the 51st Psalm by Tate and Brady. (See Hymn 45.)

126. In the hour of trial, Jesu, pray for me,
   Lest by base denial I depart from Thee;
   When Thou see'st me waver, with a look recall,
   Not for fear or favour suffer me to fall.

This Lenten hymn, by James Montgomery, is founded on the Saviour's words to St. Peter : 'I have prayed for

Account of Second Rank Hymns.

thee that thy faith fail not.' It was written in a lady's album in 1834, and was headed 'Prayers for Pilgrimage.' The first half of the last stanza is frequently omitted or varied in our modern Hymnals, although the original expresses a sublime thought in poetic language of a high order. It goes thus—

> When in dust and ashes
> To the grave I sink,
> While heaven's glory flashes
> O'er the shelving brink.

127. Jesus, where'er Thy people meet,
There they behold Thy mercy-seat;
Where'er they seek Thee Thou art found,
And every place is hallowed ground.

This favourite hymn is from the pen of William Cowper, and appeared in the *Olney Hymns*, dated 1775, under the heading, 'On opening a Place for Social Prayer.' It is thought to be the first hymn written by Cowper after his arrival at Olney in 1767. Newton and Cowper had established a prayer-meeting, and on the occasion of removing to a larger place, called 'The Great House,' in 1769, the above was written. 'There Cowper began a new course of social prayer, and there he and the little parish flock sang for the first time, "Jesus, where'er Thy people meet."' John Keble made several alterations and additions to Cowper's hymn, and in its re-cast form it appeared in the Salisbury Hymn-book of 1857.

128. O day of rest and gladness!
　　O day of joy and light!
　　O balm of care and sadness!
　　Most beautiful, most bright!

This beautiful Sabbath hymn is by Bishop Wordsworth, the learned Bishop of Lincoln. He is a nephew of William, the great Lake poet. In 1862 he published a collection of 127 hymns, called *The Holy Year*. The above is the third in the book, and is called a Sunday hymn on Psalm cxviii. 24: 'This is the day which the Lord hath made; we will rejoice, and be glad in it.'

129. O for a thousand tongues, to sing
　　My dear Redeemer's praise.

This hymn was written by Charles Wesley in 1739, and first appears in 1740 in *Hymns and Sacred Poems*. In May 1738 the author was suddenly brought into the enjoyment of perfect Christian liberty. His own words are: 'On that glad day the glorious Sun of Righteousness arose on my benighted soul and filled it with repose.' The above hymn was written a year after this event, and is entitled 'For the Anniversary Day of one's Conversion.' The original consisted of eighteen stanzas, and commenced—

　　　Glory to God, and praise, and love,
　　　　Be ever, ever given,
　　　By saints below, and saints above,
　　　　The Church in earth and heaven.

In the Methodist Hymn-book it consists of ten stanzas,

Account of Second Rank Hymns. 221

and is there placed as the first hymn in the book. This fact has caused the hymn to be more widely known.

A Moravian minister, named Peter Böhler, once remarked to Charles Wesley: 'Had I a thousand tongues, I would praise Christ with them all.' This memorable sentence made a lasting impression on the poet's mind, and we find it enshrined in this glorious hymn.

130. On Jordan's bank the Baptist's cry
　　　Proclaims aloud the Lord is nigh;
　　　Awake, and hearken, for he brings
　　　Glad tidings from the King of kings.

This hymn is a translation from a Latin hymn, 'Jordanus oras praevia,' etc., contributed by Charles Coffin to the Paris Breviary in 1736. The English rendering is by John Chandler, and first appeared in his *Hymns of the Primitive Church*, published in 1837. It has, however, been considerably modified by the compilers of *Hymns Ancient and Modern*, and is now a favourite Advent hymn.

131. Pleasant are Thy courts above,
　　　In the land of light and love.

This very sweet hymn is by Lyte, and first appeared in 1834 in his *Spirit of the Psalms*. It does justice to the 84th Psalm, on which it is founded; and no higher compliment than this can be paid to it, for the 84th Psalm is one of the sweetest of the Psalms of David. It refers to the joys and sorrows of Jewish pilgrims as they journey from the hill-country of Judæa on their way to the Temple of Jerusalem. The toils of the journey were considerably lightened by sacred song, for the happy pilgrims, longing for the courts of the sanctuary, sang joyfully in unison as they marched along the road; and at the pools of living water on the way they halted and quenched their thirst, until at length they arrived at the holy hill of Zion.

Near to Brixham, nestling by the water and under the shadow of richly-wooded hills, was the cottage where Lyte communed with Nature and his God. His love for God's house, and the souls to whom he ministered, was the sustaining and inspiring power which helped him to sing on his way amidst his bodily weakness—

> Pleasant are Thy courts above,
> In the land of light and love;
> Pleasant are Thy courts below,
> In this land of sin and woe.

132. Saviour, breathe an evening blessing,
    Ere repose our spirits seal;
Sin and want we come confessing :
    Thou canst save and Thou canst heal.

James Edmeston, author of this hymn, was a London architect, who died in 1867. He is said to have been the author of two thousand hymns. The above was printed in his *Sacred Lyrics* in 1820, and was suggested by the following sentence that occurred in Salt's *Travels through Abyssinia:* 'At night their short evening hymn, "Jesu, forgive us," stole through the camp.'

133. There is a fountain filled with blood
    Drawn from Immanuel's veins ;
  And sinners, plunged beneath that flood,
    Lose all their guilty stains.

This well-known hymn is from the pen of William Cowper, and appeared in 1779. It is founded on Zechariah xiii. 1 : 'There shall be a fountain opened for sin and for uncleanness.'

134. Ye boundless realms of joy,
    Exalt your Maker's fame,
  His praise your song employ
    Above the starry frame.

This sublime hymn is the metrical version of the 148th Psalm by Tate and Brady. (See Hymn 45.)

135. According to Thy gracious word,
    In meek humility.

This sacramental hymn, by James Montgomery, appeared in 1825. It has attained great popularity, and is now regarded as one of our standard hymns.

Its plaintive, tender thoughts recall to mind the spiritual aspirations of St. Bernard of Clairvaux.

136. Come, Holy Spirit, from above,
    With all Thy quickening power.

This hymn, by Watts, is entitled, 'Breathing after God's Spirit.' The original consists of five stanzas; but some of the phrases are objectionable, and for the most part appear altered in modern Hymnals. Another hymn, by Simon Browne, commences in the same words as first line, and therefore requires to be distinguished from that of Watts.

137. I heard the voice of Jesus say,
    'Come unto Me, and rest;
  Lay down, thou weary one, lay down
    Thy head upon My breast.'

This hymn, 'so beautiful in its severe simplicity,' is by Horatius Bonar. It first appeared in 1850, and subsequently reappeared in 1856 in Bonar's *Hymns of Faith and Hope*. It is founded on the Saviour's words, 'He that cometh to Me shall never hunger, and he that believeth in Me shall never thirst.' (See Hymn 117.)

138. Jesus, meek and gentle,
    Son of God Most High,
  Pitying, loving Saviour,
    Hear Thy children's cry.

This favourite hymn is by the Rev. G. R. Prynne, M.A., Vicar of St. Peter's, Plymouth. It was written

Account of Second Rank Hymns. 225

in 1856, and appeared in his *Hymnal suited for the Services of the Church*, published in 1858. The hymn is fast becoming a universal favourite, especially among young people.

> 139. Jesus calls us ; o'er the tumult
> Of our life's wild, restless sea,
> Day by day His sweet voice soundeth,
> Saying, ' Christian, follow Me.'

This hymn was written in 1853 by Mrs. Alexander, the accomplished wife of the Lord Bishop of Derry. It first appears as a hymn for St. Andrew's Day, in *Psalms and Hymns for Public Worship*, S.P.C.K. (See Hymn 98.)

> 140. Not all the blood of beasts
> On Jewish altars slain,
> Could give the guilty conscience peace,
> Or wash away the stain.

This well-known hymn is by Dr. Watts, and appeared in 1709. It is founded on the passage, ' The blood of Jesus Christ His Son cleanseth us from all sin.'

> 141. Sweet is the work, my God, my King,
> To praise Thy name, give thanks, and sing ;
> To show Thy love by morning light,
> And talk of all Thy truth at night.

This hymn, by Dr. Isaac Watts, is the first part of his paraphrase of the 92d Psalm, beginning, 'It is a good thing to give thanks unto the Lord, and to sing praises unto Thy name, O most High.' The original appeared in 1719.

142. The Head that once was crowned with thorns
    Is crowned with glory now;
  A royal diadem adorns
    The mighty Victor's brow.

Thomas Kelly, the author of this hymn, was a celebrated Irish hymn-writer. It was composed in 1804, and seems to be founded on Hebrews ii. 9: 'We see Jesus crowned with glory and honour.' (See Hymn 54.)

143. There is a book, who runs may read,
    Which heavenly truth imparts,
  And all the lore its scholars need,
    Pure eyes and Christian hearts.

This is part of a well-known poem of twelve stanzas in *The Christian Year*. It is designed for Septuagesima Sunday, and is founded on Genesis i., the chapter read on that day. All creation speaks of God, and 'the invisible things of Him from the creation of the world are clearly seen, being understood by the things that are made.'

144. Who are these, like stars appearing,
    These, before God's Throne who stand?
  Each a golden crown is wearing,
    Who are all this glorious band?

> Alleluia, hark! they sing,
> Praising loud their heavenly King.

This magnificent hymn is part of a translation of fourteen stanzas from the German, by Miss F. E. Cox, and appeared in her *Sacred Hymns from the German*, published in 1841. The original is by Theodore Schenk, a native of Hesse. Few particulars are known of his life. He became a schoolmaster, and subsequently Lutheran pastor at Giessen, and died in 1727.

The hymn is founded on Rev. vii. 13: 'What are these which are arrayed in white robes? and whence came they?' Another well-known translation of Schenk's original is by Miss Winkworth, and begins, 'Who are those before God's throne?'

> 145. Blest are the pure in heart,
> For they shall see our God;
> The secret of the Lord is theirs,
> Their soul is Christ's abode.

This hymn is a cento from Keble's poem for the Feast of the Purification, in *The Christian Year*, 1827. Only two stanzas are Keble's, viz., the above and the following:—

> He to the lowly soul
> Doth still Himself impart;
> And for His dwelling and His throne
> Chooseth the pure in heart.

The other stanzas were added to form a complete hymn for *A Hymnal for the use of the English Church*, published 1852, and edited by the Rev. F. H. Murray,

Rector of Chislehurst. The original, written by Keble in 1819, is founded on the words, 'Blessed are the pure in heart: for they shall see God.' Several slight alterations have been made on the hymn as it appeared in 1852 by the compilers of *Hymns Ancient and Modern*.

>146. Hark! the song of Jubilee;
>   Loud as mighty thunders roar,
>Or the fulness of the sea,
>   When it breaks upon the shore.

This jubilant hymn of praise was written by James Montgomery in 1819. The three double stanzas are of great poetic power, and celebrate the final triumph of the Messiah when 'He shall have dominion from sea to sea, and from the river unto the ends of the earth.'

>147. O God of hosts, the mighty Lord,
>   How lovely is the place
>Where Thou, enthroned in glory, show'st
>   The brightness of Thy face!

This well-known hymn is the metrical version of the 84th Psalm by Tate and Brady. (See Hymn 45.)

>148. O Jesu, Lord of heavenly grace,
>Thou brightness of the Father's face.
>
>*Splendor paternae gloriae.*

This hymn is a translation by the Rev. John Chandler, who died in 1876, aged seventy, from Latin

Account of Second Rank Hymns.

verses by Ambrose. It first appeared in 1837, in Chandler's selection of Latin hymns called *Hymns of the Primitive Church*. The original consists of nine stanzas, attributed by Fulgentius of the fifth century to St. Ambrose, the illustrious Bishop of Milan. This is confirmed by the author of *Hymni et Collectae* in 1585, and by John H. Newman. This Ambrosian hymn, according to the Roman Breviary, is appointed for Lauds on Monday morning, and for daily use in Benedictine and Carthusian Breviaries.

149. O Spirit of the living God,
    In all the fulness of Thy grace,
Where'er the foot of man hath trod,
    Descend on our apostate race.

This noble missionary hymn, by James Montgomery, first appeared in 1825 in *The Christian Psalmist*. It there consists of six stanzas, written in vigorous language of high poetic merit, and is entitled 'The Spirit accompanying the Word of God.' The hymn is founded on the words, 'That Thy way may be known upon earth, Thy saving health among all nations.'

150. The Lord of might, from Sinai's brow,
    Gave forth the voice of thunder.

This grand hymn is by Heber, and appeared in 1812. In his collection of 1827 it is appointed for the sixth Sunday in Lent. The Gospel for that day shows the ignominy to which our Saviour was subjected in His trial and crucifixion ; and the hymn contrasts the terrors of Sinai with the meekness displayed on Calvary.

 151. To bless Thy chosen race,
  In mercy, Lord, incline ;
  And cause the brightness of Thy face
  On all Thy saints to shine.

This hymn is the metrical version of the 67th Psalm by Tate and Brady. (See Hymn 45.)

 152. When God of old came down from heaven,
  In power and wrath He came ;
  Before His feet the clouds were riven,
  Half darkness and half flame.

The above, by John Keble, occurs as a poem for Whitsunday in his *Christian Year.* The original consists of eleven stanzas, from which selections are made for modern Hymnals. (See Hymn 9.)

 153. Ye servants of God, your Master proclaim,
  And publish abroad His wonderful name,
  The name all victorious of Jesus extol,
  His kingdom is glorious and rules over all.

This hymn, by Charles Wesley, first appeared in his *Hymns for Times of Trouble and Persecution,* printed in 1744. Four hymns at the end of the book are entitled

Account of Second Rank Hymns. 231

'Hymns to be sung in a tumult,' and the above is the first of the four. The allusions in it to Psalm xciii. are apparent.

> 154. Christ is our corner-stone,
>   On Him alone we build;
>   With His true saints alone
>   The courts of heaven are filled.

This hymn is a translation from the Latin by John Chandler. It occurs in *Hymns of the Primitive Church*, published in 1837. (See Hymn 148.)

There are other well-known hymns by the same author. (See p. 40.)

> 155. Far from my heavenly home,
>   Far from my Father's breast.

This plaintive hymn by Lyte first appeared in 1834, in his *Spirit of the Psalms*, a metrical version of the Book of Psalms. In issuing this work Lyte says: 'I endeavoured to give the spirit of each Psalm, and to furnish sometimes, when the length of the original would admit of it, an almost literal translation—sometimes a kind of spiritual paraphrase; at others even a brief commentary on the whole Psalm.'

This hymn is a touching spiritual paraphrase of the 137th Psalm: 'By the rivers of Babylon, there we sat down; yea, we wept, when we remembered Zion,' etc. As in this Psalm the Jewish exiles sat weeping by the banks of the stream of Euphrates, and with longing eyes looked across the Syrian desert in the direction of the much-beloved Mount Zion, so in this spiritual hymn, God's people, exiles from the home of their souls, droop and yearn for the celestial Zion, and that heavenly Jerusalem, whose Builder and Maker is God.

>156. Father, whate'er of earthly bliss
>   Thy sovereign will denies,
>   Accepted at Thy throne of grace
>   Let this petition rise.

Anne Steele, the author of this hymn, was a permanent invalid, but bore her sufferings with calm resignation. The above, entitled 'Desiring Resignation and Thankfulness,' was written about 1760, and originally consisted of ten stanzas.

>157. Hark! my soul, it is the Lord;
>   'Tis thy Saviour, hear His word;
>   Jesus speaks, and speaks to thee,
>   'Say, poor sinner, lov'st thou Me?'

This favourite hymn, by Cowper, first appeared in the *Gospel Magazine* in 1771. It breathes a happier spirit than other hymns by the same author. The original consists of six stanzas, of which stanza 4 contains a sublime description of Divine love—

>Mine is an unchanging love,
>Higher than the heights above,
>Deeper than the depths beneath,
>Free and faithful, strong as death.

Account of Second Rank Hymns. 233

158. Hark! the sound of holy voices, chanting at
the crystal sea,
Alleluia! Alleluia! Alleluia! Lord, to Thee.

This triumphant song, setting forth the final gathering of the redeemed, is by Bishop Christopher Wordsworth, and appeared in his *Holy Year*, in 1862, as the hymn for All Saints' Day.

It is founded upon the latter part of the seventh chapter of Revelation, beginning with the words, ' After this I beheld, and, lo, a great multitude, which no man could number, stood before the throne,' etc.

159. Lord, it belongs not to our care
Whether we die or live;
To love and serve Thee is our share,
And this Thy grace must give.

Richard Baxter, writer of this hymn, and the eminent author of *The Saints' Everlasting Rest*, was born at Rowton, Shropshire, in 1615. He entered the ministry, and laboured at Dudley, Bridgnorth, and other places. For twenty years he was curate at Kidderminster, and his active ministerial work was attended with much success. During this long pastorate he wrote about sixty works. On the Restoration in 1660, Baxter was appointed a chaplain to Charles II., but in consequence of the passing of the Act of Uniformity he left the Church, and became a Nonconformist preacher. His death in 1691, at the age of seventy-six, was peaceful and resigned. During his last illness, on being asked how he did, he, knowing that his end was nigh at hand, replied, 'Almost well.'

In 1681, ten years before his death, he published a collection of *Poetical Fragments*, among which is a poem of sixty-four lines to strengthen the faith of his afflicted wife, entitled 'The Covenant and Confidence of Faith.' From that poem the above hymn is a cento, and it beautifully sets forth the calm resignation of God's afflicted people.

160. Lord, teach us how to pray aright,
  With reverence and with fear;
Though dust and ashes in Thy sight,
  We may, we must draw near.

This hymn, suitable for early morning service, is by James Montgomery, and appeared in 1825. The original consisted of six stanzas, but some of them have been subjected to manifold variations. It is founded on a passage in Psalm lxv.: 'O Thou that hearest prayer, unto Thee shall all flesh come.'

161. May the grace of Christ our Saviour,
  And the Father's boundless love,
With the Holy Spirit's favour,
  Rest upon us from above.

This benedictory hymn, by the Rev. John Newton,

appeared in 1779. It is founded on the Saviour's words, recorded in St. Luke vii. 50, 'Go in peace.'

162. Sweet Saviour, bless us ere we go;
    Thy word into our minds instil;
    And make our lukewarm hearts to glow
    With lowly love and fervent will,
        Through life's long day and death's dark night,
        O gentle Jesu, be our light!

Frederick William Faber, D.D., author of the above, is justly regarded as one of the most eminent sacred poets of this century. He was born in 1815, educated at Harrow, graduated at Oxford in 1838, became Fellow and College Tutor, took holy orders, and shortly afterwards, in 1846, seceded to the Church of Rome. In 1849 he came to London, and established the Brotherhood known as 'The Oratorians,' or 'Priests of the Congregation of S. Philip Neri.' In 1854 the 'Oratory,' or place of prayer for the Brotherhood, was established at Brompton, and to the success of this 'Oratory' Faber devoted his energies for nine years, till his death in 1863.

The above hymn first appeared in 1852, and was entitled 'Evening Hymn at the Oratory.' It has undergone many alterations, and received its last revision in 1861, two years before the author's death.

163. The happy morn is come;
   Triumphant o'er the grave,
   The Saviour leaves the tomb,
   Omnipotent to save.

Thomas Haweis, author of this jubilant Easter hymn, was born at Truro, Cornwall, in 1732. He was educated at Cambridge, and became chaplain to the Countess of Huntingdon, and Rector of All Saints, Aldwinkle, Northamptonshire. Haweis was a popular preacher, and one of the founders of the London Missionary Society. He died in 1820, aged eighty-two.

In 1792 was published a collection of his hymns, entitled *Carmina Christo, or Songs to Christ*. The edition of 1808 contained 256 original hymns. In the Preface he writes: 'Whether these hymns suffer the censure or meet the approbation of the Christian world, they are such as my heart indited, and they speak the things which I have believed concerning my God and King. They all point to one object and lead to one end, to a Crucified Jesus.'

164. There is a blessèd home
   Beyond this land of woe,
   Where trials never come,
   Nor tears of sorrow flow.

Sir Henry Williams Baker, author of this Ascension-tide hymn, was born in London 1821. He graduated at Cambridge, and shortly after entering holy orders he was appointed Vicar of Monkland, near Leominster.

He was one of the chief compilers to *Hymns Ancient and Modern*, and the above comforting hymn appeared in the first issue of that Hymnal in 1861, although it appears to have been composed in 1852.

> 165. Three in One, and One in Three,
> Ruler of the earth and sea,
> Hear us while we lift to Thee
> Holy chant and psalm.

Rev. Gilbert Rorison, LL.D., author of this favourite family hymn, was born in Glasgow 1821, died 1869. He was a graduate of Glasgow, and on taking holy orders became Incumbent of St. Peter's, Peterhead. In 1850 he published a small Hymnal for his own congregation, and amongst others appeared the above, written in 1849.

> 166. Alleluia! song of sweetness,
> Voice of joy that cannot die,
> Alleluia is the anthem
> Ever dear to choirs on high;
> In the house of God abiding
> Thus they sing eternally.

This hymn is a translation, by Dr. Neale, of an ancient Latin hymn commencing 'Alleluia, dulce carmen,' thought to be as old as the thirteenth century. Daniel found the original Latin in a German MS., which he believes dates from the eleventh century. This hymn, together with the 'Alleluia perenne' and the 'Alleluiatic Sequence,' is often used immediately before

Lent, because, in accordance with a very ancient custom, hymns of praise were not sung during Lent. There are many English versions of the Latin hymns, and an excellent one by the Rev. Francis Pott resembles that by Dr. Neale.

> 167. Almighty God, Thy Word is cast
>   Like seed into the ground;
>   O may it grow in humble hearts,
>   And righteous fruits abound.

John Cawood, author of this hymn, was born at Matlock, of humble parents, in 1775. By diligence and perseverance he managed to graduate at Oxford in 1801. He was ordained the same year, and in 1814 was presented to the perpetual curacy of Bewdley, Worcestershire. Here he spent the greater part of his life, and died in 1852, at the age of seventy-seven. With reference to the above hymn his son writes: 'I do not know the occasion of the above hymn, further than that it was meant to be sung after sermon. I think it must have been written about 1815, but there is no date to it in the MS.'

> 168. Bread of Heaven, on Thee we feed,
>   For Thy Flesh is meat indeed;
>   Ever let our souls be fed
>   With this true and living Bread.

Josiah Conder, author of this hymn, was born in London in 1789. He was a person of great literary ability, as publisher, editor, journalist, and author.

Throughout life he continued a firm adherent of Nonconformity. Conder wrote many devout hymns, the earliest collection of which appeared in 1824 under the title of *The Star of the East, and other Poems*. In this collection was the above hymn, which was founded on St. John vi. 32: 'My Father giveth you the true Bread from heaven.'

The author continued to write hymns up to the day of his death, which took place in 1855.

169. Come, let us to the Lord our God
    With contrite hearts return;
Our God is gracious, nor will leave
    The desolate to mourn.

John Morrison, D.D., was born in Aberdeenshire in 1749. He entered the ministry in 1780, and spent the remainder of his life as minister of Canisbay, Caithness-shire. He wrote several good hymns, and three at least were contributed to the Scotch Paraphrases. The above is the 30th Paraphrase.

170. Come, Thou long-expected Jesus,
    Born to set Thy people free,
From our fears and sins release us,
    Let us find our rest in Thee.

This jubilant hymn, by Charles Wesley, appeared in 1743. It is founded on the Messianic prophecy by the prophet Haggai, 'The Desire of all nations shall come.'

171. Eternal Father, strong to save,
   Whose arm doth bind the restless wave,
   Who bidst the mighty ocean deep
   Its own appointed limits keep.

William Whiting, author of this excellent hymn 'for those in peril on the sea,' was born at Kensington, London, 1825. For a long period he was master of the Winchester College Choristers' School. He died in 1878. The above hymn was written in 1860 for *Hymns Ancient and Modern*. The tune 'Melita,' to which it is invariably sung, was composed by Dr. Dykes, and was named from the ancient name of Malta, close by which St. Paul was shipwrecked on his journey to Rome.

172. Hark, the voice of love and mercy
   Sounds aloud from Calvary;
   See, it rends the rocks asunder,
   Shakes the earth and veils the sky.

This Passion hymn, founded on Christ's dying words, 'It is finished,' is generally supposed to be the work of Jonathan Evans, born at Coventry 1749, died 1809; but there exist conflicting views regarding its authorship.

173. Light of those whose dreary dwelling
   Borders on the shades of death,
   Come, and by Thy love revealing,
   Dissipate the clouds beneath.

This hymn, by Charles Wesley, appeared in 1745 in his *Hymns on the Nativity of our Lord*.

174. Lo! round the throne at God's right hand
The saints in countless myriads stand;
Of every tongue redeemed to God,
Array'd in garments wash'd in blood.

This hymn was composed by Mary Lundie Duncan, but appears to be founded upon a somewhat similar hymn written by the Rev. Rowland Hill.

175. O Thou, to whose all-searching sight
The darkness shineth as the light,
Search, prove my heart; it pants for Thee,
O burst these bonds, and set it free.

This well-known hymn is a translation from the German by John Wesley, the great founder of Wesleyanism, and first appeared in the collection of *Hymns and Sacred Poems*, published by John and Charles Wesley in 1739. The two brothers were often associated in the production of a hymn-book, and although Charles was an extensive hymn-writer, it does not appear that John wrote any hymns himself, although he translated several from the German. The original of the above was written by Count Zinzendorf, and early appeared in the Moravian collection. The Count was born at Dresden in 1700. He was even in youth distinguished for his personal piety, and in manhood he became the friend of the Moravians in their persecutions. He is also celebrated as a prolific hymn-

242 *Account of Second Rank Hymns.*

writer, having composed about two thousand hymns, many of which have been rendered into English by John Wesley.

> 176. Onward, Christian soldiers,
> Marching as to war,
> With the Cross of Jesus
> Going on before.

This spirited hymn is from the pen of the Rev. Sabine Baring-Gould, and first appeared in 1865 in *The Church Times.*

> 177. Salvation! O the joyful sound!
> 'Tis pleasure to our ears,
> A sovereign balm for every wound,
> A cordial for our fears.

This hymn of praise was written by Dr. Watts in 1709. The refrain at the end of each stanza is—

> Glory, honour, praise, and power
> Be unto the Lamb for ever!
> Jesus Christ is our Redeemer;
> Hallelujah! praise the Lord.

This doxology is a simple unversified translation of a Latin chorus, 'Gloria, laus, et honor,' etc., by St. Theodulph, Bishop of Orleans, in the beginning of the ninth century. This Latin chorus was rendered by Neale in his well-known translation, ' All glory, laud, and honour.'

Account of Second Rank Hymns. 243

178. See the destined day arise!
   See, a willing Sacrifice,
   Jesus, to redeem our loss,
   Hangs upon the accursèd Cross.

Richard Mant, author of this Passion hymn, was born at Southampton in 1776. He graduated at Cambridge in 1797, and on entering holy orders became curate to his father. By his ability and zeal he gradually rose to be Bishop of Dromore. He died in 1848.

179. The sun is sinking fast,
   The daylight dies;
   Let love awake, and pay
   Her evening sacrifice.

This evening hymn was translated from the Latin by the Rev. E. Caswall, and first appeared in his *Masque of Mary* in 1858. The Latin original has been lost, and consequently a reward has been offered for its recovery. It is thought to belong to the eighteenth century. (See Hymn 59.)

180. Thine for ever, God of love,
   Hear us from Thy throne above;
   Thine for ever may we be,
   Here and in eternity.

This beautiful Confirmation hymn was written by Mrs. Maude, wife of the late Rev. Joseph Maude, Vicar of

Chirk. It was written for a Confirmation class at Newport, Isle of Wight, and first appeared in a little book entitled *Twelve Letters on Confirmation*, published in 1848.

181. Thou hidden love of God, whose height,
  Whose depth unfathomed, no man knows.

This hymn is a translation from the German, made by John Wesley in 1739. The original is by Gerhard Tersteegen, a well-known German hymn-writer of the eighteenth century.

182. Come, let us join our friends above,
  That have obtained the prize.

This inimitable hymn is by Charles Wesley, and appeared in 1759 in his *Funeral Hymns*, a collection of forty-three hymns. It is founded on St. Paul's saying, 'Of whom the whole family in heaven and earth is named.' The original consists of five double stanzas, but half the original is generally omitted in modern hymnals. In some hymn-books the opening four lines have been re-cast, and run thus—

  Let saints on earth in concert sing
  With those whose work is done,
  For all the servants of our King
  In heaven and earth are one.

It has been remarked that 'the hymn embodies almost every legitimate idea which the human mind can form as to the state, employment, and happiness of departed saints, and it is clothed in language glorious, yet chaste; elegant, yet simple; impassioned, yet correct. The hymn expands the idea that saints above and saints below, the Church Militant on earth and the Church Triumphant in heaven, are all one, one family, one army; that even now the intercourse is not totally suspended, but by faith we hold communion with those that have gone before.' The figure in the hymn,

> Though now divided by the stream,
> The narrow stream of death,

was probably suggested by the line, 'Death like a narrow stream divides,' found in Isaac Watts's hymn 'There is a land of pure delight,' written in 1709. Wesley's hymn must also be distinguished from one by Watts, viz.—

> Come, let us join our cheerful songs
> With angels round the throne.

It would seem as if Wesley in this sublime composition had striven to combine the beauties of the two foregoing hymns, written by Watts fifty years before. Charles Wesley died three years before his brother John, and it is said that the latter, not long before his own departure, was one Sunday morning conducting service in the City Road Chapel. Prayers being over, 'he ascended the pulpit; but instead of immediately announcing the hymn to be sung, to the great surprise of the congregation he stood silent, with his eyes closed, for at least ten minutes, wrapt in intense thought. Having done this, with a feeling which at once told where his spirit had been communing, he solemnly read his brother's hymn—

> Come, let us join our friends above,
> That have obtained the prize.

All felt as if they were about to witness the meeting again of the two brothers; and the two companies—the Church Militant and the Church Triumphant—seemed all but to join as the congregation sang—

> One family, we dwell in Him,
> One Church, above, beneath,
> Though now divided by the stream,
> The narrow stream of death.
> One army of the living God,
> To His command we bow;
> Part of His host have crossed the flood,
> And part are crossing now.'

183. Come, my soul, thy suit prepare,
Jesus loves to answer prayer;
He Himself has bid thee pray;
Therefore will not say thee nay.

This hopeful hymn, by Rev. John Newton, appeared in the *Olney Hymns*, published in 1779. (See Hymn 15.)

184. Jerusalem on high
My song and city is,
My home whene'er I die,
The centre of my bliss.

This popular hymn is by Samuel Crossman, B.D., Prebendary of Bristol. He was born 1624, and died

Account of Second Rank Hymns. 247

1683. The above appeared in 1664, in a small devotional book entitled *The Young Man's Meditation*. It is the second part of a poem, of fourteen stanzas, called 'Heaven,' beginning 'Sweet place, sweet place alone!' (See Hymn 16, page 98.)

In his *English Hymnody* Lord Selborne says that 'seven of the original stanzas are extremely fine, and not unsuitable for general use.'

185. Lead, kindly Light, amid the encircling gloom,
    Lead Thou me on.

This much-prized hymn was composed in 1833, by the Rev. John Henry Newman, D.D. The author was born in London in 1801; he was educated at Oxford, and became Fellow and Tutor of his College. With Dr. Pusey he shared the leadership of the 'Tractarian Movement,' commenced in 1833, and exercised an extraordinary influence over religious thought in Oxford. In 1845 he seceded from the English Church, and became a Roman Catholic. Dr. Newman is now Father Superior of the Edgbaston Oratory, Birmingham. His *Hymni Ecclesiae*, published in 1838, contains a large collection of Latin hymns.

'Lead, kindly Light,' etc., was written in 1833, when the author was making a voyage on the Mediterranean. 'He had just been overtaken by illness; his soul was passing through remarkable experiences, and he was watching with deep interest the religious movement going on at home.' The following paragraph from Newman's *Apologia pro Vitâ suâ* shows that the hymn possesses great autobiographic interest :—' I went down at once to Sicily, and fell ill of a fever. My servant thought I was dying, and begged for my last directions. I gave them, as he wished, but said, "I shall not die." I repeated, "I shall not die, for I have not sinned against light, I have not sinned against light." I never have been able to make out at all what I meant. I was laid up for nearly three weeks. Towards the end of May I set off for Palermo, taking three days for the journey. Before starting from my inn in the morning, I sat down on my bed and began to sob bitterly. My servant, who had acted as my nurse, asked what ailed me. I could only answer, "I have a work to do in England." I was aching to get home, yet for want of a vessel I was kept at Palermo for three weeks. I began to visit the churches, and they calmed my impatience. At last I got off in an orange-boat bound for Marseilles. We were becalmed a whole week in the Straits of Bonifacio. Then it was I wrote the lines "Lead, kindly Light," which have since become well known.'

'Lux benigna,' the tune to which it is usually sung, was composed for this hymn by Dr. Dykes.

186. Lord, pour Thy Spirit from on high.

This Ordination hymn was composed by James Montgomery in 1825. (See Hymn 26.)

187. O where shall rest be found
   Rest for the weary soul?
'Twere vain the ocean depths to sound,
   Or pierce to either pole.

This hymn of warning is by James Montgomery, and is thought by many to be one of the author's finest sacred pieces. The original appeared in 1819, and consisted of six stanzas. It is founded on a passage in Hebrews iv.: 'There remaineth therefore a rest to the people of God. ... Let us labour therefore to enter into that rest.'

188. The Church's one foundation
   Is Jesus Christ her Lord;
She is His new creation
   By water and by blood.

This standard hymn was written by the Rev. Samuel John Stone, M.A., Vicar of St. Paul's, Haggerstone, London.

It first appeared in 1865 in a series of twelve hymns on the Apostles' Creed, and entitled *Lyra Fidelium*.

The original heading to it was, 'I believe in the Holy Catholic Church.'

189. The God of Abraham praise,
   Who reigns enthroned above.

Thomas Olivers, the author of this very grand hymn, was born in 1725 at Tregonan, Montgomeryshire.

'As the lark, ascending from the hidden depths of the grassy hollow, rises high, and sings low and sweetly, so Olivers, coming of humble parentage, was at length known and honoured as a sweet singer in Israel.' He lost both his parents when only four years of age, and was consequently brought up by a distant relative, a farmer in the orphan's native county. At the age of eighteen he was bound apprentice to a shoemaker, but his manner of living was that of a young profligate, and to escape public indignation through his sad misconduct he was obliged to leave the neighbourhood. After wandering from place to place he came to Bristol, reduced to wretchedness and abject poverty, and there he chanced to hear George Whitefield, the celebrated revivalist, preach from the text, 'Is not this a brand plucked out of the fire?' The sermon was the means of producing a spiritual quickening in Oliver's mind, and henceforth he became a consistent Christian. On the first Sunday after he says: 'I went to the Cathedral at six in the morning. When the *Te Deum* was read I felt as if I had done with earth, and was praising God before His throne. No words can set forth the joy, the rapture, the awe and reverence I felt.' He soon afterwards joined the Wesleyan Society, and John Wesley observing his zeal enlisted his services as a travelling preacher in Cornwall. He also preached in many parts of England and Ireland, and for twenty-five years he rode on the same horse. Upon this horse he journeyed about 100,000 miles, and encountered at times fierce opposition on his travels from place to place.

Account of Second Rank Hymns. 251

He married a Scotch lady of good family, named Miss Green, who, from her deep piety, proved to be a fitting helpmate for the itinerant preacher. Olivers suffered much bodily affliction in his declining years, and died at London in 1799, aged seventy-four years. He had been an intimate friend of the Wesleys, and his dust was deposited in Wesley's own tomb.

Olivers' educational advantages were small, and yet as a hymnist two at least of his sacred songs would do credit to a person of the very highest education. The hymn 'The God of Abraham praise' was written in 1770, when the author was forty-five years of age. The hymn at first consisted of twelve stanzas, and, according to the author, was a rendering from an old Hebrew sacred ode. It soon became very popular, and at the present time deservedly takes high rank amongst our English hymns. Speaking of it, Montgomery says: 'This noble ode, though the essay of an unlettered man, claims special honour. There is not in our language a lyric of more majestic style, more elevated thought, or more glorious imagery; its structure indeed is unattractive, and on account of the short lines occasionally uncouth; but, like a stately pile of architecture, severe and simple in design, it strikes less on the first view than after deliberate examination, when its proportions become more graceful, its dimensions expand, and the mind itself grows greater in contemplating it.' Such high praise, from one whom all regard as a great authority on sacred song, speaks volumes for the excellence of the hymn. In 1805 Henry Martyn, the renowned missionary, set out for the scene of his labours with mingled feelings of regret and anxious hope, but he testifies that when he was about to leave his home, friends, and native land, Olivers' hymn was a great comfort to his soul. Lord Selborne, no mean judge, calls it 'an ode of singular power and beauty.'

Olivers was a musician as well as a poet, and composed several good hymn-tunes. While on a visit to London he happened to attend divine service at a Jewish synagogue, and was so much struck with the solemnity and grandeur of the music, that on return to the house of his friend, John Bakewell, living at Westminster, he composed the hymn 'The God of Abraham praise' to suit the music he had just heard. Shortly afterwards he called on Leoni, the Jewish High Priest, and obtained from him a copy of the ancient Hebrew melody. On showing the hymn to a brother minister Olivers said : ' Look at this ; I have rendered it from the Hebrew, giving it, as far as I could, a Christian character, and I have called on Leoni the Jew, who has given me a synagogue melody to suit it; here is the tune, and it is to be called "Leoni."'

He wrote also a well-known judgment hymn, consisting of thirty-six stanzas of six lines each. The fourth stanza begins—

> Lo! He comes, with clouds descending,
> Hark! the trump of God is blown.

It is remarkable that Charles Wesley's magnificent judgment hymn is not only akin to Olivers', both in thought and metre, but contains also the line, 'Lo!

He comes, with clouds descending.' 'Whether Wesley caught the key-note from Olivers, or Olivers from Wesley, they evidently breathed the same inspiration. Each hymnist has the same vivid realisation of the overwhelming majesty of the last scene, and neither of the two hymns can be devoutly sung without an ever-deepening feeling of solemn awe and reverent hope.

It appears that Olivers composed the well-known tune called 'Helmsley' to be sung to his 'judgment hymn.' The melody was suggested by the music of a song he heard sung on the street, and the tune is now almost invariably sung to Charles Wesley's noble Advent hymn.

> 190. The strife is o'er, the battle done,
> The victory of life is won,
> The song of triumph has begun.
> Alleluia!

This excellent Easter hymn is a translation by the Rev. Francis Pott, made in 1859. The original Latin was thought by the late Dr. Neale to date from the twelfth century.

> 191. We love the place, O God,
> Wherein Thine honour dwells;
> The joy of Thine abode
> All earthly joy excels!

This favourite hymn was composed by Dean Bullock of Nova Scotia, and first appeared in his collection of hymns, entitled *Songs of the Church*, published in 1854.

Sir H. W. Baker varied the hymn considerably for *Hymns Ancient and Modern* in 1860, and added three verses, respectively beginning—

> ' We love the Word of life,'
> ' We love to sing below,'
> ' Lord Jesus, give us grace.'

192. Approach, my soul, the mercy-seat,
    Where Jesus answers prayer ;
  There humbly fall before His feet,
    For none can perish there.

This penitential hymn, by the Rev. John Newton, appeared in 1779.

It is founded on Christ's promise : ' Him that cometh unto Me I will in no wise cast out ; ' and David's prayer in Psalm li. : ' Create in me a clean heart, and renew a right spirit within me.'

193. Arm of the Lord, awake, awake !
  Put on Thy strength, the nations shake ;
  And let the world adoring see
  Triumphs of mercy wrought by Thee !

This stirring missionary hymn was written by William Shrubsole, born at Sheerness 1759, died in London 1829.

The above first appeared in *Missionary Hymns*, in 1795.

Account of Second Rank Hymns. 255

194. As now the sun's declining rays
    At even-tide descend;
    So life's brief day is sinking down
    To its appointed end.

This hymn is a translation from the Latin by John Chandler, 1837. The original Latin was by Charles Coffin, and was contributed to the Paris Breviary in 1736, where it stands as the hymn for Nones (afternoon service).

195. Blow ye the trumpet, blow
    The gladly solemn sound;
    Let all the nations know,
    To earth's remotest bound.

This bold Easter hymn, by Charles Wesley, first appeared in his *Hymns for the New Year*, 1743. It is founded on the year of jubilee as set forth in Lev. xxv.: 'Then shalt thou cause the trumpet of the jubilee to sound, . . . and ye shall hallow the fiftieth year, and proclaim liberty throughout all the land unto all the inhabitants thereof: it shall be a jubilee unto you.'

The hymn extols the liberty of Christ in the Gospel as nobler than the deliverance of the year of jubilee under the Levitical dispensation.

196. Bread of the world, in mercy broken,
    Wine of the world, in mercy shed;
    By Whom the words of life were spoken,
    And in Whose death our sins are dead.

This short but favourite hymn of two stanzas is by

Bishop Heber, and appeared in 1827 in the collection of hymns published by his widow. (See Hymn 33.)

197. Day of judgment, day of wonders,
    Hark! the trumpet's awful sound,
  Louder than a thousand thunders,
    Shakes the vast creation round.

This noble Advent hymn is by John Newton, and appeared in the *Olney Hymns*, published in 1779. (See Hymn 15.)

198. Hail! Thou once despisèd Jesus,
    Hail! Thou great and glorious King!
  Thou didst suffer to release us,
    Thou didst free salvation bring.

John Bakewell, author of the above, was born at Brailsford, Derbyshire, in 1721. For many years he was a Wesleyan local preacher, and as such a friend of the Wesleys, Toplady, Madan, and other eminent Nonconformists of that period. While he lived at Westminster it is said that Thomas Olivers wrote the celebrated hymn, 'The God of Abraham praise,' in Bakewell's house. For a considerable period he conducted the Greenwich Royal Park Academy. His long life was distinguished for eminent piety and devoted earnestness in the cause of religion. He died at Lewisham in 1819, in his ninety-eighth year, and was buried in the City Road Chapel ground, close by the tomb of John Wesley. On his tombstone it is recorded: 'He adorned the doctrine of God our Saviour eighty years,

and preached His glorious Gospel about seventy years.'
Bakewell was the author of several hymns, but the
above is the best known. Parts of it appeared in
1757, and in an abridged form was published in
Madan's collection, 1760. The entire hymn was
given by the author to Toplady, who, after making
several verbal alterations, published it in his collection,
1776.

> 199. Hark! what mean those holy voices
>   Sweetly warbling in the skies?
> Sure th' angelic host rejoices,
>   Loudest hallelujahs rise.

This hymn for Christmas Day is by John Cawood, Perpetual Curate of Bewdley, Worcestershire. He died in 1852, aged seventy-seven. (See Hymn 167.)

> 200. Lord of the harvest, once again.

This harvest hymn was written by John Anstice in 1836, the year of his death.
'The hymns were all dictated to his wife during the last few weeks of his life.'

> 201. My faith looks up to Thee.

This hymn is by Dr. Ray Palmer, an American sacred poet, and bears date 1830. (See Hymn 110.)

202. O holy Saviour, Friend unseen.

The above is by Charlotte Elliott, the well-known hymn-writer, who died at an advanced age in 1871. (See Hymn 24.)

203. This is the day the Lord hath made,
    He calls the hours His own.

This is Watts's metrical rendering of part of the 118th Psalm, beginning 'This is the day which the Lord hath made, we will rejoice and be glad in it.' The original consists of five stanzas, all of which frequently appear in our modern Hymnals, and forms a suitable hymn for Sunday morning.

204. At the Lamb's high feast we sing
    Praise to our victorious King,
    Who hath wash'd us in the tide
    Flowing from His piercèd side.

This hymn is a translation by the late Robert Campbell, a member of the Scottish bar, who died in Edinburgh, 1868.

The original Latin, beginning 'Ad coenam Agni providi,' is said by Dean Koch to date from the sixth century, although the original was re-cast in the seventeenth century for the Revised Roman Breviary. The above translation appeared in 1850.

Account of Second Rank Hymns. 259

205. Christian, dost thou see them
    On the holy ground,
    How the troops of Midian
    Prowl and prowl around?

   οὐ γὰρ βλέπεις τοὺς ταράττοντας.

The above is a translation of Dr. Neale from the Greek of St. Andrew of Crete, and appeared in 1862 in his *Hymns of the Eastern Church.*

St. Andrew was born at Damascus in 660. Early in life he entered a monastery in Jerusalem, and from this circumstance he is sometimes called 'St. Andrew of Jerusalem.' When about fifty years old he was raised to be Archbishop of Crete, and continued to hold that high office till his death in the year 732 A.D. Seventeen of his homilies are still extant, and as a hymnist he is celebrated as the author of the sacred composition called *The Great Canon*, a penitential hymn for Mid Lent Week, consisting of three hundred stanzas, which is highly esteemed by the Greek Church, being usually regarded as the 'King of Canons.' The above hymn is extracted from this great sacred composition.

206. Ere another Sabbath's close,
    Ere again we seek repose,
    Lord, our song ascends to Thee,
    At Thy feet we bow the knee.

The author of this beautiful Sunday evening hymn is not known. It appeared in 1832 in a collection of hymns compiled by the Hon. and Rev. Baptist W. Noel.

207. O Christ, who hast prepared a place
   For us around Thy throne of grace,
   We pray Thee lift our hearts above,
   And draw them with the cords of love.

This is a translation by John Chandler from a Latin hymn of the seventeenth century, written by Jean Baptiste de Santeuil, a native of Paris. The translation, as above, appeared in 1837 in *Hymns of the Primitive Church*.

208. O happy band of pilgrims,
   If onward ye will tread,
   With Jesus as your Fellow,
   To Jesus as your Head!

This hymn, known as 'The Pilgrims of Jesus,' by Dr. Neale, was suggested by some Greek verses of St. Joseph of the Studium.

Joseph was a native of Sicily, born about the end of the eighth century. He embraced the monastic life, and was raised to be Archbishop of Thessalonica. He spent part of his life in Constantinople, Rome, and Crete. The Studium, from which he is named 'St. Joseph of the Studium,' was the greatest abbey in Constantinople, the first in the city, and perhaps the most influential abbey that ever existed in the world. Joseph was the first poet of the third period of Greek hymnology, which dates from the close of the Iconoclastic persecution. He was a most laborious writer, and his sacred compositions are almost innumerable. His best work is thought to be the 'Canon for Ascension Day,' but as a rule his sacred song does not commend itself to Western tastes, and very few of his hymns find their way into our Hymnals.

> 209. O Lord of heaven and earth and sea,
> To Thee all praise and glory be;
> How shall we show our love to Thee,
> Giver of all?

This beautiful offertory hymn is by Bishop Christopher Wordsworth, and appeared in his *Holy Year* in 1863.

> 210. O Love divine, how sweet Thou art!
> When shall I find my willing heart.

This glorious hymn, by Charles Wesley, is thought to be one of his best. It was written in 1743, and appeared in 1749 in *Hymns and Sacred Poems*. The original consisted of seven stanzas, of which the last three are usually omitted in modern Hymnals. At the latter part of stanza 1 there is a glowing climax expressive of ardent affection, which is considered a sublime strain. It runs thus—

> I thirst, and faint, and die to prove
> The greatness of redeeming love.

One writer says, 'This is one of Wesley's best hymns. For its delight in interior spiritual blessedness, and its warm, impassioned expressions of desire after the love of God, it may be compared with the best productions of S. Bernard.' 'The hymn contains an extraordinary depth of feeling and desire, eager, impatient, resolute, combined with an extended view of the love of God, such as only a poet of much heart-experience, like Charles Wesley, could write.'

It is of this hymn that Isaac Taylor writes: 'To estimate duly what was the influence of this rare gift of song, and to measure its importance, one should be able to recall scenes and times gone by, when this glorious hymn woke up all ears, eyes, hearts, in the crowded sanctuary. It was a spectacle worth gazing upon. It was a service well to have joined in, when words of such power, flowing in rich cadence, and conveying with an intensity of emphasis the loftiest, the deepest, and the most tender emotions of the Divine life, were taken up feelingly by an assembly of men and women, to whom very lately whatever was not of the earth earthy had neither charm nor meaning.'

211. O Thou, the contrite sinner's Friend,
    Who, loving, lov'st them to the end,
    On this alone my hopes depend,
      That Thou wilt plead for me.

This penitential hymn was written by Charlotte Elliott in 1837.

212. Saviour, blessed Saviour, listen while we sing,
    Hearts and voices raising praises to our King.

This jubilant hymn, by Godfrey Thring, first appeared in 1862, and is likely to take high rank in the future.

Account of Second Rank Hymns. 263

213. Thee we adore, O hidden Saviour, Thee,
　　Who in Thy Feast art pleased with us to be ;
　　Both flesh and spirit at Thy presence fail,
　　Yet here Thy presence we devoutly hail.

　This hymn is a translation by Bishop Woodford of Ely, and first appeared in 1853. The original Latin from which it is taken is by Thomas Aquinas, the 'Angelic Doctor' of the thirteenth century.

214. To the Name of our salvation,
　　　Laud and honour let us pay,
　　Which for many a generation,
　　　Hid in God's foreknowledge lay.

　This hymn is a translation from the Latin, made in 1851 by Dr. Mason Neale. The Latin original, beginning 'Salvatoris gloriosi,' was written in Germany by an unknown author, who probably lived in the fifteenth century. Another translation was made by Rev. John Ellerton in 1871 for *Church Hymns*.

215. When Christ the Lord would come on earth,
　　　His messenger before Him went,
　　The greatest born of mortal birth,
　　　And charged with words of deep intent.

　This hymn was written by Dean Alford, and first appeared in 1844, and subsequently published in his *Year of Praise* in 1867, as a hymn for the third Sunday in Advent.

CHAPTER IV.

Third Rank Hymns.

INDEX, SUMMARY, AND ACCOUNT OF EACH.

INDEX OF THIRD RANK HYMNS.

List of the 110 *Third Rank Hymns*, arranged in order of merit, with Names of Authors, Dates, and Marks of Approval.

Order.	Hymns.	Authors.		Marks.
216.	Christian, seek not yet repose,	Elliott,	1839.	19
217.	Come, Thou Fount of every blessing,	Countess of Huntingdon,	1759.	19
218.	Far from these narrow scenes of night,	Steele,	1760.	19
219.	Fountain of mercy, God of love,	Flowerdew,	1811.	19
220.	Glory to Thee, O Lord,	Toke,	1853.	19
221.	God of mercy, throned on high,	Neele,	1832.	19
222.	High let us swell our tuneful notes,	Doddridge,	1755.	19
223.	Jesu, my Lord, my God, my all,	Collins,	1852.	19
224.	Let us, with a gladsome mind,	Milton,	1624.	19
225.	O Paradise ! O Paradise !	Faber,	1852.	19
226.	O praise ye the Lord,	Tate and Brady,	1703.	19
227.	Of the Father's love begotten,	Baker, 1862, *from* Prudentius, 4th century.		19
228.	One there is, above all others,	Nunn,	born 1779.	19
229.	Saviour, again to Thy dear Name we raise,	Ellerton,	1866.	19
230.	The Church has waited long,	Bonar,	*circa* 1844.	19
231.	To-morrow, Lord, is Thine,	Doddridge,	1755.	19
232.	We saw Thee not when Thou didst come,	Gurney,	1838.	19
233.	What various hindrances we meet,	Cowper,	1779.	19
234.	At even, ere the sun was set,	Twells,	born 1823.	18
235.	Come, ye who love the Lord,	Walls,	1709.	18
236.	Fountain of good, to own Thy love,	Doddridge,	1755.	18
237.	Gracious Spirit, love Divine,	Stocker,	1776.	18

Index of Third Rank Hymns.

Order.	Hymns.	Authors.		Marks.
238.	Great King of nations, hear our prayer,	Gurney,	1838.	18
239.	Hark! a thrilling voice is sounding,	Caswall, 1849, *from* Ambrose, 4th century.		18
240.	I was a wandering sheep,	Bonar,	1844.	18
241.	Jesu, Thy blood and righteousness,	J. Wesley, 1743, *from* Zinzendorf.		18
242.	Lord, in Thy name Thy servants plead,	Keble,	1857.	18
243.	Lord of the Sabbath, hear us pray,	Doddridge,	1755.	18
244.	O come and mourn with me a while,	Faber,	1849.	18
245.	O Lord, how happy should we be,	Anstice,	1836.	18
246.	O what, if we are Christ's,	Baker,	1852.	18
247.	Prayer is the soul's sincere desire,	Montgomery,	1818.	18
248.	Round the Lord in glory seated,	Bp. Mant,	1776-1848.	18
249.	Sing Alleluia forth in duteous praise,	Ellerton,	1865.	18
250.	Spirit of Truth, on this Thy day,	Heber,	1827.	18
251.	Thou Judge of quick and dead,	Wesley,	1749.	18
252.	We give immortal praise,	Watts,	1709.	18
253.	We give Thee but Thine own,	How,	1854.	18
254.	We've no abiding city here,	Kelly,	1804.	18
255.	When this passing world is done,	M'Cheyne,	1837.	18
256.	When wounded sore, the stricken soul,	Alexander,	1858.	18
257.	Bound upon the accursèd tree,	Milman,	1837.	17
258.	Christ is made the sure foundation,	Neale, 1837, *from* Latin Hymn, 8th century.		17
259.	Creator of the stars of night,	Campbell, 1850, *from* Roman Breviary.		17
260.	Crown Him with many crowns,	Bridges,	1852.	17
261.	Fair waved the golden corn,	Gurney,	1853.	17
262.	For all Thy saints, O Lord,	Mant,	*circa* 1837.	17
263.	Forty days and forty nights,	Smyttan,	1856.	17
264.	Lord God, the Holy Ghost,	Montgomery,	1825.	17
265.	My God, how wonderful Thou art,	Faber,	1849.	17
266.	My God, I love Thee, not because,	Caswall, 1849, *from* Xavier, 1506-1552.		17
267.	O come, loud anthems let us sing,	Tate and Brady,	1703.	17
268.	O Jesu, King most wonderful,	Caswall, 1849, *from* St. Bernard.		17
269.	O Lord, how joyful 'tis to see,	Chandler, 1837, *from* Paris Breviary.		17
270.	Sons of men, behold from far,	Wesley,	1743.	17
271.	Take up thy cross, the Saviour said,	Anon.,	1833.	17
272.	Thou art gone to the grave, but we will not deplore thee,	Heber,	1827.	17

Index of Third Rank Hymns.

Order.	Hymns.	Authors.		Marks.
273.	Weary of earth, and laden with my sin,	Stone,	born 1839.	17
274.	When, His salvation bringing,	King,	1830.	17
275.	While with ceaseless course the sun,	Newton,	1779.	17
276.	Awake, my soul, stretch every nerve,	Doddridge,	1755.	16
277.	Christ the Lord is risen again,	Winkworth, 1858, *from* Weiss,	1531.	16
278.	Father, by Thy love and power,	Anstice,	1836.	16
279.	Father, I know that all my life,	Waring,	1850.	16
280.	From every stormy wind that blows,	Stowell,	1832.	16
281.	Hail! Thou Source of every blessing,	Woodd,	1760.	16
282.	Hark, hark, my soul! angelic songs are swelling,	Faber,	1862.	16
283.	He is risen! He is risen,	Alexander,	1858.	16
284.	Head of the Church triumphant,	Wesley,	1745.	16
285.	Hosanna, raise the pealing hymn,	W. H. Havergal,	1833.	16
286.	I lay my sins on Jesus,	Bonar,	1845.	16
287.	Jesus, I my cross have taken,	Lyte,	1847.	16
288.	Let me be with Thee where Thou art,	Elliott,	1836.	16
289.	Lord of the harvest, Thee we hail,	Gurney,	1853.	16
290.	Now, my soul, thy voice upraising,	Baker, 1837, *from* Paris Breviary.		16
291.	O render thanks to God above,	Tate and Brady,	1703.	16
292.	Praise, O praise our God and King.	Baker,	1861.	16
293.	The advent of our King,	Chandler, 1837, *from* the Paris Breviary.		16
294.	The race that long in darkness pined,	Morrison,	1781.	16
295.	There is a happy land,	Young,	1838.	16
296.	There's a Friend for little children,	Midlane,	1860.	16
297.	This stone to Thee in faith we lay,	Montgomery,	1825.	16
298.	To Thy temple I repair,	Montgomery,	1825.	16
299.	When I can read my title clear,	Watts,	1709.	16
300.	With glory clad, and strength arrayed,	Tate and Brady,	1703.	16
301.	With joy we meditate the grace,	Watts,	1709.	16
302.	As when the weary traveller gains,	Newton,	1779.	15
303.	Behold! the mountain of the Lord,	Bruce,	1781.	15
304.	Blessed city! heavenly Salem,	Neale, 1851, *from* Latin hymn, 8th century.		15
305.	Breast the wave, Christian,	Stammers,	born 1801.	15
306.	Dread Jehovah, God of nations,	C. F.,	1804.	15
307.	Father, again in Jesus' name we meet,	Whitmore.		15
308.	Fierce was the wild billow,	Neale, 1862, *from* Anatolius, 5th century.		15
309.	From Egypt lately come,	Kelly,	1804.	15

Summary of Third Rank Hymns.

Order.	Hymns.	Authors.		Marks.
310.	Gracious Saviour, gentle Shepherd,	Wesley,		15
311.	Gracious Spirit, Holy Ghost,	Wordsworth,	1865.	15
312.	I need Thee, precious Jesus,	Whitfield,	1864.	15
313.	In the Lord's atoning grief,	Oakeley, *from* Bonaventura, 1221-1274.		15
314.	It came upon the midnight clear,	Sears,	*circa* 1838.	15
315.	Jesu! the very thought is sweet,	Neale, 1862, *from* St. Bernard,	1150.	15
316.	Joy to the world! the Lord is come,	Watts,	1709.	15
317.	My God, how endless is Thy love,	Watts,	1709.	15
318.	O love, how deep, how broad, how high,	Neale,	1862.	15
319.	O Saviour, is Thy promise fled,	Heber,	1827.	15
320.	Once more the solemn season calls,	Chandler, 1837, *from* Paris Breviary.		15
321.	Saviour, who Thy flock art feeding,	Muhlenberg,	1826.	15
322.	Son of God, to Thee we cry,	Mant,	1776-1848.	15
323.	The Day of Resurrection,	Neale, *from* St. John Damascene, 8th cent.		15
324.	This is the day of light,	Ellerton,	born 1826.	15
325.	Ye choirs of New Jerusalem,	Campbell, 1850, *from* Latin hymn, 11th cent.		15

SUMMARY OF THIRD RANK HYMNS.

All hymns found in fifteen Hymnals and upwards, and in fewer than twenty, have been classified as hymns of the *third* rank.

Of these there are 110, composed by 60 hymn-writers, of whom—

39 authors contribute	1 hymn each =	39 hymns.
6	,,	2	,,	12	,,
6	,,	3	,,	18	,,
6	,,	4	,,	24	,,
1	,,	5	,,	5	,,
2	,,	6	,,	12	,,
60 authors.				110 hymns.	

Summary of Third Rank Hymns.

Arranging the hymn-writers according to the number of hymns contributed, they stand thus—

Neale,	6	Newton,	2	Neele,	1
Watts,	6	Anon.,	1	Nunn,	1
Doddridge,	5	Bridges,	1	Oakeley,	1
Baker, Sir H.,	4	Bruce,	1	Sears,	1
Faber,	4	C. F.,	1	Smyttan,	1
Gurney,	4	Collins,	1	Stammers,	1
Montgomery,	4	Cowper,	1	Steele,	1
Tate and Brady,	4	Flowerdew,	1	Stocker,	1
Wesley, C.,	4	W. H. Havergal,	1	Stone,	1
Bonar,	3	How,	1	Stowell,	1
Caswall,	3	Huntingdon,	1	Toke,	1
Chandler,	3	Keble,	1	Twells,	1
Ellerton,	3	King,	1	Waring,	1
Heber,	3	Lyte,	1	J. Wesley,	1
Mant,	3	M'Cheyne,	1	Whitfield,	1
C. F. Alexander,	2	Midlane,	1	Whitmore,	1
Anstice,	2	Milman,	1	Winkworth,	1
Robert Campbell,	2	Milton,	1	Woodd,	1
C. Elliott,	2	Morrison,	1	Bp. Wordsworth,	1
Kelly,	2	Muhlenberg,	1	Young,	1

Of the above sixty hymn-writers, several contribute to First Rank hymns; several also contribute to Second Rank hymns, and fourteen contribute to First, Second, and Third Rank hymns.

Number of Third Rank Hymns found in the chief Hymnals.

Of the 110 hymns included in the Third Rank—

1. The Hymnal Companion . contains 78, and omits 32
2. Church Hymnal (Irish) . . ,, 58 ,, 52
3. The Church of England Hymn-Book ,, 52 ,, 58
4. Church Hymns (S.P.C.K.) . ,, 51 ,, 59
5. Hymns Ancient and Modern . ,, 48 ,, 62
6. The Westminster Abbey Hymn-Book ,, 40 ,, 70

216. 'Christian, seek not yet repose,'
   Hear thy guardian angel say;
'Thou art in the midst of foes,
   Watch and pray.'

This well-known hymn, consisting of six stanzas, is from the pen of Miss Charlotte Elliott, and first appeared as a Wednesday morning hymn in her *Hymns for a Week*, published in 1839. Each stanza consists of three long lines, and a short one consisting of the words 'Watch and pray,' which form a refrain at the end of each stanza. This form of metre, although somewhat rare, is adopted by Miss Elliott in many of her hymns.

The above is founded on the words, 'Watch and pray, lest ye enter into temptation.'

217. Come, Thou Fount of every blessing,
   Tune my heart to grateful lays.

This hymn of praise is generally assigned to the Countess of Huntingdon (1759), but there are reasons for thinking that it was written in 1758 by Robert Robinson, a celebrated Baptist minister, who died in 1790. Sometimes the first line is written, 'Saviour! Fount of every blessing.' The hymn ought carefully to be distinguished from one beginning 'Hail, Thou Source of every blessing,' written by B. Woodd in the beginning of this century.

218. Far from these narrow scenes of night
    Unbounded glories rise,
    And realms of infinite delight,
    Unknown to mortal eyes.

This hymn was written in 1760 by Miss Anne Steele, daughter of a Baptist minister at Broughton, Hampshire. The above hymn in the original consists of eleven stanzas, and is entitled 'The Promised Land.' It is founded on Isaiah xxxiii. 17 : 'Thine eyes shall see the King in His beauty, and shall behold the land that is very far off.' (See Hymn 119.)

219. Fountain of mercy, God of love,
    How rich Thy bounties are !

This harvest thanksgiving hymn is by Mrs. Alice Flowerdew, and first appeared in 1811. It is founded on a hymn written in 1768 by John Needham, a Baptist minister in Bristol. Mrs. Flowerdew, being left a widow, took up a ladies' boarding-school in Islington. She wrote several hymns, of which she says : 'They were written at different periods of life, some indeed at a very early age, and others under the severe pressure of misfortune, when my pen had frequently given that relief which could not be derived from other employments.' She died at Ipswich in 1830, aged seventy-one.

220. Glory to Thee, O Lord,
   Who from this world of sin.

This hymn, founded on the slaughter of the Holy Innocents, was written by Mrs. Emma Toke, and was contributed to the S.P.C.K. Hymnal of 1852.

221. God of mercy, throned on high,
   Listen from Thy lofty seat.

This useful hymn for children was written in 1818 by Henry Neele, and is founded on Jeremiah iii. 4: 'My Father, Thou art the guide of my youth.'

222. High let us swell our tuneful notes,
   And join the angelic throng.

This Christmas hymn was written about 1737 by Philip Doddridge. It was originally entitled 'The Angels' Song at Christ's Birth,' and is founded on St. Luke ii. 14: 'Glory to God in the highest, and on earth peace, good will-toward men.'

223. Jesu, my Lord, my God, my All,
   Hear me, blest Saviour, when I call.

This hymn was written in 1852 by Henry Collins, a London clergyman, who seceded to the Church of Rome in 1857, and died lately as a Cistercian monk. The refrain, 'Oh! make me love Thee more and more,' is adapted from Faber's hymn 'Corpus Christi.'

224. Let us, with a gladsome mind,
    Praise the Lord, for He is kind:
    For His mercies aye endure,
    Ever faithful, ever sure.

John Milton, author of the above, is accounted our greatest epic poet, and the equal of Homer and Dante. He was born in London 1608, educated at St. Paul's School, graduated at Cambridge, where he distinguished himself for the excellence of Latin verses. When a mere youth Milton gave promise of his poetical talent by writing metrical versions of some of the Psalms. The above hymn is part of his rendering of the 136th Psalm, and was composed when the author was a scholar at St. Paul's School, and only fifteen years of age.

Thirty years after he began to write his incomparable poem 'Paradise Lost,' and in 1667 appeared his 'Paradise Regained.' Milton died in 1674, at the age of sixty-six, and was buried in St. Giles', Cripplegate.

225. O Paradise! O Paradise!
    Who doth not crave for rest?

This hymn, founded on the text, ' Having a desire to depart, and to be with Christ, which is far better,' was written by Faber, and appeared in his collected hymns in 1862. In that year Faber completed his collection of 150 hymns, and then he determined to stop, in order that his hymns might equal the Psalms in number. The above is 149 in the general collection.

226. O praise ye the Lord!
   Prepare your glad voice.

This is the metrical version of the 149th Psalm by Tate and Brady, published in 1703.

227. Of the Father's love begotten
   Ere the worlds began to be.
   <small>Corde natus ex parentis,
   Ante mundi exordium.</small>

The translation of this hymn is by Dr. Mason Neale, and first appeared in 1852. It was slightly altered for *Hymns Ancient and Modern* by the late Sir H. W. Baker. The original is a cento from a sacred ode by Prudentius, entitled, 'Hymnus omnis horae,' which celebrates the whole life of our Saviour from His Nativity to His Ascension.

228. One there is, above all others,
   O how He loves.

This excellent hymn for children, founded on the text, 'There is a friend that sticketh closer than a brother,' is a varied form of a hymn written by Miss Marianne Nunn (1779-1847). In the year of her birth, 1779, John Newton published in his *Olney Hymns* one commencing with the same words as the above.

229. Saviour, again to Thy dear Name we raise
   With one accord our parting hymn of praise.

This beautiful evening hymn is from the pen of the Rev. John Ellerton, Rector of Barnes, a living hymnist, who writes many excellent hymns. The above was written for a Festival of Parochial Choirs held at Nantwich in 1866, and was subsequently, in 1868, inserted in the Appendix to *Hymns Ancient and Modern*.

230. The Church has waited long
Her absent Lord to see.

This Advent hymn was written by Dr. Horatius Bonar in 1844, and reprinted in his *Hymns of Faith and Hope* in 1856.

231. To-morrow, Lord, is Thine,
Lodged in Thy sovereign hand,
And, if its sun arise and shine,
It shines at Thy command.

This hymn of warning and invitation, by Philip Doddridge, is founded on the verse 'To-day, if ye will hear His voice, harden not your hearts,' and was probably written to be sung at the end of one of Doddridge's sermons on the foregoing text.

232. We saw Thee not when Thou didst come
To this poor world of sin and death,
Nor e'er beheld Thy cottage-home
In that despisèd Nazareth;
But we believe Thy footsteps trod
Its streets and plains, Thou Son of God.

This hymn is a cento based on an anonymous American hymn beginning 'We see Thee not.' The

Account of Third Rank Hymns. 275

first and third stanzas are by the Rev. Henry James Buckoll, one of the Masters of Rugby School, who first re-cast the American hymn for use in Rugby School Chapel. It was re-written in 1838 by John Hampden Gurney, Rector of St. Mary's, Marylebone, and appeared in the Marylebone collection of hymns published in 1851. Gurney composed the fourth and fifth stanzas.

233. What various hindrances we meet
In coming to the Mercy-seat;
Yet who, that knows the worth of prayer,
But wishes to be often there?

'This hymn or prayer by Cowper may seem at first sight too familiar for insertion, but those who know the high value that is set upon it by the poor will be unwilling to banish it from a Church Hymnal. Such a hymn will be an incentive to devotion in many a lonely cottage, and yet lonelier workhouse and orphanage. It is in places like these this hymn is so useful for private meditation or pastoral counsel.'

234. At even, ere the sun was set,
The sick, O Lord, around Thee lay.

This soothing evening hymn, founded on the words, 'And at even, when the sun did set, they brought unto Him all that were diseased, and He healed many that were sick of divers diseases,' was written by the Rev. Henry Twells, Rector of Waltham, Leicestershire, and appeared in 1868 in *Hymns Ancient and Modern.*

235. Come, ye who love the Lord,
   And let your joys be known,
Join in a song with sweet accord,
   And thus surround the Throne.

This hymn of praise was written by Dr. Watts in 1709.

The original consists of ten stanzas, of which only about half appear in our modern Hymnals. The hymn is founded on the opening verses of the 100th Psalm: 'Make a joyful noise unto the Lord, all ye lands. Serve the Lord with gladness; come before His presence with singing.'

236. Fountain of good, to own Thy love
   Our thankful hearts incline.

This hymn, for almsgiving, is founded on the words, 'Inasmuch as ye have done it unto one of the least of these My brethren, ye have done it unto Me.' It is based on a hymn by Doddridge, beginning 'Jesus, my Lord, how rich Thy grace!' The adaptation was chiefly effected by Edward Osler, and first appeared in 1836 in Hall's *Psalms and Hymns*.

237. Gracious Spirit! Love Divine!
   Let Thy light around us shine.

This hymn, suitable for Whitsuntide, appeared first in the *Gospel Magazine* in 1777. It bore the signature of John Stocker, but all that is known of this author is

Account of Third Rank Hymns.

that he belonged to Honiton, Devon, and contributed nine hymns to the same Magazine, all characterised by considerable religious fervour.

238. Great King of nations, hear our prayer,
    While at Thy feet we fall.

This hymn, for a day of national humiliation, was written by John Hampden Gurney, and appeared in 1838 in his collection of Hymns for Public Worship.

239. Hark! a thrilling voice is sounding.
    En clara vox redarguit.

This is a translation from some Latin stanzas, thought by some to be the work of St. Ambrose. The rendering is by the Rev. Edward Caswall, born 1814, seceded to the Church of Rome in 1847, and died a priest of the Oratory, Birmingham, 1877. The Latin is a re-cast made by order of Pope Urban VIII., in the seventeenth century, of a hymn of the fifth century, beginning 'Vox clara ecce intonat.'

The hymn itself is designed for Advent, and its language is mainly drawn from the Epistle of the first Sunday and the Gospel of the second Sunday of that season.

240. I was a wandering sheep,
    I did not love the fold.

This hymn, so touching in its simplicity, is founded on the parable of the Lost Sheep, and was written by Dr. Bonar in 1844.

241. Jesu, Thy blood and righteousness
  My beauty are, my glorious dress;
  'Midst flaming worlds in these array'd
  With joy shall I lift up my head.

This hymn is a translation from the German of Count Zinzendorf by John Wesley, and is founded on Isaiah lxi. 10: 'He hath covered me with the robe of righteousness.' Wesley's translation consists of ten stanzas, but the original consists of twenty-four stanzas. The first verse, however, quoted above, is part of a hymn by Paul Eber, a friend and amanuensis of Melanchthon. The original German was written by Zinzendorf in 1739, in the island of Eustatius, when the Count was returning from visiting some missionaries who had gone forth from Germany to preach the Gospel in the West Indies.

242. Lord, in Thy name Thy servants plead,
  And Thou hast sworn to hear.

This was written in 1856, at Malvern, as a harvest-hymn, by John Keble, and inserted the following year, 1857, in the Salisbury Hymn-book.

243. Lord of the Sabbath, hear us pray,
  In this Thy house, on this Thy day.

This hymn, suitable for Sunday morning, is by Dr. Doddridge, and bears date 1736-7. It is entitled by the author 'The Eternal Sabbath,' and is founded on Hebrews iv. 9 : 'There remaineth therefore a rest for the people of God.'

244. O come and mourn with me a while,
    O come ye to the Saviour's side.

This touching Passion hymn was written by Faber in 1849.

The refrain, 'Jesus my Love is crucified,' at the end of each stanza, is evidently taken from the words of Ignatius, who on the way to his martyrdom frequently exclaimed, 'My Love is crucified.'

245. O Lord, how happy should we be
    If we could cast our care on Thee.

This beautiful hymn, founded on the words, 'Casting all your care upon Him, for He careth for you,' was written by Professor Anstice in 1836, just a few weeks before his death.

246. O what, if we are Christ's,
    Is earthly shame or loss?

This hymn, founded on the words, 'I reckon that the sufferings of this present time are not worthy to be compared with the glory which shall be revealed in us,' was contributed by Sir H. W. Baker, in 1861, to *Hymns Ancient and Modern*.

247. Prayer is the soul's sincere desire,
   Uttered or unexpressed.

This hymn was written by James Montgomery in 1818, at the request of the late Edward Bickersteth, for his treatise on Prayer. It is so perfect an exposition of that heavenly exercise, and rises so beautifully at its close into direct supplication, that it may well find a place in a Church Hymnal.

248. Round the Lord in glory seated,
   Cherubim and Seraphim.

This hymn is by Bishop Mant, and appeared in his *Ancient Hymns from the Roman Breviary*. This, however, is original, and the first stanza, generally omitted, though very beautiful, begins—

   Bright the vision that delighted
   Once the sight of Judah's seer.

249. Sing Alleluia forth in duteous praise,
   O citizens of Heaven; in sweet notes raise
   An endless Alleluia.

This hymn of praise, known from the refrain as 'The Endless Alleluia,' is a translation of an old Latin hymn assigned by Mone to the fifth century. The original, beginning 'Alleluia piis edite laudibus,' is found in the Mozarabic (Spanish) Breviary, and was sung in the first week of Lent. The translation is by the Rev. John Ellerton, and first appeared in the

Churchman's Family Magazine for April 1865. It was revised for the Appendix to *Hymns Ancient and Modern* in 1868.

250. Spirit of Truth, on this Thy day,
 To Thee for help we cry.

This hymn, for Whitsuntide, was written by Bishop Heber, and appeared in his collection of hymns published in 1827, after his death.

251. Thou Judge of quick and dead,
 Before whose bar severe.

This hymn, founded on the words, 'Take ye heed, watch and pray,' was written by Charles Wesley in 1749.

252. We give immortal praise
 To God the Father's love.

This hymn, founded on the words, 'Of Him, and through Him, and to Him are all things; to whom be glory for ever. Amen,' was written by Dr. Watts, and appeared in 1709.

253. We give Thee but Thine own,
 Whate'er the gift may be.

This hymn is by Bishop Walsham How, and appeared first in 1854, in Morrell and How's Psalms and Hymns.

254. We've no abiding city here:
    This may distress the worldling's mind,
    But should not cost the saint a tear,
    Who hopes a better rest to find.

This favourite hymn, by Thomas Kelly, appeared in 1804. It is founded on the words in Heb. xiii. 14: 'Here have we no continuing city, but we seek one to come.'

255. When this passing world is done,
    When has sunk yon glaring sun.

This hymn is by the sainted M'Cheyne, born in Edinburgh in 1813, died in 1843. The above appeared in 1837 in his *Songs of Zion.* 'Like the course of the falling star, that after delighting us for a moment seems to hasten quickly away to some more congenial sphere, so was the brief but beautiful career of this eminent servant of God.'

256. When wounded sore, the stricken soul
    Lies bleeding and unbound.

This Lenten hymn, founded on the words, 'He healeth the broken in heart,' was written by Mrs. C. F. Alexander, and first appeared in 1858 in her *Hymns Descriptive and Devotional.*

257. Bound upon the accursèd tree,
    Faint and bleeding, who is He?

This Passion hymn was written by Dean Milman, and appeared in 1837.

Account of Third Rank Hymns.

258. Christ is made the sure foundation,
    Christ the head and corner-stone.

This is a rendering of a Latin hymn beginning 'Angulare Fundamentum,' by Dr. Neale, made in 1851. Some think the original is Ambrosian, but it is generally believed to be the work of an unknown author of the eighth century. From the same source is Neale's rendering, 'Blessed city, heavenly Salem.'

259. Creator of the stars of night,
    Thy people's everlasting light.

This is a translation of a Latin hymn of the sixth century, beginning 'Conditor alme siderum,' by Robert Campbell. Translations of the same Latin hymns have been made by Neale, Thring, and others.

260. Crown Him with many crowns,
    The Lamb upon His throne.

This hymn, founded on the words, 'and on His head were many crowns,' is by Matthew Bridges, who, about 1848, became a Roman Catholic. The above appeared in 1852 in a small work of his called *The Passion of Jesus*. The hymn has lately been re-cast by the Rev. Godfrey Thring, and printed in his *Church of England Hymn-Book*.

261. Fair waved the golden corn
    In Canaan's pleasant land.

This excellent hymn for children is by J. H. Gurney, and first appeared in 1838 in his *Psalms and Hymns*.

262. For all Thy saints, O Lord,
    Who strove in Thee to live.

This hymn, suitable for Saints' Days, is founded on the words, 'Be ye followers of them, who through faith and patience inherit the promises,' and was written by Bishop Mant about 1837. It first appeared in his *Ancient Hymns from the Roman Breviary.*

263. Forty days and forty nights
    Thou wast fasting in the wild.

This Lenten hymn first appeared in the *Penny Post* in March 1856, and was reprinted in 1860 in *Hymns Ancient and Modern.* It is by the Rev. George Hunt Smytton, appointed Rector of Hawksworth, Nottinghamshire, in 1850.

264. Lord God, the Holy Ghost,
    In this accepted hour.

This excellent hymn, suitable for Whitsuntide, is founded on the words, 'And suddenly there came a sound as of a rushing mighty wind, . . . and they were all filled with the Holy Ghost.' It was written by James Montgomery, and appeared in 1825.

265. My God, how wonderful Thou art,
    Thy majesty how bright.

This general hymn is by Frederick William Faber, and first appeared in 1849. It was also embodied in Faber's collection of 1862, and is hymn No. 9.

266. My God, I love Thee, not because
   I hope for heaven thereby.

This is a translation from a Latin hymn by Francis Xavier, the famous Jesuit missionary to the East, who died near Canton, China, in 1552. The translation was made by Edward Caswall, and appeared in 1849 in his *Lyra Catholica*.

267. O come, loud anthems let us sing,
   Loud thanks to our Almighty King!
   And high our grateful voices raise,
   As our salvation's Rock we praise.

This hymn is the metrical version of the 95th Psalm, beginning 'O come, let us sing unto the Lord; let us heartily rejoice in the strength of our salvation.' It is taken from the Psalter known as the 'New Version,' by Tate and Brady, and appeared in 1703.

268. O Jesu, King most wonderful!
   Thou Conqueror renowned.

> Jesu! rex admirabilis,
> Et triumphator nobilis.

A portion of the Latin poem of St. Bernard of Clairvaux, written 1140 A.D., rendered into English by Edward Caswall, M.A., in 1849. See 'Jesu! the very thought of Thee.'

269. O Lord, how joyful 'tis to see
    The brethren join in love to Thee.

This hymn is a rendering by John Chandler, in 1837, from the Paris Breviary. The original Latin is a hymn for Vespers on Tuesdays, composed by Charles Coffin in 1736.

270. Sons of men, behold from far,
    Hail the long-expected Star!
    Jacob's Star, that gilds the night,
    Guides bewildered nature right.

This hymn for the Epiphany is by Charles Wesley. It appeared in his *Hymns and Sacred Poems*, published in 1739. The hymn is founded on Balaam's prediction, uttered on the top of one of the mountains of Moab: 'I shall see Him, but not now: I shall behold Him, but not nigh: there shall come a Star out of Jacob, and a Sceptre shall rise out of Israel.'

271. Take up thy cross, the Saviour said,
    If thou wouldst My disciple be.

This hymn, founded on the words, 'If any man will come after Me, let him deny himself, and take up his cross, and follow Me,' is by the Rev. Charles William Everest, M.A., an American clergyman, and first appeared in 1833.

272. Thou art gone to the grave, but we will not
deplore thee,
Though sorrows and darkness encompass
the tomb.

This, suitable for 'The Order for the Burial of the Dead,' is by Bishop Heber, and appeared in a collection of his hymns published in 1827. Heber had only one child, but at the early age of six months the beloved babe died. Speaking of her death, he says, 'I am myself more cut down than I thought I should be, but I hope not impatient. I do not forget that to have possessed her at all, and to have enjoyed the pleasure of looking at her, and caressing her, for six months, was God's free gift, and still less do I forget that He who has taken her will at length, I hope, restore her to us.'

The above hymn probably refers to the death of this dear little babe.

273. Weary of earth, and laden with my sin,
I look at heaven, and long to enter in.

This hymn is by the Rev. Samuel John Stone, author of 'The Church's one foundation.' (See Hymn 188.) The above appeared in his *Lyra Fidelium*, which consisted of twelve poems on the articles of the Creed. It was published in 1865 under the article, 'I believe in the Forgiveness of Sins.'

274. When, His salvation bringing,
　　To Zion Jesus came.

This favourite hymn for children was written by Joshua King about 1830. It is founded on the scene at the triumphal entry of Christ into Jerusalem: 'And the children crying in the temple, and saying, Hosanna to the Son of David.'

275. While with ceaseless course the sun
　　Hasted through the passing year.

This hymn, suitable for the close of the year, is by John Newton, and appeared in the *Olney Hymns* in 1779.

276. Awake, my soul, stretch every nerve,
　　And press with vigour on.

This hymn, suitable for Confirmation, is founded on the words, 'I press toward the mark for the prize of the high calling of God.' It was written by Dr. Doddridge, and appeared in 1755.

277. Christ the Lord is risen again,
　　Christ hath broken every chain.

This Easter hymn is a translation from a German hymn written in 1531 by Michael Weiss, a pastor of the Bohemian Brethren, who died in 1540. It was founded upon an old German Sequence of the thirteenth century. The above translation was made by Miss Catharine Winkworth in 1858.

278. Father, by Thy love and power,
    Comes again the evening hour.

This sweet evening hymn was written by the Rev. Joseph Anstice in 1836. All his hymns were dictated to his wife during the last few weeks before his death, and were privately printed in 1836, immediately after his decease.

279. Father, I know that all my life
    Is portioned out for me.

This hymn, consisting in the original of eight stanzas, was written by Anna Lætitia Waring, and appeared in 1850. 'Her beautiful spiritual hymns cannot be mingled and lost amongst the numerous productions of ordinary writers. Their intrinsic excellence as Christian hymns has given them a hold upon the public religious mind.'

280. From every stormy wind that blows,
    From every swelling tide of woes.

This very beautiful hymn is founded on the words, 'There I will meet with thee, and I will commune with thee from above the mercy-seat.' It was written in 1832 by Canon Hugh Stowell, Rural Dean of Salford, who died in 1865.

281. Hail! Thou Source of every blessing,
    Sovereign Father of mankind.

This Epiphany hymn, founded on the words, 'That the Gentiles should be fellow-heirs, and of the same body, and partakers of His promise in Christ by the

T

Gospel,' was written in 1799 by the Rev. Basil Woodd, for forty-six years minister of Portland Chapel, Marylebone. The above is often confounded with a well-known hymn beginning, 'Come, Thou Fount of every blessing,' but the similarity of the two ceases with the first line of each.

 282. Hark, hark, my soul! Angelic songs are swelling
   O'er earth's green fields and ocean's wave-beat shore.

This favourite hymn is by Faber, and appears in his collection of 1862, where it is entitled 'The Pilgrims of the Night.'

Bishop Alexander quaintly says: 'This hymn combines every conceivable violation of every conceivable rule with every conceivable beauty.'

It combines, however, noble poetry with deep spirituality, and has found its way to Christian hearts.

 283. He is risen! He is risen!
   Tell it with a joyful voice.

This Easter hymn is by Mrs. Cecil Frances Alexander, and appeared in 1858 in her *Hymns Descriptive and Devotional*.

 284. Head of the Church triumphant,
   We joyfully adore Thee!

This noble hymn was written by Charles Wesley in 1745, and appeared in his *Hymns for Times of Trouble*

Account of Third Rank Hymns. 291

and Persecution. These hymns derive additional interest from the circumstances under which they were written. England was not only at war with France and Spain, but the country was disturbed by the Rebellion of the Pretender, and many outrages were being committed throughout the land. Preachers of the Gospel were often subjected to shameful usage, and this rough treatment is alluded to in the following expressions from the above hymn—

> While in affliction's furnace,
> And passing through the fire.

In the account of the last days of Bishop Heber there is an interesting passage bearing upon this hymn. The writer of the narrative says : ' On returning from church in the morning I was so ill as to be obliged to go to bed, and, with his usual affectionate consideration, the Bishop came and sat the greater part of the afternoon with me. Our conversation turned chiefly on the blessedness of heaven, and the best means of preparing for its enjoyment. He repeated several lines of an old hymn by Charles Wesley, which he said, in spite of one or two expressions, he admired as one of the most beautiful in our language for a rich and elevated tone of devotional feeling—

> Head of the Church triumphant,
> We joyfully adore Thee.'

This estimate of the above, by one who is justly regarded as one of the sweetest hymn-writers, is of great value, and gives additional interest to the hymn itself.

285. Hosanna, raise the pealing hymn
   To David's Son and Lord!

This hymn for children, founded on the words, 'The children crying in the temple, and saying, Hosanna to the Son of David,' was written in 1838 by Canon Havergal, a hymn-writer and distinguished composer of music. For many years he was Rector of Shareshill, near Wolverhampton. His youngest daughter was the late Frances Ridley Havergal.

286. I lay my sins on Jesus,
   The spotless Lamb of God.

This hymn is by Dr. Bonar, and appeared in 1857 in his *Hymns of Faith and Hope*. It was, however, written in 1844, and was founded on an old Latin hymn beginning—

> Jesu, plene caritate
> Manus tuae perforatae,
> Laxent mea crimina.

287. Jesus, I my cross have taken,
   All to leave and follow Thee.

This hymn, founded on the words, 'God forbid that I should glory, save in the cross of our Lord Jesus Christ,' is by H. F. Lyte, and was written in 1825.

288. Let me be with Thee where Thou art,
   My Saviour, my eternal Rest!
Then only will this longing heart
Be fully and completely blest!

This short hymn, consisting of four stanzas, was written by Miss Charlotte Elliott in 1836, and appears as the hymn for Friday evening in her *Hymns for a Week*. It is founded on the words of the Saviour addressed to His disciples, 'Where I am, there shall also My servant be.'

289. Lord of the harvest, Thee we hail,
   Thine ancient promise doth not fail!

This harvest hymn is by John Hampden Gurney, and appeared in 1851 in his *Psalms and Hymns for Public Worship*, although written some time before this collection appeared.

290. Now, my soul, thy voice upraising,
   Tell in sweet and mournful strains.

This hymn is a translation made in 1861 by Sir H. Baker from the Paris Breviary. It differs very little from a rendering made by John Chandler in 1837.

The original Latin hymn in the Paris Breviary is by Santolius Maglorianus, who died two centuries ago.

291. O render thanks to God above,
    The Fountain of eternal love,
    Whose mercy firm through ages past
    Has stood, and shall for ever last!

This hymn, usually consisting of five stanzas, is part of the metrical rendering of the 106th Psalm by Tate and Brady. The original appeared in the New Version in 1703, and consisted of forty-eight stanzas, thus equal to the verses of the Psalm, which begins: 'Praise ye the Lord. O give thanks unto the Lord; for He is good: for His mercy endureth for ever.'

292. Praise, O praise our God and King,
    Hymns of adoration sing!

This excellent harvest thanksgiving hymn is by Sir H. W. Baker, and appeared in 1861 in *Hymns Ancient and Modern*. The refrain in each stanza—

    For His mercies still endure,
    Ever faithful, ever sure,

—is evidently a paraphrase of 'for His mercy endureth for ever,' found in each verse of the 136th Psalm.

293. The advent of our King,
    Behold, the Lord is near!

This Advent hymn, founded on the words, 'Tell ye the daughter of Sion, Behold, thy King cometh unto thee,' is a translation from a Latin hymn contributed to the Paris Breviary by Charles Coffin in 1736, and first appeared in the Sarum Hymnal.

The hymn seems but a variation of a translation of the same Latin piece made by John Chandler in 1837, beginning—

> The Advent of our King
> Our prayers must now employ.

294. The race that long in darkness pined
    Have seen a glorious light.

This hymn is founded on Isaiah ix. 2, 3 : 'The people that walked in darkness have seen a great light: they that dwell in the land of the shadow of death, upon them hath the light shined.'

It is by the Rev. John Morrison, born 1749, and for many years minister of Canisbay, Caithness-shire, until his death in 1798. The hymn was inserted in the Scotch Paraphrases in 1781.

295. There is a happy land,
    Far, far away!

This favourite Sunday-school hymn was written by Mr. Andrew Young, an Edinburgh gentleman, about 1838. Mr. Young was a student of Edinburgh University, and after devoting a great many years to scholastic duties, he settled in Edinburgh, where he has now resided for many years.

296. There's a Friend for little children
    Above the bright blue sky.

This very popular children's hymn is by Albert Midlane, a layman, living at Newport, Isle of Wight. It first appeared in 1860, in a little book entitled *Good News for the Little Ones.*

297.   This stone to Thee in faith we lay,
   We build the temple, Lord, to Thee;
  Thine eye be open night and day
   To guard this house and sanctuary.

This beautiful hymn, suitable for the consecration of a church, is from the pen of James Montgomery, and appeared in 1825. It is founded on Solomon's prayer at the dedication of the Temple: 'O God of Israel, have Thou respect unto the prayer of Thy servant, that Thine eyes may be open toward this house night and day, even toward the place of which Thou hast said, My Name shall be there.'

298.   To Thy temple I repair,
   Lord, I love to worship there;
  When within the veil I meet
  Christ before the mercy-seat.

This hymn, well adapted for public worship, was written by James Montgomery, and appeared in 1825. The original consisted of seven stanzas, of which the following seldom appears in modern Hymnals :—

   While I hearken to Thy law,
   Fill my soul with humble awe;
   Till Thy Gospel bring to me
   Life and immortality!

299. When I can read my title clear
   To mansions in the skies.

This hymn of faith is by Dr. Watts, and appeared in 1709. The allusions in this hymn to aspects of the sea, such as 'wild deluge,' 'storms,' 'seas of rest,' 'bathe,' 'wave,' 'peaceful,' etc., were probably suggested by the views of 'Southampton Water' as seen from the residence of the poet.

300. With glory clad, with strength array'd,
   The Lord that o'er all nature reigns.

This hymn is a paraphrase of the 93d Psalm, by Tate and Brady, and first appeared in their New Version of the Psalms in 1696.

301. With joy we meditate the grace
   Of our High Priest above!

This hymn, founded on the words, 'We have not an high priest which cannot be touched with the feeling of our infirmities,' is by Dr. Watts, and appeared in 1709.

302. As when the weary traveller gains
   The height of some o'erlooking hill,
   His heart revives, if, 'cross the plains,
   He eyes his home, though distant still.

This favourite hymn, by John Newton, appeared in the Olney collection in 1779. It is founded on the passage in Hebrews where the Patriarchs of old are spoken of as pilgrims journeying towards their home in the heavens: 'These all died in faith, not having received the promises, but having seen them afar off, and were persuaded of them, and embraced them, and confessed that they were strangers and pilgrims on the earth.'

> 303. Behold! the mountain of the Lord
> In latter days shall rise.

This beautiful hymn, suitable for Epiphany, was written by Michael Bruce, born 1746, died 1767, a talented Scottish poet, who died in youth of a rapid consumption. The above was embodied in the Scottish Paraphrases in 1781, and is really a paraphrase of Isaiah ii. 2-6: 'It shall come to pass in the last days, that the mountain of the Lord's house shall be established in the top of the mountains, and shall be exalted above the hills; and all nations shall flow unto it.'

> 304. Blessed city, heavenly Salem,
> Vision dear of peace and love.

This is a translation made by Dr. Neale of a grand old Latin hymn of the eighth century, beginning 'Urbs beata Hierusalem.'

> 305. Breast the wave, Christian, when it is strongest,
> Watch for day, Christian, when the night's longest.

This hymn was written about 1830 by Joseph Stammers, born at Bury St. Edmunds in 1801. He still continues to pursue the profession of a barrister.

Account of Third Rank Hymns. 299

306. Dread Jehovah, God of nations,
    From Thy temple in the skies.

This noble hymn, suitable for a day of national supplication, appeared in 1804. The author is unknown, but it was signed with the initials 'C. F.'

307. Father, again in Jesus' name we meet,
    And bow in penitence beneath Thy feet.

This hymn, suitable for Lent, is by Lady Whitmore, daughter of the Earl of Bradford; born 1792, died 1840. The hymn appeared in 1824 in a volume of Family Prayers, and was slightly altered in 1861 by Rev. Francis Pott.

308. Fierce was the wild billow
    Dark was the night,
  Oars laboured heavily,
    Foam glimmered white.
  Trembled the mariners,
    Peril was nigh:
  Then said the God of God,
    'Peace! it is I.'

This is one of Dr. Neale's happiest translations of a Greek hymn by S. Anatolius beginning Ζοφερᾶς τρικυμίας. The hymn is founded on the passage, 'When even was now come, His disciples went down unto the sea; ... and it was now dark, and Jesus was not come unto them. And the sea arose by reason of a great wind that blew, but He saith unto them, It is I; be not afraid.' It draws a vivid picture of Christ stilling the waves of the Sea of Galilee, and then appeals to Him as the Calmer of the storms of the soul. The third stanza of Dr. Neale's translation is very happy.

> 309. From Egypt lately come,
>   Where death and darkness reign,
>   We seek our new, our better home,
>   Where we our rest shall gain.

This hymn, by Thomas Kelly, appeared as the 57th hymn in the edition of the author's hymns published in 1806. The original consists of seven stanzas, with a chorus, and is founded on the words, 'For they that say such things declare plainly that they seek a country.'

> 310. Gracious Saviour, gentle Shepherd,
>   Little ones are dear to Thee.

This child's hymn was written by the Rev. J. Whittlemore, a Baptist minister, born at Sandy, Bedfordshire, in 1802, and died in London in 1860. In his last year he published a *Supplement to all Hymn-Books*, which contained this hymn.

> 311. Gracious Spirit, Holy Ghost,
>   Taught by Thee, we covet most.

This hymn is by Bishop Wordsworth, and appeared in 1862 in his *Holy Year*. It is appointed for Quinquagesima Sunday, and founded on the words that

Account of Third Rank Hymns. 301

occur in the Epistle for that day: 'And now abideth faith, hope, charity, these three; but the greatest of these is charity.'

> 312. I need Thee, precious Jesus,
> For I am full of sin.

This hymn, founded on the words, 'Unto you who believe He is precious,' was written in 1859 by the Rev. Frederick Whitfield, formerly Vicar of Kirkby Ravensworth.

> 313. In the Lord's atoning grief,
> Be our rest and sure relief.

This Passion hymn is by Canon Oakeley, formerly a clergyman of the Anglican Church, but subsequently a member of the Church of Rome. He died in 1880. The above is a rendering of a Latin piece beginning 'In passione Domini,' supposed to be by Bonaventura, of the thirteenth century.

> 314. It came upon the midnight clear,
> That glorious song of old.

This Christmas hymn is by the Rev. Edmund Hamilton Sears, an American Unitarian minister, born 1810, died 1876. The hymn was composed for Christmas 1850.

> 315. Jesu! the very thought is sweet,
> In that dear Name all heart joys meét.

This hymn is a translation by Dr. Mason Neale of a part of the 'Jubilee Rhythm' of Bernard of Clairvaux, beginning, 'Jesu dulcis memoria.' The original dates from about 1150, and the above translation appeared in 1851. Another well-known rendering of the same is 'Jesu! the very thought of Thee,' by Edward Caswall.

316. Joy to the world! the Lord is come,
    Let earth receive her King.

This Advent hymn is by Dr. Watts, and appeared in 1709. It is a metrical version of the 98th Psalm, beginning, 'O sing unto the Lord a new song,' etc.

316. My God, how endless is Thy love,
    Thy gifts are every evening new.

This beautiful morning hymn is by Dr. Watts, and appeared in 1709. It is founded on the words, 'His compassions fail not; they are new every morning.'

318. O love, how deep, how broad, how high,
    How passing thought and fantasy.

This is a translation by Dr. Neale from a Latin hymn beginning, 'O amor quam exstaticus,' and appeared in *Hymns Ancient and Modern* in 1861.

319. O Saviour, is Thy promise fled,
    Nor longer might Thy grace endure.

This tender and exquisitely simple hymn is by Heber, and appeared first in the *Christian Observer* in 1811. In his collection of hymns published in 1827 this is assigned to the third Sunday in Advent. The Gospel

Account of Third Rank Hymns. 303

for that day represents Christ as the Great Physician fulfilling the prophecy, 'Then the eyes of the blind shall be opened, and the ears of the deaf shall be unstopped: then shall the lame man leap as an hart, and the tongue of the dumb sing.'

320. Once more the solemn season calls
A holy fast to keep.

This Lenten hymn, founded on the words, 'Rend your hearts, and not your garments, and turn unto the Lord your God,' is an improved version that appeared in 1861 of John Chandler's hymn, 'The solemn season calls us now.' The latter is a translation from the Paris Breviary, where the Latin piece is a Lenten hymn for Lauds.

321. Saviour, who Thy flock art feeding
With the Shepherd's kindest care.

This hymn, suitable for Holy Baptism, is by the Rev. William Augustus Muhlenberg, D.D., born in Pennsylvania in 1796. He was for many years Chaplain of St. Luke's Children's Hospital, New York. The above first appeared in 1826, and the tender references to children have probably primary reference to the little ones intrusted to the author's spiritual care.

322. Son of God, to Thee we cry,
By the wondrous mystery.

This hymn, suitable for Passion Week, is based on a hymn by Bishop Mant, an Irish Bishop, born 1776, died 1848. It appeared in Denton's *Church Hymnal* in 1853.

323. The Day of Resurrection! Earth, tell it out abroad.

This Easter hymn is a translation from the Greek by Dr. Neale, and first appeared in 1862 in his *Hymns of the Eastern Church.*

The Greek is by St. John Damascene, the last of the Greek Fathers, who died about 780, and the original is a hymn of victory, sung at the first hour of Easter morning.

324. This is the day of light, Let there be light to-day.

This hymn for Sunday morning is by the Rev. John Ellerton, Rector of Barnes, one of our best living hymnists. It first appeared in 1868 in the Selection of Hymns compiled for use in Chester Cathedral.

325. Ye choirs of New Jerusalem, Your sweetest notes employ.

This Easter hymn is a translation by Robert Campbell of an ancient Latin hymn, written about 1000 A.D. by St. Fulbert of Chartres. Another translation by Neale appeared in *Hymns Ancient and Modern* in 1861.

CHAPTER V.

General Summary and Index of Standard Hymns.

GENERAL SUMMARY OF STANDARD HYMNS.

The 325 Standard Hymns were composed by 117 hymn-writers, of whom

74 authors contributed	1 hymn each	=	74 hymns.
12	,,	2	,,	24	,,
8	,,	3	,,	24	,,
4	,,	4	,,	16	,,
4	,,	5	,,	20	,,
4	,,	6	,,	24	,,
2	,,	7	,,	14	,,
2	,,	8	,,	16	,,
1	,,	9	,,	9	,,
1	,,	11	,,	11	,,
1	,,	12	,,	12	,,
1	,,	16	,,	16	,,
1	,,	17	,,	17	,,
1	,,	21	,,	21	,,
1	,,	22	,,	22	,,
			Anon.	5	,,

Total, 117 authors.   325 hymns.

SUMMARY TABLE.

List of the 117 Authors who composed the 325 Standard Hymns, together with the number of Hymns in each Rank contributed by each.

Authors' Names.	First Rank.	Second Rank.	Third Rank.	Total.
C. Wesley,	10	8	4	22
Watts,	8	7	6	21
Neale,	7	4	6	17
Montgomery,	4	8	4	16
Heber,	7	2	3	12
Tate and Brady,	3	4	4	11
Doddridge,	4	...	5	9
Chandler,	...	5	3	8
Newton,	2	4	2	8
Cowper,	3	3	1	7
Keble,	2	4	1	7
Bonar,	...	3	3	6
Caswall,	2	1	3	6
Elliot,	2	2	2	6
Lyte,	2	3	1	6
Sir H. Baker,	...	1	4	5
Faber,	...	1	4	5
Gurney,	1	...	4	5
Kelly,	1	2	2	5
Alexander,	1	1	2	4
Mant,	...	1	3	4
Milman,	3	...	1	4
Wordsworth,	...	3	1	4
Addison,	1	2	...	3
Alford,	2	1	...	3
Anstice,	...	1	2	3
R. Campbell,	...	1	2	3
Ellerton,	...	...	3	3
Grant,	3	...	...	3
Steele,	...	2	1	3
J. Wesley,	...	2	1	3
Bruce,	1	...	1	2
Cawood,	...	2	...	2
Cox,	1	1	...	2

Summary Table.

Authors' Names	First Rank.	Second Rank.	Third Rank.	Total.
Edmeston,	1	1	...	2
Haweis,	1	1	...	2
Ken,	2	...	...	2
Morrison,	...	1	1	2
Oakeley,	1	...	1	2
Ray Palmer,	...	2	...	2
Shirley,	2	...	...	2
Stone,	...	1	1	2
Toke,	1	...	1	2
Adams,	1	...	...	1
Auber,	1	...	...	1
Baker, F.,	1	...	...	1
Bakewell,	...	1	...	1
Barbauld,	...	1	...	1
Baring-Gould,	...	1	...	1
Baxter,	...	1	...	1
Bridges,	...	...	1	1
Bullock,	...	1	...	1
Byrom,	1	...	...	1
Browne,	1	...	...	1
C. F.,	...	...	1	1
Cameron,	1	...	...	1
Carlyle,	1	...	...	1
Cennick,	1	...	...	1
Collins,	...	...	1	1
Conder,	...	1	...	1
Cooper,	1	...	...	1
Cosin,	1	...	...	1
Crossman,	...	1	...	1
Dix,	1	...	...	1
Doane,	1	...	...	1
Downton,	1	...	...	1
Dryden,	...	1	...	1
Evans,	...	1	...	1
Flowerdew,	...	...	1	1
Hammond,	...	1	...	1
Hart,	...	1	...	1
Havergal,	...	...	1	1
Hill,	...	1	...	1
How,	...	...	1	1

Summary Table.

Authors' Names.	First Rank.	Second Rank.	Third Rank.	Total.
Huntingdon,	...	...	1	1
Irons,	...	1	...	1
Kethe,	1	...	...	1
Kirke White,	1	...	...	1
King,	...	...	1	1
Mardley,	1	...	...	1
Marriott,	1	...	...	1
Maude,	...	1	...	1
M'Cheyne,	...	...	1	1
Midlane,	...	...	1	1
Milton,	...	...	1	1
Muhlenberg,	...	...	1	1
Newman,	...	1	...	1
Neele,	...	...	1	1
Nunn,	...	...	1	1
Olivers,	...	1	...	1
Osler,	1	...	...	1
Perronet,	1	...	...	1
Pott,	...	1	...	1
Prynne,	...	1	...	1
Rorison,	...	1	...	1
Ringwaldt,	1	...	...	1
Rinkart,	1	...	...	1
Scott,	1	...	...	1
Sears,	...	...	1	1
Shrubsole,	...	1	...	1
Smyttan,	...	...	1	1
Stammers,	...	...	1	1
Stocker,	...	...	1	1
Stowell,	...	...	1	1
Thring,	...	1	...	1
Toplady,	1	...	...	1
Twells,	...	...	1	1
Waring,	...	...	1	1
Whitfield,	...	...	1	1
Whiting,	...	1	...	1
Whitmore,	...	...	1	1
Williams, I.,	1	...	...	1
Williams, W.,	1	...	...	1
Winkworth,	...	...	1	1

Summary Table.

Authors' Names.	First Rank.	Second Rank.	Third Rank.	Total.
Woodd,	...	...	1	1
Woodford,	...	1	...	1
Young,	...	...	1	1
Anon.,	2	2	1	5
117 authors.	105	110	110	325

Of the 117 standard hymn-writers it ought to be noted that—

28 authors contribute to first rank hymns only.
25 ,, second rank ,,
27 ,, third rank ,,
5 ,, first and second rank hymns only.
6 ,, first and third rank ,,
12 ,, second and third rank ,,
14 ,, first, second, and third ,,
117 authors.

The fourteen hymn-writers who contribute hymns to the First, Second, and Third Rank are:—Alexander, Caswall, Cowper, Elliott, Heber, Keble, Kelly, Lyte, Montgomery, Neale, Newton, Tate and Brady, Watts, Wesley.

The following general summary shows that the six Hymnals, arranged according to the number of classified hymns contained in each, stand thus—

	First Rank.	Second Rank.	Third Rank.	Total.	Omitted.
	105.	110.	110.	325.	
1. The Hymnal Companion contains	103	96	78	277	48
2. Church Hymnal (Irish) ,,	99	85	58	242	83
3. The Church of England Hymn-Book . . . contains	102	73	52	227	98
4. Church Hymns (S.P.C.K.) ,,	97	62	51	210	115
5. The Westminster Abbey Hymn-Book . . . contains	98	66	40	204	121
6. Hymns Ancient and Modern ,,	90	54	48	192	133

STANDARD HYMNS OF THE FUTURE.

Some beautiful hymns of comparatively recent date have not found a place among 'Standard Hymns,' simply because they lack age. They are, however, rapidly finding their way into modern Hymnals, and in the future will probably occupy a high position.

To obtain general sympathy a hymn should be terse in thought and expression, Scriptural in phraseology, catholic in doctrine, and clothed in poetic language.

The following thirty hymns of recent date fulfil more or less the above conditions, and seem likely to attain to the rank of 'Standard Hymns' of the future—

Hymns.	Authors.	Date.	Marks.
Behold the Lamb of God, O Thou, etc.,	Matthew Bridges,	1848	12
Brightly gleams our banner,	T. J. Potter,	1862	13
Come unto Me, ye weary,	W. C. Dix,	1864	13
Conquering kings their titles take,	John Chandler, 1837.	1861 (altered).	13
Days and moments quickly flying,	Edward Caswall,	1858	10
Earth has many a noble city,	Edward Caswall, 1858.	1861 (altered).	Copyright.
Fierce raged the tempest o'er the deep,	Godfrey Thring.	1861	13
For all the saints who from their labours rest,	Bishop W. W. How,	1854	14
Forward! be our watchword,	Dean Alford,	1867	6
His are the thousand sparkling rills,	Cecil Frances Alexander,	1861	Copyright.

Standard Hymns of the Future.

Hymns.	Authors.	Date.	Marks.
I am not worthy, holy Lord,	Sir Henry W. Baker,	1861	*Copyright.*
Light's abode, celestial Salem,	John Mason Neale, 1851,	1861 (*altered*).	9
Morn of morns, and day of days,	Isaac Williams, 1839,	1861 (*altered*).	10
Now that the daylight fills the sky,	John Mason Neale,	1861 (*altered*).	13
Now the day is over,	S. Baring-Gould,	1865	12
O Jesus, I have promised,	J. E. Bode,	1860	11
O Jesu, Thou art standing,	Bishop W. W. How,		12
O sacred Head surrounded,	Sir Henry W. Baker,	1861	11
Once in royal David's city,	C. F. Alexander,	1848	10
Praise to the holiest in the height,	John Henry Newman,		10
See, the Conqueror mounts in triumph,	Bishop Wordsworth,	1862	12
Sion's daughter, weep no more,	Sir H. W. Baker,	1861	*Copyright.*
Stars of the morning, so gloriously bright,	John Mason Neale,	1862	12
Ten thousand times ten thousand,	Dean Alford,	1867	9
The King of Love my Shepherd is,	Sir H. W. Baker,	1861	*Copyright.*
There is a green hill far away,	C. F. Alexander,	1848	9
Those eternal bowers man hath never trod,	John Mason Neale,	1862	14
Thou art coming, O my Saviour,	Frances R. Havergal,		5
Through the night of doubt and sorrow,	S. Baring-Gould,	1867	12
We plough the fields, and scatter,	From the German,	1861	11

GENERAL INDEX.

FIRST RANK,	Nos. 1 to 105
SECOND RANK,	Nos. 106 to 215
THIRD RANK,	Nos. 216 to 325

Order.	Hymns.	Page
117.	A few more years shall roll,	212
5.	Abide with me,	58
135.	According to Thy gracious word,	223
100.	All glory, laud, and honour,	192
46.	All hail, the power of Jesus' name,	136
21.	All people that on earth do dwell,	104
1.	All praise to Thee, my God, this night,	47
166.	Alleluia! song of sweetness,	237
167.	Almighty God! Thy Word is cast,	238
88.	Angels from the realms of glory,	172
192.	Approach, my soul, the mercy-seat,	254
193.	Arm of the Lord, awake, awake!	254
101.	Art thou weary, art thou languid,	192
194.	As now the sun's declining ray,	255
89.	As pants the hart for cooling streams,	172
73.	As with gladness men of old,	162
302.	As when the weary traveller gains,	297
234.	At even, ere the sun was set,	275
204.	At the Lamb's high feast we sing,	258
118.	Awake and sing the song,	213
6.	Awake, my soul, and with the sun,	60
276.	Awake, my soul, stretch every nerve,	288

General Index.

Order.	Hymns.	Page
102.	Before Jehovah's awful throne,	196
303.	Behold! the mountain of the Lord,	298
304.	Blessed city, heavenly Salem,	298
145.	Blest are the pure in heart,	227
195.	Blow ye the trumpet, blow,	255
257.	Bound upon the accursèd tree,	282
168.	Bread of Heaven, on Thee we feed,	238
196.	Bread of the world, in mercy broken,	255
305.	Breast the wave, Christian, when it is strongest,	298
22.	Brief life is here our portion,	107
82.	Brightest and best of the sons of the morning,	167
55.	Children of the Heavenly King,	144
258.	Christ is made the sure foundation,	283
154.	Christ is our corner-stone,	231
277.	Christ the Lord is risen again,	288
37.	Christ the Lord is risen to-day,	126
34.	Christ, whose glory fills the skies,	124
205.	Christian, dost thou see them,	259
216.	Christian, seek not yet repose,	269
83.	Christians, awake! salute the happy morn,	168
23.	Come, Holy Ghost, our souls inspire,	111
106.	Come, Holy Spirit, come,	207
136.	Come, Holy Spirit, from above,	224
90.	Come, gracious Spirit, Heavenly Dove,	172
30.	Come, let us join our cheerful songs,	120
182.	Come, let us join our friends above,	244
169.	Come, let us to the Lord our God,	239
183.	Come, my soul, thy suit prepare,	246
217.	Come, Thou Fount of every blessing,	269
170.	Come, Thou long-expected Jesus,	239
47.	Come, ye thankful people, come,	137
235.	Come, ye who love the Lord,	276
259.	Creator of the stars of night,	283
107.	Creator Spirit, by whose aid,	207
260.	Crown Him with many crowns,	283

Order.	Hymns.	Page
197.	Day of judgment, day of wonders,	256
108.	Day of wrath, O day of mourning,	208
306.	Dread Jehovah, God of nations,	299
206.	Ere another Sabbath's close,	259
171.	Eternal Father, strong to save,	240
261.	Fair waved the golden corn,	283
155.	Far from my heavenly home,	231
218.	Far from these narrow scenes of night,	270
307.	Father, again in Jesus' name we meet,	299
278.	Father, by Thy love and power,	289
279.	Father, I know that all my life,	289
48.	Father of Heaven, whose love profound,	138
119.	Father of mercies, in Thy Word,	214
156.	Father, whate'er of earthly bliss,	232
308.	Fierce was the wild billow,	299
262.	For all Thy saints, O Lord,	284
123.	For ever with the Lord,	217
38.	For thee, O dear, dear country,	127
91.	For Thy mercy and Thy grace,	173
78.	Forth in Thy name, O Lord, I go,	165
263.	Forty days and forty nights,	284
236.	Fountain of good, to own Thy love,	276
219.	Fountain of mercy, God of love,	270
124.	From all that dwell below the skies,	218
309.	From Egypt lately come,	300
280.	From every stormy wind that blows,	289
17.	From Greenland's icy mountains,	98
31.	Glorious things of thee are spoken,	121
56.	Glory be to Jesus,	145
220.	Glory to Thee, O Lord,	271
57.	Go to dark Gethsemane,	145
49.	God moves in a mysterious way,	138
109.	God of mercy, God of grace,	208
221.	God of mercy, throned on high,	271

General Index.

Order.	Hymns.	Page
103.	God of our life, to Thee we call,	197
39.	God, that madest earth and heaven,	127
310.	Gracious Saviour, gentle Shepherd,	300
311.	Gracious Spirit, Holy Ghost,	300
237.	Gracious Spirit, love divine,	276
18.	Great God, what do I see and hear,	101
238.	Great King of nations, hear our prayer,	277
58.	Guide me, O Thou great Jehovah,	147
25.	Hail the day that sees Him rise,	114
198.	Hail! Thou once despisèd Jesus,	256
281.	Hail! Thou Source of every blessing,	289
26.	Hail to the Lord's Anointed,	116
239.	Hark! a thrilling voice is sounding,	277
282.	Hark, hark, my soul!	290
157.	Hark! my soul, it is the Lord,	232
14.	Hark! the glad sound, the Saviour comes,	81
2.	Hark! the herald angels sing,	50
146.	Hark! the song of Jubilee,	228
158.	Hark! the sound of holy voices,	233
172.	Hark! the voice of love and mercy,	240
199.	Hark! what mean those holy voices,	257
125.	Have mercy, Lord, on me,	218
283.	He is risen! He is risen!	290
284.	Head of the Church triumphant,	290
222.	High let us swell our tuneful notes,	271
11.	Holy! Holy! Holy! Lord God Almighty!	76
285.	Hosanna, raise the pealing hymn,	292
27.	Hosanna to the living Lord,	117
120.	How beauteous are their feet,	215
50.	How bright these glorious spirits shine,	139
15.	How sweet the name of Jesus sounds,	84
137.	I heard the voice of Jesus say,	224
286.	I lay my sins on Jesus,	292
312.	I need Thee, precious Jesus,	301
240.	I was a wandering sheep,	277

General Index.

Order.	Hymns.	Page
126.	In the hour of trial, Jesu,	218
313.	In the Lord's atoning grief,	301
105.	In token that thou shalt not fear,	197
314.	It came upon the midnight clear,	301
16.	Jerusalem, my happy home!	86
184.	Jerusalem on high,	246
7.	Jerusalem the golden,	62
8.	Jesu, Lover of my soul,	68
223.	Jesu, my Lord, my God, my All,	271
315.	Jesu, the very thought is sweet,	301
59.	Jesu, the very thought of Thee,	149
110.	Jesu, Thou joy of loving hearts,	209
241.	Jesu, Thy blood and righteousness,	278
139.	Jesus calls us ; o'er the tumult,	225
12.	Jesus Christ is risen to-day,	78
287.	Jesus, I my cross have taken,	292
51.	Jesus lives ! no longer now,	140
138.	Jesus, meek and gentle,	224
40.	Jesus shall reign where'er the sun,	128
127.	Jesus, where'er Thy people meet,	219
316.	Joy to the world ! the Lord is come,	302
64.	Just as I am, without one plea,	155
185.	Lead, kindly Light, amid the encircling gloom,	247
92.	Lead us, Heavenly Father, lead us,	174
288.	Let me be with Thee where Thou art,	293
224.	Let us, with a gladsome mind,	272
173.	Light of those whose dreary dwelling,	240
3.	Lo ! He comes with clouds descending,	53
174.	Lo ! round the throne at God's right hand,	241
93.	Lord ! as to Thy dear Cross we flee,	174
79.	Lord, dismiss us with Thy blessing,	165
264.	Lord God, the Holy Ghost,	284
94.	Lord, in this Thy mercy's day,	175
242.	Lord, in Thy name Thy servants plead,	278
159.	Lord, it belongs not to our care,	233

General Index.

Order.	Hymns.	Page
80.	Lord of mercy and of might,	167
200.	Lord of the harvest, once again,	257
289.	Lord of the harvest, Thee we hail,	293
243.	Lord of the Sabbath, hear us pray,	278
84.	Lord of the worlds above,	169
186.	Lord, pour Thy Spirit from on high,	248
160.	Lord, teach us how to pray aright,	234
35.	Lord, when we bend before Thy throne,	124
74.	Love Divine, all love excelling,	163
161.	May the grace of Christ our Saviour,	234
201.	My faith looks up to Thee,	257
41.	My God, and is Thy table spread?	130
316.	My God, how endless is Thy love,	302
265.	My God, how wonderful Thou art,	284
266.	My God, I love Thee, not because,	285
24.	My God, my Father, while I stray,	113
13.	Nearer, my God, to-Thee,	79
65.	New every morning is the love,	156
140.	Not all the blood of beasts,	225
290.	Now, my soul, thy voice upraising,	293
105.	Now thank we all our God,	198
207.	O Christ, who hast prepared a place,	260
75.	O come, all ye faithful,	163
244.	O come and mourn with me a while,	279
267.	O come, loud anthems let us sing,	285
128.	O day of rest and gladness,	220
85.	O for a closer walk with God,	170
111.	O for a heart to praise my God,	209
129.	O for a thousand tongues to sing,	220
60.	O God of Bethel! by whose hand,	152
147.	O God of Hosts, the mighty Lord,	228
19.	O God, our help in ages past,	103
95.	O God, unseen yet ever near,	176

General Index.

Order.	Hymns.	Page
208.	O happy band of pilgrims,	260
76.	O help us, Lord, each hour of need,	164
202.	O holy Saviour, Friend unseen,	258
268.	O Jesu, King most wonderful,	285
148.	O Jesu, Lord of heavenly grace,	228
245.	O Lord, how happy should we be,	279
269.	O Lord, how joyful 'tis to see,	286
209.	O Lord of heaven and earth and sea,	261
52.	O Lord, turn not Thy face from me,	141
210.	O Love Divine, how sweet Thou art!	261
318.	O love, how deep, how broad, how high,	302
225.	O Paradise! O Paradise!	272
226.	O praise ye the Lord!	273
291.	O render thanks to God above,	294
319.	O Saviour, is Thy promise fled?	302
149.	O Spirit of the living God,	229
42.	O Thou from whom all goodness flows,	131
211.	O Thou, the contrite sinner's Friend,	262
175.	O Thou, to whose all-searching sight,	241
187.	O where shall rest be found,	249
32.	O worship the King,	122
227.	Of the Father's love begotten,	273
28.	Oft in danger, oft in woe,	118
246.	Oh! what if we are Christ's,	279
130.	On Jordan's bank the Baptist's cry,	221
320.	Once more the solemn season calls,	303
228.	One there is above all others,	273
176.	Onward, Christian soldiers,	242
53.	Our blest Redeemer, ere He breathed,	142
131.	Pleasant are Thy courts above,	221
66.	Praise, my soul, the King of heaven,	157
292.	Praise, O praise our God and King,	294
67.	Praise the Lord; ye heavens, adore Him,	158
121.	Praise to God, immortal praise,	215
247.	Prayer is the soul's sincere desire,	280

General Index.

Order.	Hymns.	Page
86.	Rejoice, the Lord is King,	170
61.	Ride on, ride on in majesty,	153
4.	Rock of Ages, cleft for me,	55
248.	Round the Lord in glory seated,	280
177.	Salvation, O the joyful sound,	242
229.	Saviour, again to Thy dear name we raise,	273
212.	Saviour, blessed Saviour,	262
132.	Saviour, breathe an evening blessing,	222
20.	Saviour, when in dust to Thee,	103
321.	Saviour, who Thy flock art feeding,	303
178.	See the destined day arise,	243
249.	Sing Alleluia forth in duteous praise,	280
68.	Soldiers of Christ, arise,	158
322.	Son of God, to Thee I cry,	303
62.	Songs of praise the angels sang,	154
270.	Sons of men, behold from far,	286
112.	Spirit of mercy, truth, and love,	210
250.	Spirit of truth, on this Thy day,	281
9.	Sun of my soul, Thou Saviour dear,	70
141.	Sweet is the work, my God, my King,	225
162.	Sweet Saviour, bless us ere we go,	235
36.	Sweet the moments, rich in blessing,	125
271.	Take up thy cross, the Saviour said,	286
96.	That day of wrath, that dreadful day,	177
293.	The advent of our King,	294
230.	The Church has waited long,	274
188.	The Church's one foundation,	249
97.	The day is past and over,	187
323.	The day of resurrection,	304
189.	The God of Abraham praise,	249
163.	The happy morn is come,	236
142.	The head that once was crowned with thorns,	226
113.	The Lord my pasture shall prepare,	210
150.	The Lord of might from Sinai's brow,	229
87.	The Lord will come, the earth shall quake,	171

Order.	Hymns.	Page
294.	The race that long in darkness pined,	295
98.	The roseate hues of early dawn,	188
33.	The Son of God goes forth to war,	122
122.	The spacious firmament on high,	216
69.	The strain upraise of joy and praise,	159
190.	The strife is o'er, the battle done,	253
179.	The sun is sinking fast,	243
114.	The voice that breathed o'er Eden,	211
213.	Thee we adore, O hidden Saviour, Thee,	263
164.	There is a blessed home,	236
143.	There is a book, who runs may read,	226
133.	There is a fountain filled with blood,	223
295.	There is a happy land,	295
70.	There is a land of pure delight,	160
296.	There's a Friend for little children,	295
180.	Thine for ever, God of love,	243
324.	This is the day of light,	304
203.	This is the day the Lord hath made,	258
297.	This stone to Thee in faith we lay,	296
272.	Thou art gone to the grave,	287
71.	Thou art gone up on high,	161
77.	Thou art the Way; to Thee alone,	164
181.	Thou hidden love of God,	244
251.	Thou Judge of quick and dead,	281
29.	Thou whose almighty word,	120
165.	Three in One, and One in Three,	237
63.	Through all the changing scenes of life,	155
54.	Through the day Thy love hath spared us,	143
115.	Thy way, not mine, O Lord,	211
151.	To bless Thy chosen race,	230
214.	To the Name that speaks salvation,	263
298.	To Thy temple I repair,	296
231.	To-morrow, Lord, is Thine,	274
252.	We give immortal praise,	281
253.	We give Thee but Thine own,	281
191.	We love the place, O Lord,	253

General Index.

Order.	Hymns.	Page
232.	We saw Thee not when Thou didst come, .	274
116.	We sing the praise of Him who died, .	212
273.	Weary of earth, and laden with my sin,	287
254.	We've no abiding city here,	282
233.	What various hindrances we meet, .	275
99.	When all Thy mercies, O my God,	189
215.	When Christ the Lord would come on earth,	263
81.	When gathering clouds around I view,	167
152.	When God of old came down from heaven,	230
274.	When, His salvation bringing,	288
299.	When I can read my title clear,	297
10.	When I survey the wondrous cross,	73
43.	When our heads are bowed with woe,	131
255.	When this passing world is done, .	282
256.	When wounded sore, the stricken soul,	282
44.	Where high the heavenly temple stands,	132
45.	While shepherds watched their flocks by night,	134
275.	While with ceaseless course the sun,	288
144.	Who are these, like stars appearing,	226
300.	With glory clad, with strength arrayed,	297
301.	With joy we meditate the grace,	297
134.	Ye boundless realms of joy, .	223
325.	Ye choirs of New Jerusalem,	304
153.	Ye servants of God, your Master proclaim,	230
72.	Ye servants of the Lord,	162

Edinburgh University Press
THOMAS AND ARCHIBALD CONSTABLE, PRINTERS TO HER MAJESTY.

www.ingramcontent.com/pod-product-compliance
Lightning Source LLC
Chambersburg PA
CBHW031857220426
43663CB00006B/665